"Swells with unadorned heroi...

"In the best tradition of book... ...ge to community service, place, and the men and women who live there. A perfectly pitched celebration of small-town life." —*Kirkus Reviews*

"This is a quietly devastating book—intimate and disarming and lovely." —Adrienne Miller, *Esquire*

"I have been waiting for thirty years for a fresh and talented voice to rise out of the volunteer fire service in America, and finally it has arrived in Michael Perry's *Population: 485*. Perry is a firefighter/EMT and he makes you feel you are responding right along with him to fires, auto wrecks, even suicides, and his hard work is told with the thoughtfulness and gracefulness of a first responder who cares about people, his town, our country, and the world we live in. But this is more than a book about a small-town fire department. It is a literary venture told on the cusp of service to his community—all written with a soft human touch by an intuitive writer with a distinctive and refined American style. Firefighters and EMTs will be talking about this book for a long time to come. And so will all readers who have a love for American literature. This is a small-town story in the big tradition of Sherwood Anderson and James Agee."

—Dennis Smith, author of *Report from Ground Zero*

"My heart goes out to anybody who knows—and writes as well as Michael Perry does—about rural small-town life. His book is often funny, sometimes heartbreaking, but always full of life, characters, and the tangled web of small-town history, daily drama, and strain of occasional weirdness that make country living such a challenge and an adventure. New Auburn, Wisconsin, sounds a lot like Pleasant Valley, New York, except colder in the winter, so I felt immediately at home reading *Population: 485*. If there's one thing I admire more than a man who can go home again, and does, and happily, it's a volunteer firefighter. Mr. Perry's account of firefighting is scary, inspiring, and renews my gratitude toward our own, to whom I owe much. He has written a joy of a book, as gnarly, stubborn, courageous, and full of eccentricity in all its forms as country life itself." —Michael Korda

Population: 485

Also by Michael Perry

Truck: A Love Story

Off Main Street

Big Rigs, Elvis & the Grand Dragon Wayne

Why They Killed Big Boy . . . and Other Stories

Never Stand Behind a Sneezing Cow (CD)

I Got It from the Cows (CD)

Population: 485

485

Meeting Your Neighbors
One Siren at a Time

MICHAEL PERRY

HARPER  PERENNIAL

NEW YORK • LONDON • TORONTO • SYDNEY

This is a work of nonfiction. In some instances, names, locations, and other identifying details have been changed to protect individual privacy.

HARPER ● PERENNIAL

The excerpt from Frank Stanford's "Blue Yodel of the Lost Child" on pages 231–32 appears by the kind permission of Ginny Stanford.

A hardcover edition of this book was published in 2002 by HarperCollins Publishers.

P.S.™ is a trademark of HarperCollins Publishers.

HarperCollins books may be purchased for educational, business, or sales promotional use. For information please write: Special Markets Department, HarperCollins Publishers, 10 East 53rd Street, New York, NY 10022.

First Perennial edition published 2003.

First Harper Perennial edition published 2007.

Designed by Elliott Beard

Library of Congress Cataloging-in-Publication Data is available upon request.

ISBN: 978-0-06-136350-4 (pbk.)
ISBN-10: 0-06-136350-2 (pbk.)

07 08 09 10 11 ❖/RRD 10 9 8 7 6 5 4 3 2 1

For J. & S.

Acknowledgments

Thanks to:

First and foremost, my parents—anything decent is because of them, anything else is simply not their fault.

. . . the people in and around "Nobbern" who make it my favorite place in the world. Members of the NAAFD, past and present. The Chetek ambulance and fire crews, Bloomer ambulance and fire crews, and the "Silver Star" crews—it's a privilege to be out there with you. Frank, clear back to Galloway. The Bruce for early seeds, late rumbles. Magnuson, for garage rants and intercession. Jayne, cool and true. McDowell family. Mrs. Rehrauer. John Hildebrand. A, B, and C. Racy's, for much coffee. Kris and Frank, for food and football. Shimon Lindemann (Whitelaw Johnie and his Mystery Date). Bill and Wilda. Adrienne Miller, Darcy Frey, Ilena Silverman, Susan Orlean, Karen Croft, for a hand along the way. Everyone who came to the readings over the years. And in the big city, Lisa Bankoff, Alison Callahan, Patrick (he of Obscure Powers) Price, and Liz Farrell.

. . . *Esquire, Salon, Hope Magazine, Orion, Troika, Word, Brevity,*

No Depression, Discovery Online, and *The World & I,* for publishing essays from which some of the material for this book was drawn.

. . . the volunteers everywhere, and to the professionals who do it every day, setting the bar for us amateurs.

. . . the memory of Robert Jones and Waylon Jennings.

If I missed you, drop by. But do announce yerself. . . .

Contents

1	Jabowski's Corner	1
2	Beagle	18
3	Tricky	37
4	Silver Star	52
5	Structure Fire	69
6	Running the Loop	87
7	My People	108
8	Death	128
9	Call	143
10	Cat	164
11	Oops	182
12	Penultimate	197
13	Sarah	211

Population: 485

1

JABOWSKI'S CORNER

We are in trouble down here. There is blood in the dirt. We have made our call for help. Now we look to the sky.

═══════════

SUMMER HERE COMES ON like a zaftig hippie chick, jazzed on chlorophyll and flinging fistfuls of butterflies to the sun. The swamps grow spongy and pungent. Standing water goes warm and soupy, clotted with frog eggs and twitching with larvae. Along the ditches, heron-legged stalks of canary grass shoot six feet high and unfurl seed plumes. In the fields, the clover pops its blooms and corn trembles for the sky.

If you were approaching from the sky, you would see farmland neatly delineated by tilled squares and irrigated circles. The forests, mostly hardwoods and new-growth pine, butt up against fields, terminating abruptly, squared off at fence lines. The swamps and wetlands, on the other hand, respect no such boundaries, and simply meander the lay of the land, spreading organically in fecund hundred-acre stains. The whole works is done up in an infinite palette of greens.

There is a road below, a slim strip of county two-lane, where the faded blacktop runs east-west, then bends—at Jabowski's Corner—like an elbow. In the crook of the elbow, right in the space where you would cradle a baby, is a clot of people. My mother is there, and my sister, and several volunteer firefighters, and I have just joined them, and we are all on our knees, kneeling in a ring around a young girl who has been horribly injured in a car wreck. She is crying out, and we are doing what we can, but she feels death pressing at her chest. She tells us this, and we deny it, tell her no, no, help is on the way.

I do my writing in a tiny bedroom overlooking Main Street in the village of New Auburn, Wisconsin. Population: 485. Eleven streets. One four-legged silver water tower. Seasons here are extreme. We complain about the heat and brag about the cold. Summer is for stock cars and softball. Winter is for Friday-night fish fries. And snowmobiles. After a good blizzard, you'll hear their Doppler snarl all through the dark, and down at the bar, sleds will outnumber cars. In the surrounding countryside, farmsteads with little red barns have been pretty much kicked in the head, replaced with monster dairies, turkey sheds, and vinyl-sided prefabs. The farmers who came to town to grind feed and grumble in the café have faded away. The grand old buildings are gone. There is a sense of decline. Or worse, of dormancy in the wake of decline. But we are not dead here. We still have our Friday-night football games. Polka dances. Bowling. If you know who to ask, you can still get yourself some moonshine, although methamphetamine has become the favored homebrew. Every day, the village dogs howl at the train that rumbles through town, and I like to think they are echoing their ancestors, howling at that first train when it stopped here in 1883. Maybe that's all you need to know about this town—the train doesn't stop here anymore.

Mostly I write at night, when most of this wee town—except for

the one-man night shift at the plastics factory, and the most dedi-
cated drinkers, and the mothers with colicky babies, and the odd in-
somniac widower, and the young couples tossing and turning over
charge card balances and home pregnancy tests—is asleep. This is
my hometown, and in these early hours, when time is gathering itself, I can kill the lights, crack the blinds, and, looking down on
Main Street, see the ghost of my teenage self, snake-dancing beneath
the streetlight, celebrating some football game twenty years gone. I
was a farm boy then, rarely in town for anything other than school
activities. I didn't see Main Street unless I was in a parade or on a
school bus.

But now Main Street is in my front yard. On a May evening nineteen years ago I walked out of the school gym in a blue gown and left
this place. Now I have returned, to a house I remember only from the
perspective of a school bus seat. In a place from the past, I am looking
for a place in the present. This, as they say, is where my roots are. The
trick is in reattaching. About a month after I moved back, I dropped
by the monthly meeting of the volunteer fire department.

The New Auburn fire department was formed in 1905. The little village was just thirty years old, but it had already seen its share
of change. The sawmill that spawned the settlement ran out of pine
trees and shut down before the turn of the century. Forests gave way
to farmland and New Auburn became a potato shipping center.
Large, hutlike charcoal kilns sprang up beside the rail depot. In
time, the village has been home to a wagon wheel factory, a brick
factory, and a pickle factory. There was always something coming
and going. But then, in 1974, the state converted the two lanes of
Highway 53 to four lanes and routed them west of town, and the
coming and going pretty much went. We have a gas station, two
cafés, a couple of bars, and a handful of small businesses, but the
closest thing to industry is the plastics factory, which employs two
men per shift, rolling plastic pellets into plastic picnic table covers.
Most of the steady work, the good-paying stuff, is thirty or forty
miles away. During the day, the streets are still. It is from this shal-

low pool that the community must skim its firefighters. If we get a fire call during a weekday, we are likely to have more fire trucks than volunteer firefighters to drive them.

During that first meeting, a motion was made and seconded to consider my application as a member. The motion carried on a voice vote, and I was admitted on probationary status. After the meeting concluded, the chief led me to the truck bay. He is a stout man, burly but friendly. By day he dispatches freight trucks. "Try on these boots," he said. "We've got a helmet around here somewhere." Someone handed me a stiff pair of old fire pants—bunkers, they're called. A farmer in a bar jacket showed me how to shift the pumper, his cigarette a sing-along dot dancing from word to word. That was it. I was now a member of the NAAFD—the New Auburn Area Fire Department.

Among my fellow volunteers are a pair of butchers, two truckers, a farmer, a carpenter, a mailman, and a mother of four. A guy like me ends up on the fire department for two reasons: (a) I have a pulse, and (b) I am frequently home during the day. I've put in seven years now, and am no longer on probation. I've been to house fires, barn fires, brush fires, and car fires, and I've had enough training to tell a halligan from a hydrant wrench. When one of the old-timers sends me after a water hammer, I don't take the bait. I have attended firefighting classes at the tech school, where I learned that water hammer is a situation, not a tool. Still, my primary qualifications remain availability and a valid driver's license.

Seven years since the accident, and this is what freezes me, late at night: There was a moment—a still, horrible moment—when the car came squalling to a halt, the violent kinetics spent, and the girl was pinned in silence. One moment gravel is in the air like shrapnel, steel is tumbling, rubber tearing, glass imploding, and then . . . utter stillness. As if peace is the only answer to destruction. The meadowlark sings, the land drops away south to the hazy tamarack bowl of the Big Swamp . . . all around the land is rank with life. The girl is terribly, terribly alone in a beautiful, beautiful world.

As long as I can remember, Stanislaw Jabowski was all stove up. Foggy autumn mornings, the school bus would stop where the county road cut between his house and barn, and we'd see him stumping along the path, pails in hand, shoulders rocking side to side with his hitch-along gait. Spare, he was. Short, and lean as a tendon. A walking Joshua tree, with a posture less tribute to adversity overcome than adversity withstood.

The farm was a rock patch. And where the rocks stopped, the swamps began. It was a tough place to subsist, let alone thrive. During one nine-year stretch, when five of the ten Jabowski kids were in braces, Stanislaw worked night and swing shifts at the munitions plant in Eau Claire, Wisconsin, arranging his farm work around the full-time job. He'd feed the sheep and cows, do the milking, drive forty miles to the munitions plant, pull a full shift, drive home, and do all the chores again before sleeping. Night shift or swing shift, the cows swung with him. Somewhere in there—I can't imagine—he planted crops and put up hay and sleepwalked through the month-long twenty-four-hour-a-day grind of lambing season. I regret to report that there was a shamefully mirror-intensive period in my life in which I engaged briefly and quite ineffectively in the sport of body-building, and one of the reasons I just couldn't keep at it was because I'd watch my bulging, lubricated compadres admiring the cut of their triceps, or the belly of their biceps, and I'd think of Stanislaw Jabowski, with his bowed shoulders and little strap-iron muscles, and how, within four days of head-to-head choring and bomb-building, he would leave those baked-fish-nibbling showpieces whimpering in a damp corner of the milkhouse. Somehow, pectorals the size of beef roasts seemed pointless.

Catholics, the Jabowskis. Seven girls, three boys. And for them, Stanislaw worked himself to a nub. They were smart kids, and one pail of milk at a time, Stanislaw fed them, clothed them, and earned every one of them a chance at college—and the Pope always got his cut. The economics are flabbergasting. The kids lent a hand, but Stanislaw didn't encourage it. "If I was a lawyer or a doctor," he'd say, "I wouldn't expect my kids to work in my office." It was a hard-scrabble campaign, but Stanislaw had a secret weapon. He married Renata when she was nineteen and he was twenty-four. They tried for four years to have children, without success. So they arranged to adopt, and it was as if the decision released something, because almost immediately, Renata grew large with child, and others arrived regularly for over a decade. She washed mountains of clothes, cooked food in shifts, did some of the plowing, took outside work to supplement the milk check, and even found time to finish her social service degree and get elected to the school board. She was cheerful and fair, but she was fierce in the way only a mother can be. Aboard the Jabowski family ship, Stanislaw toiled belowdecks; Renata stood at the prow.

The youngest Jabowski boy, Hadrian, and I were the same age. We shared a classroom for thirteen years. As children, we played in his basement, wrapping potatoes in tinfoil and baking them to a cinder in the woodstove coals. During a game of hide-and-seek, I raced around behind the little white house and collided with a pipe thrust out of the ground at such a height that the full force of the impact registered directly on my maturing privates. I recall a blinding flash of pain, and little or no sympathy from Hadrian as I clutched myself and convulsed on the lawn.

The last Jabowski graduated from New Auburn High School in 1987. The cows are gone. The barnyard is thick with weeds. With property taxes going through the roof, the Jabowskis are selling off chunks of the homestead. Stanislaw, having had a head start on looking worn out, now looks a pretty good seventy-six. He still crosses the road to the barn once in a while. Last year I asked him why he built the house on the east side of the road, when everything else was on the west side. He looked at me. "Didn't want the chickens in the yard!"

When Stanislaw was a child, a man walked up that road and

asked for a tire pump. Stanislaw fetched one, and studied the man's face as he patched the spare on his dusty four-door. There were other men in the car, and they didn't say much. When he was finished, the man returned the pump and gave the boy fifty cents. Against the standard of the day, it was a princely sum. These were the Depression years. Al Capone was in jail, but gangsters still ran to the Wisconsin woods to hide, and to this day Stanislaw remembers that face, and reckons he's the little boy who helped John Dillinger fix a flat.

———

It was always a worry, that road. To raise ten kids on a farm where the house is separated from the outbuildings by a county highway. Renata invented a rhyme, and taught her children to stop at the shoulder and recite: "Before you cross, count to seven; otherwise you go to Heaven." There were some close calls, and once a dump truck rear-ended a pickup waiting behind the school bus, but truth be told, the real trouble always happened just downhill from the house, on the corner overlooking the Big Swamp. Over the years, the corner has claimed a litany of wayward vehicles. Sometimes the walking wounded wound up on Renata's couch. Sometimes there were bodies in the corn. The corner is tricky. There's something deceiving about the sweep and dip of it. People come in too fast, and confronted with the overshoot, either overcorrect or plunge headlong into the sheep pasture below. In the plat book, it is just another bend in County M, but around here, it's known as Jabowski's Corner, and it is infamous. Renata was at the dining room table when the girl crashed, and, hearing the noise of the tumbling vehicle, she went out to check. Someone else was already running up the road to call an ambulance.

My uncle Shotsy was a UPS driver. He used to tell me that you could take any corner at exactly twice its posted speed. The second time he rolled his big brown van, UPS let him go. I still think of him whenever I see a yellow curve sign and do the math. Uncle Shotsy was a victim of optimistic physics. They are not posted, but every corner in the county has its parameters. Exceed them, and you pay. Best-case scenario, you pay up in tire smoke and cold sweat. Worst-case scenario, you entwine your name with that corner for six or seven generations.

I have only one recollection of Janis Bourne: My classmates and I are in Mrs. Carlson's little music room, sitting cross-legged on the floor. We are grade-schoolers, looking up to Janis the high-schooler. She is sitting in a straight-backed chair, wearing dark blue corduroy bell-bottoms, accompanying herself on electric bass and singing the Barbara Fairchild hit:

> *I wish I was*
> *a teddy bear*
> *Not livin' or lovin'*
> *not goin' nowhere . . .*

I sang the song for weeks after that. The exact chronology is unclear, but some time later, Janis was killed when her car went straight on a curve just north of town. I heard about it in school. Someone said she went way out in the brush. For the past five years, I have driven through that curve at least twice a week. Every time, I think of Janis, and her big bass guitar, and that song. This summer, we were called to a hay fire in the middle of the night. I was driving a tanker, which meant I had nine tons of water at my back, and I hit that corner too fast. I knew it right before the centerline began to bend. It was too late to make adjustments. The variables were set, the physics were immutable. All I could do was hold the wheel and ride. The truck heaved and pitched leeward, the headlights sweeping across the brush as we pushed into the deep edge of the curve. I thought of Janis, like always. The headlights swept out of the brush, dipped at the ditch, and then locked on the centerline. The truck settled back on keel.

So, technically, I wasn't going too fast. Whatever variables I fed into the baroque formula governing that truck and me, the answer came up "play again." My heart was pounding. I felt the cold breath of Janis Bourne's ghost at my temples. Somewhere, Uncle Shotsy is grinning like an outlaw.

Used to be, when I was driving my beat-up old pickup up from college to visit the home farm, I could drop the hammer at the edge of town, and by the time I hit the spot where Old Highway 53 peeled away to the northeast, I'd be wound out in high gear. I'd shoot straight at the split, roaring up Five Mile Road through the salty-sweet air of Keesey Swamp, headed for home. In one beautiful kinetic moment, the truck would leave the banked curve of the highway, dip down and to the right, and for just a second, everything would float. Then the wheels bounced back and I'd be rocketing northbound. When I hit the split, the air became familiar. The split was my portal to reentry, and to breach it at speed was magical.

Then one night the split was gone, replaced with a carefully reengineered ninety-degree turn to be entered at the apex of the curve. I had to downshift and motor sedately through the turn lane to Five Mile Road. The intersection is safer now, of course. More sensible. But lately I see that some truck-driving youths have been making the straight shot again. They've worn twin tracks in the weeds, right where the old road ran. I still have that old truck. It isn't running, but I could work on it. Drop the hammer and do a little time traveling.

I don't mean to intimate that New Auburn is located on the frontier. A major highway runs right past the village. The people we meet on fire and ambulance calls are a mix of townies, farmers, upper-crusters with lake property, and trailered recluses. It ain't the frontier, and it ain't the ghetto, but there is a seam of raggedness throughout. There are women here who put on their makeup like rust-proofing. Preschoolers toddle through the trailer park mud puddles, splashing and pimp-cussing. Teenage girls in sweat pants and ratty NASCAR T-shirts smoke over parked strollers, hips set at a permanent baby-propping cant. The afternoons oxidize like trailer tin. Still, there are boyfriends, and emotions worth screaming over, fistfuls of affections rained down behind closed doors. At the bar up the block, the closing-time domestics wind up on Main Street, playing out beneath the one streetlight, the fuck you/fuck *you* execrations concluding with a door slam and squealing tires, the roar of the engine pocked by a missing cylinder. You can call the cops, but since the local constable quit, the closest county deputy may be an hour away. Other areas are far more remote, but we have our pockets of darkness, and because trouble is a volunteer fire department's summons, we're often the first to discover them. First on the scene at a raging trailer house fire, my brother—also a volunteer fireman—is met by a man walking down the driveway toting a gas can. He asks my brother, "Is it against the law to burn your own house?"

———

The girl is still lying there, trapped but alive and conscious, two miles outside of town, when the siren on the water tower goes off, rising and falling three times. Help is still a ways off. There is no ambulance in New Auburn. Depending on the location of the telephone pole you clip, an ambulance will be dispatched from a town nine miles to the north or nine miles to the south of our village. Today the ambulance will be coming from the south, from Bloomer. From the time the call comes in until the ambulance arrives, fifteen minutes will pass. In the meantime, we'll respond with two fire trucks and a rescue van. A few of us on the department are EMTs and first responders—we arrive with a pack of rudimentary medical supplies and do our best to stabilize the situation until more definitive help arrives. Sometimes that means crawling into a tangled car in an attempt to keep an unconscious victim breathing. Sometimes it means simply holding the hand of a sickly grandmother or a suicidal farmer.

Today, the pumper will drive to the vehicle in case a fire should break out, or a gasoline spill needs to be contained and controlled. The van and the tanker will be used to control traffic. Securing the scene, it's called. Shutting traffic down makes a lot of people cranky, but it is vital for the safety of the victims and those helping the victims.

And so the girl waits. But we are on our way now, coming from all sides of town, converging on the little white fire hall. Inside, the light is dim and the brick walls are cool. The coats and boots wait in their rows, the trucks are still.

It was never my dream to be a firefighter, or to scream around the country in an ambulance. It all began when I graduated from nursing school and found myself frustrated by the fact that here I was, freshly armed with a bachelor's degree in the caring arts, steeped in holism and paradigms and able, if need be, to catheterize you in a trice, but I knew nothing of how to extricate someone safely from a pancaked Yugo, or splint a dislocated elbow. My first nursing job was for a surgeon in Rice Lake, Wisconsin. After moving to Rice Lake, I enrolled in a 115-hour emergency medical technician class through the regional technical school and subsequently passed the National Registry exam. When a new nursing job took me to Eau Claire, Wisconsin, I hired on part-time with a private ambulance service in that town. We served a large metropolitan and rural area, as well as a long stretch of I-94. When I reported for my first day of work, the first-out rig was gone to a nasty accident on the interstate. A van had driven full speed into the back of a parked semi. When the rig finally returned, the lead EMT looked me over, fresh in my new uniform. "We were out scraping up an *ohsh*," he said. Long *o*, short *sh*.

"An *ohsh*?"

"An *ohsh*," he repeated. "Guy in the van only left six feet of skid marks."

I still didn't get it. The veteran EMT chuckled. "An *ohsh* is when you look up at the last second, see the rear end of that semi, scream, '*Oh, shit!,*' but only make it to '*Oh, sh . . . !*'"

Within a year, I'd been on more than two hundred calls. I could drop the *ohsh* thing on newbies. I stayed on as a part-timer for more than five years, and when I moved back to New Auburn, it just seemed natural to continue some association with emergency services. But I have long since lost the ability to be flip about things like the *ohsh*.

Today, when I see the girl there on the blacktop, all that seasoned veteran hoo-hah will go right out the window, because she is delicate and frightened and conscious, and most of all, she is one of us. When we gather around her we are firefighters and first responders and EMTs, but we are also neighbors, classmates, family. If she doesn't make it, I'm going to see her parents around town. It happens. Last year we had a heart attack call, found the woman too far gone, with signs she'd been dead awhile. Not long, but too long. The woman's teenage daughter was there, teary and expectant, but there was nothing we could do. The following weekend, I was sitting at a folding table in front of the gas station selling raffle tickets for our fire department fund-raiser when the girl drove in with a friend. I had to look her in the eye, ask her how it was going. Me, worthless in her mother's hour of death, now selling two-dollar chances to win a trip to Orlando, a beer cooler, a deer rifle, a four-pack of insulated Packer mugs. We do this whole pitch. How each ticket sold helps us raise money for critical equipment, equipment that helps us improve our service to the community. The spiel takes on a whole different significance when you're speaking to the daughter of someone you were utterly unable to help. Another time, my brother and I drove the ambulance up a long back road where a woman was having a stroke. Her adult granddaughter rode with us to the hospital. Three days later, in the grocery store, I exited the fruit-juice aisle and came face-to-face with the granddaughter, all made up and wearing a discreet black dress.

I inquired after Grandma.

"We just came from the funeral mass," said the woman.

And yet she was kind, praising my brother and me for the gentle way we had handled Grandma, for the way we had accommodated the family.

━━━━━

The girl is lying on the road because she came into the curve a little too fast, or a little too wide, or both, it only matters that she overcorrected, and instead of flying over the embankment, the car boomeranged across the centerline, skidding and rolling and shuddering to rest below some Norway pines on the inside shoulder of the curve, which seems counterintuitive to physics. Somewhere in the tumbling, she was thrown from the car, then dragged beneath its great weight. The blacktop is scored with evidence.

I remember pulling up in the pumper, leaving it parked by Jabowski's. Wally, another new guy on the department, was riding shotgun, and he stayed back to stop traffic. I remember gallumphing down the hill toward the clot of people, blue medical kit over one shoulder, bunkers slapping at my legs, the cleated heels of my steel-toed rubber boots thudding on the pavement. I remember the cluster of rescuers, and I remember the chief standing on the asphalt, directing people and traffic, poking the air with his radio antenna like a conductor waving a baton. My mother took the EMT class with me all those years ago, and she is there, as is my sister. My sister will begin her junior year of high school at summer's end. She was preparing for a friend's wedding shower when the call came, and rode along in case my mother needed an extra pair of hands. Looking down when she arrives, she recognizes the girl on the road. Tracy Rimes is a year older than my sister, due to start her senior year, but they used to gossip in the same study hall. With three EMTs in the family, my sister has been the "victim" of many training exercises, and when my mother shows her how to hold Tracy's head in careful alignment, she knows what to do. While my mother unzips her oxygen kit and hooks up a breathing mask, my sister talks to Tracy, and Tracy answers. Later, when the day is older, and we are all back in our homes, I will marvel at my sister's composure. She was a toddler when I left home. Here she looks shaken but steady. It is a test, and she is strong in the face of it.

There is so much to do. I relieve my sister, our hands touching as we perform the delicate handoff of Tracy's head. From here I can get my bearings, see what we're facing, what needs to be done. I can see that Tracy's right leg is badly injured. The femur, the large bone in her upper leg, is fractured. This is dangerous. You can bleed enough from this injury alone to die. The hemorrhaging is all internal, between the spaces of the muscles. Compartmental bleeding, it's called. She has other injuries as well. One look at her, and the chief ordered a medical helicopter. Even if the ambulance runs like hell, it will take nearly forty-five minutes to get her to the nearest trauma center. From the time you begin your training as an EMT you are drilled and drilled on the concept of the "Golden Hour," in which the odds of a patients surviving a severe traumatic event decline precipitously if they do not receive definitive treatment within sixty minutes. By the time the ambulance arrives, fifteen to twenty minutes of that hour will already be spent. So thirty miles away, a chopper has risen into the air and is headed our way.

Back by Jabowski's, and around the bend to the east, traffic has been stopped, and firefighters become flagpersons, turning travelers back, sending them on a twelve-mile detour. Other firefighters are preparing a landing zone, marking it out back in the curve right about at the spot where the car first left the road. Meanwhile, we are doing what we can for Tracy. Communication is critical and we think aloud. Jack Most, a feed mill operator who was my math tutor in fifth grade, readies a reserve tank of oxygen. His brother Bob, a butcher, puts a plastic collar around Tracy's neck. The ambulance arrives with more equipment, and we keep working, wanting to have her ready to go—"packaged," it's called in EMS terms—when the chopper arrives. Her leg is causing her great pain, so we apply a traction splint, a racklike device that attaches at the ankle and, with a ratcheting action, pulls the leg straight. This draws the bone ends apart. With Tracy, the relief is instantaneous.

Still, Tracy is growing more and more apprehensive, and her color is getting worse. Her lung sounds are diminishing on the left side. Pneumothorax. Each time she takes a breath, air rushes through a hole in her lung. Left unchecked, this air will fill the space between the chest wall and the lung, pushing the lung out of place until it collapses. This is a true emergency, and must be treated quickly, with equipment we do not have. I look at her eyes and see fear. We talk to her, reassure her that help is on the way. I do not tell her everything will be all right. I have never been able to tell my patients everything will be all right.

We have her strapped to a hard plastic litter now, packaged and ready for the chopper. For a moment, there is time to reassess. We keep checking her vital signs—blood pressure, pulse, respirations—shine a light in her eyes to check the reaction of her pupils. We talk to one another, ask if we've missed anything. Recheck the splint, recheck the straps, double-check the amount of oxygen left in the tank, fetch another one for backup. Tracy's breathing is getting worse. We are all sneaking peeks to the sky, looking for the chopper. Now a man is kneeling by the girl's shoulder, speaking to her intently, his face tight with fear. She reaches to him. It is her father. "I love you, Tracy," he says. "You be strong."

Suddenly there it is. The chopper, cresting a pine copse. It approaches with a thunderous buzz, an iron blue dragonfly, circling, hovering, then, in a wash of wind and grit, settling to the centerline.

Two flight nurses exit the chopper, stooped over and running with tackle boxes; the first nurse takes one look at the girl there, gasping and losing color, and says, "We need a chest tube." Out come iodine swabs, forceps, tubing, a shockingly huge needle. Within seconds she drives the needle between Tracy's ribs. Air rushes out, and almost immediately, the girl's breathing and color improve. A few other tasks are quickly dispatched—an IV line, another set of vital signs—and then we are hunched over, feeding the stretcher into the thrumming chopper. Shielding our eyes from the downwash, we scuttle away as the chopper rises, banks, and is gone over the treetops. The chief turns the scene over to the captain and hustles away to drive the father to the hospital. The father was once the chief of the department. The two men have history.

Later, walking back to the pumper, I reflect on the call. It went well. We handled it well. We talked our way through the confusion and fear and mess, and it seems we did all the right things, limited though they might be. A long line of cars was waiting atop the hill, and suddenly a woman jumped out of one and called my name. She ran up and hugged me. It was a high-school girlfriend. I hadn't seen her for years. It was a fine moment, standing there sweaty in my T-shirt and bunkers, with this beautiful woman hugging me, and me remembering her spearmint kisses that first night on the basketball bus. After we said good-bye again, I wondered if the deadly crotch-high pipe still stood behind Jabowski's house, and I began to realize how this fire department was a means of reentry, of rediscovering the place I had left a decade before, of recapturing my sense of place one tragedy at a time. I was realizing that this service is a privilege, a way to weave myself back into the fabric of a place. Today we had tragedy, but it was our tragedy, and we dealt with it not only as public citizens, but also as friends and neighbors. I am not an optimistic sort, but I felt good that day, driving that tanker back toward a little town that was reemerging from memory, across land I feel in my guts. To feel at home is a rare, precious thing, and I began to feel at home that day.

● ● ●

The word came back through town. Tracy didn't survive the night. To the ghosts of this land, we add another ghost.

That was seven years ago. Last night I biked out to Highway M, around Jabowski's Corner. The afternoon had been stormy. Rain was rising from the asphalt, the steam fat with the black smell of tar. The pavement is aromatic because it is new; since Tracy died, the corner has been recut and reshaped, the roadbed raised and the camber adjusted. I cycle through the flattened curve, following as the highway straightens and drops eastward, a soft declining line bisecting the leafy plenty of August. The land is settling into an easy evening, and into that season where everything that has risen up prepares to fade and fall, this death blanketing last year's death. The land is at ease with the idea of mortality. But the sky . . . cumulonimbus clouds are stacked and banked to the stratosphere, and the lowering sun has bronzed and brassed and blushed them. These are clouds to make you long for wings. These are clouds that leave you not knowing what to believe.

2

BEAGLE

You'd jump too, if you yanked the fire-hall door open at three A.M. and found the One-Eyed Beagle in your face. The Beagle is a butcher, and he looks it. His knuckles are knife-scarred. His forearms and biceps are thick with years of hoisting half-beefs from the meat hook to the cutting table. A Fu Manchu mustache brackets his mouth, the gray whiskers dropping straight to his jawline. His lip—even at three A.M., *especially* at three A.M.—is always jammed with chaw. But with the Beagle, it's the eyes that put the startle in you. Several years ago, the Beagle donated a kidney to his niece. He came out of surgery with one eye inexplicably crossed. He jokes about it. His given name is Bob, but he'll be the first to hip you to the One-Eyed Beagle thing.

The eye isn't just crossed, it is out to lunch. If Beagle points his nose south, his right eye shoots due east. Any more easterly, and it is headed back around the bend. And so you understand that when I got to the hall, after running from my house through backyards in the dark, thinking I was the first one there, when Bob rared up right off the end of my snoot, I went a little pop-eyed.

"Scared ya there, Mikey!"

• • •

The Beagle has been on the department for more than twenty-five years. Only the chief has more seniority. The Beagle can tell you some stories. He remembers when the old pumper was the new pumper. He once broke his ankle in the line of duty. He was running to the hall in his cowboy boots and landed wrong when he jumped the ditch. The cowboy boots are trouble. He'll hit a patch of ice, and his feet get to *zip-zip-zipping*—it looks like a hairy version of *Riverdance*. Lately he has switched to slip-on tennies. Gives him an edge, he says. The Beagle and I are pretty much equidistant to the fire-hall door. We're usually the first ones there, and it's always a little race to see who gets to drive the van.

Two things you can count on when you jump in a rig with the Beagle: you're going to get a whiff of wintergreen, and you're going to get a detailed report of exactly where he was and what he was doing when the page went off. Every call starts that way. Somewhere in that first half mile he'll give you the update. "Damn, I was just sittin' down to eat, and I heard Bloomer paged over the scanner and I said, 'That's our area,' so I started gettin' my shoes on, and sure enough here come the page!" "Hell, I was in the shower, and I thought I heard the damn pager go off . . ." "Me and the ol' lady . . ."

The whiff of wintergreen you get because the Beagle doesn't make a move without a fresh plug of Kodiak. After all these years, the cud slips in between his cheek and gum like an afterthought and stays there. You think he'd take it out at mealtime, but he says no. "I could eat an apple, I got that big a pouch in there," he says.

You'll smell the wintergreen, but you'll never see the Beagle spit. He is of the man-enough-to-chew, man-enough-to-swallow school. My pancreas cramps at the thought of it. He says his dad called him the other day, told him to bring over a tin of Kodiak. The Beagle found this strange, because his dad is always getting on him to quit the chew. Turns out Dad's dog had worms, and he wanted the tobacco for a dewormer. The Beagle said it was a tussle, but they got a wad of snoose down Shep's gullet.

"That dog shit worms for a week!" said the Beagle. We were sitting around the fire hall at four in the morning, back from some call.

"And what does that tell you, Beagle?" I had to say it, to set him up.

"I sure as hell ain't got worms!"

━━━━━━━━

You create a fire department out of citizen volunteers, you're going to get some characters. A while back, we had a car fire during the day. The siren went off, and when we converged at the hall, there were exactly four of us. The assistant chief, who left his small-engine repair business unattended. Beagle, the cross-eyed butcher. Lane, a lean, wiry man who lives to ride rodeo bulls. And me. Lane recently had the muscles of his right forearm stripped from the bone in a factory accident. His arm is splinted, his hand feels nothing. We head out into the country, find the fire, put it out. Afterward we joke with the chief. About how he got stuck on a command consisting of one firefighter with one eye, one firefighter with one arm, and one firefighter who became the first volunteer in village history to miss the monthly meeting because of a poetry reading.

The organization of citizen fire brigades around disparate yokels like us seems a noble extension of civilized society, but it has not always been perceived as such. Back in A.D. 112, Pliny the Younger had been witness to a devastating fire in that portion of Asia Minor under his governance. In a letter to the Emperor Trajan, Pliny bemoaned the lack of firefighters and firefighting apparatus and requested that he be allowed to form a company of 150 firemen.

No dice, replied Emperor Trajan. "If people assemble for a common purpose," he wrote, "whatever name we give them and for whatever reason, they soon turn into a political club." He didn't mind making firefighting equipment and training available to the general public, but feared that any sort of sanctioned firefighting organization would end up fomenting political disturbances. History has proven, of course, that mostly we just foment water fights, raffles, and chicken feeds.

Our little volunteer department is actually a compromise drawn on the concepts of both Pliny and Trajan. We are organized and are a part of the local political scene inasmuch as we subsist in part on taxes, but because none of us is a career firefighter, we are for the most part descendants of Trajan's general public, trained to use equipment owned by the community at large.

The first firefighting equipment of record in New Auburn is referenced in the handwritten minutes of a village board meeting held April 2, 1902. *"Farmer's Store Cos. Bill for $2.28 for pails used at Hoard's fire, recommended to the consideration of the board. Accepted, carried."*

Not so fast there, Smokey. Four days later, April 6, 1902: *"Pail bill disallowed."* No reason given.

For the next three years, there are no more mentions of firefighting, but apparently, forward-thinking citizens realized borrowed pails weren't going to cut it in the long run. On June 3, 1905, the village board minutes contain the following entry, an entry which years hence would put me face-to-face with the One-Eyed Beagle:

A typewritten report from the Committee on fire protection and apparatus of their recommendations of May 27th and June 2nd, '05, was read and report filed with Clerk.

Moved and seconded that we approve of the recommendations of said Committee on fire protection in procuring fire fighting apparatus that will comply with the requirements of the insurance companies in raising our village from a fifth rate to a fourth rate town. Carried.

Duly note we are not just some fifth-rate town.

Moved and seconded that the Chairmen of the finance and street committees and the president of the village board negotiate with the American La France Fire Engine Company and procure their best terms and purchase one double 35 gallon Chemical Engine [rather than using a pump, the water pressure in a chemical engine was generated by combining water, soda, and acid in a sealed tank] *as per specifications furnished by their agent T. R. Johnstone under date of June 3rd and exhibited in writing. Carried.*

If you're going to have a fire truck, you better have a fire chief. And he'll need minions and underlings. We move to July 1, 1905:

Moved and seconded that for the purpose of organizing a volunteer fire company we hereby appoint Thomas W. Peterson as Fire Chief he to select his own assistants. Carried.

On August 2, 1905, it was time to kick the tires:

The Chemical Engine which was shipped by the LaFrance Company having arrived the president appointed a committee to check over invoice of paraphernalia and to see that the village gets a good demonstration of what the engine will do.

Three days pass. In minutes dated August 5, 1905, it appears agent T. R. Johnstone had a bad day:

The exhibition given by the agent was not satisfactory to the board and they asked Mr. Johnstone to give them a further demonstration to show what a chemical engine could accomplish.

The representative of the company agreed to do this on Monday, August 7, and the board adjourned to await the call of the president.

So they chewed the whole thing over for a few days. I imagine T. R. Johnstone in a room at the Hotel Auburn, downing stomach powders and calculating lost commissions. I don't think he ever had anything to worry about. Small-town folk want to appear skeptic and shrewd, but more than that, we really, really want the newfangled doodad. I imagine the board members met around town and did some dismissive bloviating, but you can hear corollary expositions in the local café to this very day, when some local goes on at length and volume about the frivolous vacuity of satellite television or Indian casinos, then hurries home to watch *Silk Stalkings* before catching the courtesy bus to bingo night. We know we're rubes, we just don't want to be *taken* for rubes. So they made old T.R. sweat some, and they performed some procedural gymnastics, but on August 10, 1905, New Auburn got itself a fire truck:

> *Board met in special session at call of President to make settlement of the matter of the chemical engine . . . the committee on Engine reported that they did not prepare another demonstration feeling that it would not satisfy all, there being so much sentiment against the engine, and thus they would save extra cost. The committee was satisfied that the first exhibition was not a fair test. Committee's report was on motion, seconded. Adopted.*
>
> *Moved and seconded to postpone the acceptance and settlement till some future time. Motion lost.*
>
> *Motion made that we reject this engine. Motion lost.*
>
> *Motion and second that we accept the engine and that the President and Clerk be authorized to draw an order for ($200) two hundred dollars to make first payment on contract and to sign all necessary warrants in settlement of the same. Carried by unanimous vote. Moved and carried to adjourn.*

Really, the village board deserves a little credit. In the space of three months, our burg went from appropriated buckets to a full-blown department. From fifth rate to fourth rate.

The chief arranged to store the fire engine at the village hall. The local marshal hauled it to fire scenes at a buck a shot. (The same minutes that indicate the marshal was paid $4 for hauling the fire engine to four different fires also indicated that he was paid $2.60 "for care of tramps.") There remained the difficulty of alerting fire-fighters to the presence of a fire. The solution came about on January 6, 1906, in the form of fortuitous fallout from a controversy involving school equipment:

> To set aside future misunderstanding it was moved and carried that the ownership of the school bell be transferred to school district No. 11, the Village to reserve the right of the use of the bell by the Fire department for fire and practice call.

Just over three years later, in the minutes of February 3, 1909, it was recorded that an order for $200 was drawn "to pay the final note on the Village fire engine." Six months later, on August 4, 1909, the minutes state that "a representative of a hook and ladder company was present and laid a proposition before the Board for them to consider the purchase of a hook and ladder truck."

This is the thing about firefighters. You give them toys, and they want more toys. Today we have seven trucks. Two pumpers, three tankers, one rapid-attack pumper, and a rescue van. One of the pumpers is twenty-seven years old. We use it mostly to fight wildfires. The Beagle is one of the few people on the department able to run it with confidence. The new pumper is fourteen years old. It has an open, rear-facing cab unit in which three firefighters can ride. In the winter, by the time you get to the scene, your fingers are so cold you can't work the buckles on the air packs. The tankers hold roughly 2,300 gallons of water each. Because we rarely have access to fire hydrants, we use a shuttle system, running water to the fire scene in a constant rotation of tankers. The rapid-attack pumper is our newest vehicle. We got it primarily for fighting brush fires (it has four-wheel drive and winches fore and aft), but with its on-board water and twin inch-and-a-half hose reels, it can be invaluable in getting an early jump on a house fire while the main pumper is being set up. The rescue van is a 1985 Ford panel van. We bolted an old school-bus seat to the floor and use it mainly for responding to medical emergencies.

All of the rigs carry extra equipment. Two of the tankers are equipped with small outboard pumps and can be used to fight grass fires. The main pumper is crammed with gear—air packs, fire axes, an array of nozzles and couplers, 1,200 feet of hose, chimney fire equipment, powerful flashlights, a roof saw, a collapsible water reservoir, hose wrenches, suction apparatus, a generator, a rackful of ladders. Our most recent acquisition is a thermal imager. It can see through smoke, detect heat inside a wall, show the outline of a body in the darkness. It is, in short, magic. It fits in a case half the size of a pillow. It cost $15,000.

Some of the money we have to raise on our own. It's not all covered by the tax rolls. Fund-raisers are a way of life in most volunteer departments. We'll have a pancake breakfast now and then, or sell some barbecued chicken. We have a raffle almost every year. For as long as I can remember, two of the top five prizes have been firearms. I always get a kick out of that. All the efforts to do away with guns, and here we are giving them away.

Our most well-worn money-maker is the Jamboree Days beer tent. We run it for three days in conjunction with a softball tournament. The softball tournament kicks off on Friday night with an exhibition game between our fire department and the fire department from the city of Chetek, nine miles to the north. A lot of the guys on the Chetek department play league ball. A lot of the guys on our department play pinochle. It shows. We get trounced on a yearly basis, but it's a real good time. Not too serious, a lot of hollering and shenanigans. Beer cups in the outfield. It pays off in little ways throughout the year when the two departments fulfill their mutual aid agreements by helping each other out on big calls. You're in a ditch somewhere, or packing up to head into a burning barn, and you recognize the person helping you as the same guy that blew a shoe rounding third, or who lent you his glove in the outfield. It gives you a little human common ground. The chiefs and government representatives hash out the specifics of the mutual aid contract at big tables during long meetings. The spirit of the contract works itself out on the softball field.

The real softball tournament kicks off at eight A.M. on Saturday, runs 'til dark, and picks up again Sunday morning. Teams come from all over. The softball field is directly adjacent to the beer tent, which is no accident—amateur softball players are your prime suds demographic. We always hope for hot weather. When it rains, the teams still show up, but beer sales tank.

The Beagle feels he is past his softball prime, so he spends most of the weekend tending the beer-tent bar. He'll usually punch out early Saturday night so he can drink and dance some, but the rest of the weekend, you can find him behind the plywood stand, filling pitchers. Last year the Beagle and I got down to the park early Sunday morning to do a little cleanup before the crowds arrived. It wasn't even nine A.M. and the first softball game of the day was already under way. We were picking up plastic cups and straightening tables when this guy walked into the tent and asked if he could get a beer. "I guess there's no law against it," said the Beagle. He went behind the bar and got a clean cup. The guy propped his elbows on the plywood. I didn't recognize him, but he wasn't dressed for softball. Bob took his money and passed him the beer. The guy raised the cup, and just when it was at his lips, someone smacked a long fly ball. At the crack of the bat, the man's head snapped to the right. His beer stayed right where it was, fixed in midair. He scanned the field for a minute, watched the outfielder make the catch, then brought his lips back in line with the cup, which hadn't moved. Ducking forward to take a pull at the foam, he rolled his eyes at the Beagle and shook his head.

"Little early in the mornin' for softball!"

• • •

The only equipment some of your early colonial firefighters had were leather buckets made by Dutch shoemakers. The firefighters worked in pairs, the buckets suspended between them on two parallel poles. A good team could hustle eighteen buckets. This being prior to the age of personalized license plates, many of the firefighters gussied up their buckets with embroidery and gold leaf. Without a pickup window in which to strategically hang their helmet and turnout gear, you probably had your guys who ran around town with their personalized bucket dangling off their mule. Operative theory being, chicks dig firefighters, and why should colonial chicks be any different?

Before I moved back and joined the department, someone out in the county called in a garage fire. Bryan Swanson and my brother Jed were working in that neck of the woods, and got there first. The flames were just taking hold. Bryan grabbed a plastic bucket, filled it in the ditch, and handed it up to Jed. Jed flung the water on the flames. It was touch and go for a while, but when the fire trucks rolled up, Bryan and Jed were standing there in their gear with their buckets and the flames were flat. "Get the wet stuff on the red stuff," the old-timers say, and sometimes the old ways will do.

Right now, the Beagle needs a little extra cash. Wife Number Two hit the road a while back, but it will take a thousand bucks to do the divorce and make it official. He'll get the money in November, he says, off all the overtime he accumulates butchering during deer season. The deer come in nonstop then, stiff in the back of pickups, slung over trunks, stacked in trailers. The Beagle will cut up fifteen, twenty deer a day. He is at work by four A.M., and he leaves for home, bone-tired and nicked up, at eight P.M. It goes on like that for several weeks. My family and I butcher our own deer, but I dropped off a few extras for the Hunters Against Hunger program last year, and it was strange to see the Beagle in his apron, with his knife and steel, strange in that off-center little way it always is when we see acquaintances outside the usual context. The deer—over 200 of them—were all dragged in headfirst and laid out four wide along the chutes leading to the killing floor. The effect was riverine. One thought of logjams. Most of the deer were hung from trees or rafters after they were shot, and had frozen with their back legs and necks extended, and their forelegs bent at the knee. All those deer in that position, it looked like the mass start of a deer triathlon, everybody doing the backstroke. I know what it is to skin and bone a deer— my family and I do probably twenty a year—and when the Beagle tells me he sees the river of upturned deer legs in his sleep, I believe him. But this year, for every hide that hits the floor, another couple of dollars go in the divorce kitty.

We talked about it on our way back from a call in the rescue van, just me and him. An old lady had fallen in her bathroom and become wedged between the toilet and the tub. She had been there all night. She was cold to the touch and unable to talk. She had terrified eyes. We took her vital signs and gave her oxygen, and then the Beagle covered her with a blanket and I held her hand, talking to her until the ambulance came. Sometimes the best thing we can do is give someone a little comfort. On the ride back, we got to talking about women, and the Beagle said he knew this last marriage was in trouble when his wife wouldn't let him look at the checkbook. I agreed that might be one of your Top Five Signs. Other disagreements—about bills, about stepchildren—followed, until eventually the Beagle reckoned it was time—once again—to split the blanket. The One-Eyed Beagle, *el lobo solo*. But I had heard he was already seeing another woman. The Beagle never stays lonely long. We were crossing the overpass when I said as much. I asked him what his secret was. I was in the passenger seat, and he turned and grinned at me. "I got a big sign on my forehead," he said. "Blinking red lights. It says, *dumb bastard*!" He turns his eye back to the road, and laughs like it's the best joke ever. What the Beagle has is equanimity.

Back in the mid-1600s, certain prominent citizens of New Amsterdam were assigned by the city government to patrol the streets at night with large wooden rattles. Upon spotting a fire, they spun the rattles, waking the locals, who jumped out of bed and formed bucket brigades. According to historian and *Firehouse* contributing editor Paul Hashagan, the "rattle watch" is generally recognized as the first organized attempt at fighting fire in America. You'll read here and there that Benjamin Franklin founded the first volunteer fire department in America. That's inaccurate, but it is widely agreed that when he formed Philadelphia's Union Fire Company in 1736, he set the organizational standard for all volunteer brigades to follow. Franklin's fire company would put your fire out no matter who you were; prior to this, many fire "clubs" and "societies" existed only to protect paying members. The Friendship Veterans Fire Engine Company of Alexandria, Virginia, counted among its members a surveyor named George Washington. In 1774, he bought the city its first fire engine. Thomas Jefferson, Sam Adams, John Hancock, Paul Revere, Alexander Hamilton, Aaron Burr, Benedict Arnold, James Buchanan, and Millard Fillmore were all volunteer firefighters. The first female volunteer firefighter of record was a slave named Molly Williams. The juxtaposition of "volunteer" and "slave" produces a certain irony.

If I could swing the time-travel thing, it would be a kick to convene Ben Franklin and the Beagle over some beers and venison sausage. Maybe a basket of deep-fried cheese curds. It would be a ripping chat. They would speak of firefighting, of course. Of all that has changed, and all that remains the same. It is difficult to know what the Beagle would have made of the Franklin chestnut "Keep your eyes wide open before marriage, half shut afterwards." There is much there of pertinence to a cross-eyed double-divorcé. Franklin filled *Poor Richard's Almanack* with that sort of wit, but here too the Beagle would be more than able to return serve. The Beagle can turn a phrase. One frosty morning we work half an hour to extricate a young man from a mangled car. Later, the Beagle declares, "Hell, you couldn't a got that guy outta there with a shoehorn and a plunger!" When rotund Tee Norman and skinny Dude Fawcett get to horsing around next to the portable reservoir during a training session and Tee pulls Dude into the water, I try to describe the thrashing and splashing to someone back at the fire hall, and the Beagle breaks in. "What it looked like," he says, "was a water snake wrasslin' a walrus!" Once the Beagle and I made a call after dark on a godforsaken logging trail and got jumped by some cheesehead *Deliverance* feeb. The Beagle was cool, but later, when we were safely home, he turned that eye on me. "Hell, Mikey, I was nervous as a whore in church!"

Ben Franklin was fond of promoting a list of thirteen virtues. Temperance, moderation, and chastity among them. Historical records and assorted offspring suggest he knocked holes in the list on a regular basis, perhaps leading him to write, "A benevolent man should allow a few faults in himself, to keep his friends in countenance." Your top-grade aphorist covers all the angles. Truly, though, what you're hearing there is equanimity again. I crave equanimity. I have more than I did as a young man, and am beginning to suspect—rather hopefully—it is a product of age. Equanimity is the only thing that will save you from this world, and it doesn't come easy. Or cheap. And you can't fake it for long. Guys like Ben and the Beagle, they do not succumb to false hope, but neither do they cave in to absolute despair. Don't expect much, but don't give up. "People ask me," says the Beagle, "they say, 'You must be upset about the divorce.' I say, 'Nope. It's over. That simple.'" I ask the Beagle why he stays on the fire department. "I do it because I enjoy it," he says. Matter-of-fact. "Same reason I've been cutting meat for twenty-five years—I enjoy it." A little pause. "Course when I'm an old man, my hands will be so bent up I won't be able to scratch my ass." A big laugh. "Who is rich?" wrote Franklin. "He that rejoices in his Portion."

We get paged at two in the morning. A semi full of bananas has rolled over on the interstate. The dispatcher says the truck is north of the overpass, in the median. I won the race to the hall, so I'm driving the van, and the Beagle is riding shotgun. I hammer down the on-ramp and slide over to run in the passing lane so that we can scan the median. We're cruising at about seventy when this pickup roars up the right side of us. The driver is gesticulating and pointing back down the road. The Beagle has his sleepy face to the window, peering, trying to figure out what the guy wants. The brim of his helmet keeps bumping the glass. After some charades, we realize the driver is trying to tell us the accident is *south* of the overpass. The dispatcher sent us the wrong way. We hit the crossover and backtrack, and sure enough, we find the semi, and the tumbled mound of bananas. The semi is destroyed but the driver is OK. I'm just wishing I could hear the conversation in that northbound pickup truck. What they must have thought—first all those ba-nanas, then the wrong-way rescuers, speeding directly away from the scene, and then this drowsy cross-eyed guy goggling at them from beneath his slantways fire helmet. The Beagle and I are not al-ways able to support the image of Ace Rescuers.

You try. You do feel a responsibility. You are, after all, working on behalf of the community, using equipment the community helped pay for. It's fun to play at this, to give each other the needle and treat the whole thing like fun with cool toys, but there's a seri-ousness at the base of it all.

When polls are conducted asking people who they most trust and admire, firefighters consistently finish at the top. It's nice to pig-gyback to that, even as a citizen volunteer, but the blessing isn't a given. A single misstep and you break a trust that can take decades to repair. Every year there are reports of volunteer firefighters start-ing fires so that they can go out on calls. This being related to human nature, it is nothing new. In *Fire and Civilization*, Johan Goudsblom mentions historical instances of firefighters committing arson recorded as far back as A.D. 64. He cites motives including looting, self-aggrandizement, and pyromania. You want to be a hero bad enough, you make your own disasters. There have been cases of firefighters starting fires so they could earn extra money. You'd have to burn down a lot of stuff around here to make it financially viable.

You're on call twenty-four hours a day for free. You get ten dollars an hour for fighting a fire or making a medical call. You get seven dollars for attending the monthly meeting, and seven dollars an hour for training, with the training not to exceed two hours. The average New Auburn firefighter took home around $400 last year; the largest check was for $1,561. I'll get some justifiable argument from professional firefighters, but in our situation, I prefer low pay. Weeds people out. Keeps your motivations pure. If you get big enough to where you need full-time professionals, pay them accordingly. In our case, I prefer to believe that my neighbors are showing up simply to help, not to pad their Christmas fund.

The Roman Marcus Crassus, who operated until 53 B.C., used to show up at fires with a corps of five hundred slaves trained as builders. With his men standing by, Crassus would find the owners of the burning buildings and those adjacent and make an offer to buy the structures at a ridiculously low price. Once the owners agreed, Crassus would order his men to put the fire out. As soon as the smoke cleared, Crassus would set his crews to rebuilding. He then resold the properties at a grand profit. I told the chief maybe we wanted to think about some sort of similar program. Our motto would be, First You Pay, Then We Spray.

Rusty, one of the firefighters who keeps our trucks tuned, just donated a kidney to his son-in-law. He and the Beagle have something in common now, although Rusty's eyes still track. Twenty-four firefighters on our roster, and two have given away kidneys. I wonder how that stacks up against the general population. I don't think it's a coincidence. It's easy to look at the Beagle simply as a character—in the "he's quite a character" sense—and he comes well armed. But when his first ex-wife's new husband got serious facial and inhalation burns from an exploding heater, it was the Beagle who separated from the responding crew and knelt at the guy's head, giving him the best care he knew how. Down there on his knees, his cud working, his eye shooting off south, doing the neighborly thing. I would trust the Beagle with my life. Not would, *do*. He'll be goofy, but he'll be *there*.

Selflessness has its drawbacks, and the Beagle will point them out. We get dispatched to a forest fire after midnight. One of the decisions you make when calls come in at that time of night is whether or not to stop and pee. Tonight nobody did. The forest fire turns out to be a small brush fire, and after an hour on scene, we're on our way back to the hall. There are four of us jammed in the cab. "Jeez, I gotta take a leak," says Matt Jeffski.

"How ya think I feel?" pipes up the Beagle. "I only got one kidney!"

The Beagle has other problems. Both his ex-wives work at the only gas station and convenience store in town. So he's gotten to where he avoids the Gas-N-Go. Drives to Bloomer for his gas and morning coffee. Sometimes he'll send his new girlfriend in to get him a can of chew. The ex's have been known to give her the evil eye, and sometimes they slap the Kodiak down a little sharply. "They don't like it," says the Beagle, "but they know my brand!" Big guffaw.

The year has cycled around, and it's Jamboree Days again. It's Saturday night, late. We've got a nice little husband/wife band in, they do country and rock covers, old and new, and under the big white tent, the dance floor is jammed. The Beagle had his twenty-five-year class reunion today. He has just arrived from the party and, frankly, he's happily loaded. He's got his girlfriend with him. She's a stout girl with smiling eyes, looks like she could toss some hay bales. The Beagle has his groove on. He dances song after song, twisting and shucking and jiving and doing this move where he twiddles his butt and pops his knees up and down in sequence, like a beefy marionette. Every now and then he gives his sweetie a little belly bump. Me and the Chief, we're not drinking. We're sitting in lawn chairs in the grass on the outskirts, and the dancing Beagle has us cracked up. We reckon it's like watching some sort of courtship ritual on *Animal Planet* or the Discovery channel. When he finally leaves us, it is with a grin and a salute, and someone to keep him company. Monday morning he'll be hoisting sides of beef before the sun comes up, but tonight he is a dancer and a lover, and he is tripping the Beagle light fantastic.

I'm a teetotal non-dancer, but I have come to love the nights under the Jamboree Days beer tent. All the happy sweaty faces, all the goofing after midnight, all the loud shooting of the breeze over yesterday's favorites and today's greatest hits. Every year I recognize more faces. I'll sit in my lawn chair with my radio by my ear so I can hear if we get a call, and I'll be seized by how glorious it is in this tumultuous world to be so simply free and happy. A softball toss from the beer tent, there is a little rise, and atop the rise is a little cemetery. It was surveyed and platted in 1882 by David W. Cartwright, the man who founded this town. His grave is up there. The tombstone is a simple rectangle. Cartwright was a strict Seventh-Day Baptist who took his name off this town when the council approved its first liquor license, so I figure he wouldn't be too happy about the drinking, but it's nice to think of his bones up there, maybe catching a little vibration from all the dancing feet that followed him to this town. I think he'd be glad to see us happy here. Cartwright's presence gives me a sense of history, reminds me that even Saturday nights in a beer tent take their place in the course of human events.

The lady down at the Gas-N-Go let me look through her collection of old pictures and newspaper clippings last year, and I came across an article in the Thursday, June 17, 1976, issue of the *Chetek Alert* recognizing a firefighter named Ivan Boldon for fifty years of service to the New Auburn Area Fire Department. The article said when Ivan joined the department in 1926, they were still using the old chemical pumper. The tanks were mounted on a trailer cart hitched to a Model T Ford. There were several pictures, including a group photo of the department members. The Beagle is right up there in the front row. He had just joined up, right out of high school. I like the idea that this chain—me knowing the Beagle, the Beagle knowing Ivan Boldon, Ivan Boldon having used the old chemical pumper—puts us in almost tangible contact with the very first days of the department. The Beagle wouldn't put it in these terms, but he knows that out here, rescue is less about throwing ropes or stanching blood or running into burning buildings than it is about assuming a role in a quirky narrative that weaves itself through generations. The events arrange themselves along a communal timeline. The community is the constant. Volunteer firefighters come and go. The old-timers hand down equipment and stories, show up occasionally when we're shorthanded, but most of all they help us recognize that time—*our time*—is transient.

Whenever we finish up a call, the officer in charge fills out a run report. The report includes a roster, arranged in order of seniority. If you pull a report from a run the Beagle and I have been on, you will find a check beside Beagle's Christian name, right up there at the top, and down near the bottom, working its way up, a check beside mine. Proof in ink that we were present at the making of history, no matter how small the event. A little detail within the brief parentheses that is our existence.

The Beagle says he'll keep answering the pager until he can't make it down here anymore. Gonna get himself a wheelchair with flashing lights on it, he says. In the picture from the *Chetek Alert*, he is long-haired and slim, clean-shaven except for a set of muttonchop sideburns. He's looking straight ahead, with both eyes.

Maybe you could meet the Beagle someday. He knows his eye can make a person uncomfortable, and so he has this story he'll tell to break the ice. We've all seen it several times. A newcomer will be looking up, down, sideways, anything so as not to seem to be staring. The Beagle smiles, says, "You probably noticed my eye."

The person might shrug, or demur, but the Beagle continues, matter-of-fact.

"Deal is, I was born without an eyelid."

Now he has their attention.

"Yah, strangest thing. No eyelid on that eye. Doc said he'd never seen nothin' like it. He told my parents it was a long shot, but there was one thing they could try."

By now the person is usually leaning right in.

"What they did is, when they circumcised me, they took the extra skin and they made an eyelid from it."

The listener usually gulps, but is invariably staring hard at the crossed eye.

"Yep," says the Beagle, "been cockeyed ever since!"

3

TRICKY

NEW AUBURN DRAWS its name from an eighteenth-century elegiac pastorale. This might not be your first thought if you come to town, say, on a November Saturday evening when all the pickup trucks are lined up at the Gas-N-Go with dead deer hanging over the tailgate, or if you exit the highway behind a spreader truck full of turkey manure. If you approach from the north, past Slinger Joe's automobile graveyard, past the Packer green and gold of Pat's Pub, past the abandoned laundromat—still half-toppled and wrapped in yellow crime-scene tape since the rainy evening a year ago when Tricky Jackson sideswiped it running seventy in a thirty-five—if you notice there are four defunct service stations and a desolate train siding, you may strain at the relevance of lyric verse. But the name on our old silver water tower originated from the Oliver Goldsmith poem "The Deserted Village," written in 1770 and opening with the line, "Sweet Auburn! loveliest village of the plain . . ." More than a century after it was coined, we took that name for our own. It didn't take easily. Frankly, it was the fourth choice.

Even the staunchest civic booster would have to admit that the bloom is off the rose here in New Auburn. Our eleven streets are tree-lined and peaceful. There are a number of trim houses on neat lawns. But rust and desperation are never more than a backyard away. The family next door to me is hard to sort. Many children, several women, two men. The fighting frequently spills out into the yard, which has steadily disappeared under a welter of absurd possessions: a tangle of thirty unworkable bicycles; a mossy camper; a selection of detached automobile seats; an inoperative ride-on lawn mower wrapped—Christo-like—in a blue tarp; a huge rotting speedboat. The village board sent someone around to recite nuisance ordinances chapter and verse, but beyond rearranging the bikes and aligning the camper with the speedboat—feng shui *primitif*—nothing has changed. You take what you can get in this life. Someone calls you white trash, you go with it, and fight like hell to keep your trash. You understand it is only a matter of distinctions: yuppies with their shiny trash, church ladies with their hand-stitched trash, solid citizens with their secret trash. In a yard just outside town, a spray-painted piece of frayed plywood leans against a tree. It reads Trans Ams: 2 for $2000. It has been there for two years.

The old man and his adult son tinker on the speedboat now and then. They pop the cowling, poke around with wrenches, stare, cuss. The old man stands inside the hull and yanks on the pull rope, and the huge motor rumbles and smokes, then dies with a dry cough. The speedboat has never left the yard. The slipcover is mildewed and undone, and the deck is layered with decaying leaves. Out on the street, the summer traffic is rarely more than desultory, but it does pick up a little on the weekends, with people cutting through town on their way to summer cottages and lake properties to the north. Many of them are towing beautiful boats. The man and son talk as they work, and if I am doing dishes at the sink, I catch fragments through the screen, but it is their persistence and glances toward the road that speak most clearly, and the message is, life is a box o' shit, but by God we've got a speedboat, and one of these days we'll get that son of a tatcher runnin', and we'll go out some Sunday fuckin' afternoon and we'll blow them Ill-*annoy* tourist bastards right outta the water. They work awhile, the old man and the kid, then disappear into the house for days.

Four tries it took, to name this village. In 1875, a man named David W. Cartwright located a clearing in the great pines and put up a sawmill. With the first boards off the saw deck, he enclosed the mill. Then he built a house. Then his employees built their own houses around the mill, forming a settlement that became known as Cartwright Mills. In 1882, for the convenience of the postal service, the name was shortened to Cartwright. In 1902, a saloon keeper approached the village board and requested a liquor license. Cartwright—a devout Seventh-Day Baptist—declared that as long as the town bore his name, liquor licenses were out of the question. The board voted to change the name to Auburn. Unfortunately, the adjacent township was already named Auburn, and so in 1904, pleading confusion, the Chicago Railroad requested that the town change its name once more. The board tacked on "New," and so it is we became New Auburn.

David W. Cartwright was a late arrival. Glaciers were the original visitors, ebbing and flowing throughout the Pleistocene epoch. The ice made its last big push 25,000 years ago, advancing until two-thirds of the land now known as the state of Wisconsin were blanketed. My backyard was a mile deep in ice. When the glacier finally withdrew, it did so reluctantly, and 10,000 years ago, on the cusp of the Holocene epoch, the Chippewa Lobe of the great Laurentide Ice Sheet made one last charge south, stopping just short of New Auburn before retreating for good. In its wake, we were left a raw, poetic topography of kettles and moraines, kames and eskers, and drumlins.

Wildlife thrived in the post-glacial period, and humans followed. A copper lance point found outside town in the late 1900s suggests that Paleo-Indian hunters were in the area 6,000 years ago. At some point, Sioux Indians arrived. Later, Ojibwa Indians filtered down from the north. By the 1760s, the two tribes were warring over the territory. After many battles—one of which took place on the shores of a local lake now studded with summer homes—the Ojibwa drove out the Sioux for good.

White men first appeared in the form of fur-trading Frenchmen. In 1767, Jonathan Carver, a captain in the New England militia, passed through on his way to Lake Superior. He would later report that because of his "deep friendship" with the Indian chiefs of the area, they had deeded him a vast tract of land comprising a very large part of what is now northwestern Wisconsin—including what is now Chippewa (from Ojibwa) County, in which New Auburn resides. Carver's claim was ultimately denied by both the British and post-revolutionary American governments, but the white incursion had begun. By the time the lumberjacks swept through in the mid to late 1800s, settlement of the area was well under way, fueled by the usual mincemeat of destiny and deception. Save for a few stragglers, the Indians were gone, leaving behind arrowheads and wild rice beds. Today, when I see the cornfields sprouting duplexes and hear my neighbors mourning the loss of the family farm—a decimation which began in the 1980s and is now virtually complete—my gut sympathies lie foursquare with the displaced farmers, but I can't help but think that this land has been lost before.

The night Tricky Jackson wiped out the laundromat, I was six miles out of town and on my way home when the pager went off, so I just kicked the accelerator a little. It was raining, and the ruts on the old county highway were brimming with water. I straddled the ruts to avoid hydroplaning. I switched my handheld radio over to scan mode and heard the fire department respond, as well as the Bloomer ambulance.

Just north of the village limits, the county highway and Five Mile Road converge at a narrow angle. About a quarter mile out, I looked east across the fields to Five Mile Road, and there's my mom, hammer down in her big old Lincoln, bearing through the rain like a mini-destroyer. We are on intersecting vectors. I figure it's Mom behind the wheel, because it's unusual to see the Lincoln operating at these speeds. Usually Dad is driving, and it is a rare thing for him to redline the old car. He drives farmer-style: middle of the road, attention focused sideways on the state of the crops, all day to get there. He frequently chauffeurs Mom to calls, napping in the car until the carnage is cleared. But tonight he has stayed home to baby-sit one of the legion foster children they care for (nearly 60, my mother hasn't stopped changing diapers since she had me, her first-born), and when the Lincoln pulls in front of me at the intersection, sure enough, there's Mom's gray hair, up in a bun, just visible over the head rest. They got the Lincoln well worn from some traveling salesman—it's a square, non-aerodynamic barge, missing a few hub-caps. I believe Dad's theory is to surround the woman he loves with a lot of steel. It's a far cry from the days when he toted the variable baker's half dozen of us (our family, while always large, fluctuated constantly) around in a VW bus.

So there I am, flying in formation behind my mother, on our way to another accident. My mother, my brother John, and I all took the EMT course together back in 1988. I was left with an abiding image when I looked across the vocational college shop floor during our extrication training to see my mother—she is a petite five foot three, given to pinning her hair up and wearing modest skirts, and I have never known her to utter even the slightest off-color comment—clad in a hard hat and goggles, armed with the Jaws of Life, ripping the door off a Gremlin. I shouldn't have been surprised, I suppose. The toughness was always there. She used to wear construction boots under her maxi skirts.

The wreck is right on the main drag, and it looks as if most of the town has turned out to have a look. Normally I get righteously cranky about gawkers—what if it was you or your mother lying there?—but tonight I really can't blame them. It's quite a scene. Tricky's car is crosswise on the centerline, facing backward. The laundromat—an apartment, actually, but it was a laundromat when I was a kid, and so it is forever more—looks as if someone rolled a one-ton bowling ball along the street-side wall. The pale yellow siding is smeared and folded inward, and the eave teeters precariously over the sidewalk. The interior is visible through gaps in the wall. The man who rents the place is outside, telling anyone who will listen that he was lying on the couch, "and all of a sudden, the wall started coming at me." He's glad he put the couch where he did.

Witnesses said the car came howling down the wet pavement, hydroplaned, got backward, hit the laundromat, ricocheted into a parked car, and slid to where it sat. Tricky denies all this, says he was northbound, not southbound, that the parked car wasn't parked at all, but rather pulled out in front of him, and that the driver fled immediately after the crash. Even the most perfunctory review of the evidence on scene—from the skid marks to the debris trail—establishes this as utter hogwash, but Tricky is adamant, and keeps running through the crowd, exhorting everyone to "find the son of a bitch that was driving that other car."

Three people piled out of the car when it came to a stop, and two remained in the backseat. Out and about are Tricky and his friends, Bill and Elmo. Still in the car are Travis and Shirley. Travis is badly injured and semiconscious. Shirley is shaking Travis, and slapping his face. Somewhere along the line, Tricky says, "He was unconscious when we put him in the car."

It might seem obvious, but what Tricky Jackson has done here is, he has created a scene. And in the parlance of rescue, what we're trying to do now is establish scene control. Entire emergency-service seminars are devoted to the topic. It begins with the scene size-up, which in this case probably began the moment the chief rounded the corner and thought, "Aw, geez." The size-up is critical. It's that moment you take to look for hazards—downed electrical lines, leaking boxcars, spilled gasoline, sad or crazy mopes with guns. It will be drummed into your head from your first EMT class to your most recent firefighting lecture: Do not go in until you are certain the scene is secure. "Dead heroes cannot save lives," writes Nancy L. Caroline in the third edition of *Emergency Care in the Streets*. We are especially careful when called to domestic disputes, and never enter the house without a police officer first clearing the way. Rushing in too quickly can get you into trouble. The most benign-looking delivery truck may be leaking invisible killer gases, and suddenly your fender-bender is a hazardous-materials scene. We are taught to hang back, uphill and upwind, until we know what we're dealing with. Still, you get wound up and forget. Cops forget, too, and because they are often first on scene, you judge how close to get by where the first cop is lying. At a recent haz-mat course, the instructor called this phenomenon the "cop-o-meter."

In this case, there are no downed power lines or leaking chemical tanks, but it looks like Tricky's gas tank might be leaking, so the chief sends the attack pumper in to charge a line so we have water at the ready, just a nozzle-flip away. The next most obvious hazard will be traffic, since Tricky is right in the middle of the old highway. To this end, the chief dispatches firemen with traffic wands to either end of town, to reroute traffic a few blocks over. Cross-street access is blocked off by the main pumper. The next step is to identify and assess the victims. Not so easy in this case, as three out of the five are out of the car, mixing in with the onlookers.

Scene control is an amorphous art. You have to adapt your control to the scene. In this case, we've got onlookers who might wander into harm's way, we've got belligerent patients, we've got seriously injured patients, we've got noise and confusion. We've also got lots of help, which is essential, but can lead to trouble if there isn't some sort of co-ordinated command and control. We need to find a focus. So we fan out. Some are preparing the cutting tools. Some are tending to Travis. Our concerns are over the severity of his injury and his altered level of consciousness, or LOC. He's drifting in and out, and he looks pale in the backseat. He's clutching his deformed leg. We manage to convince Shirley that slapping Travis won't help, and she has exited the vehicle. Beagle reaches through the broken window and takes C-spine traction on Travis, holding his head in line with his spine. Someone else

cuts away his pant leg to expose the injured thigh. The foot on that leg
is wedged under the driver's seat, holding it at an absurd angle. The
car is a two-door, and in order to safely remove him, we'll have to cut
the roof away. I am not dressed for this. If I had responded with the
fire trucks, I would have my protective turnout gear on. As it is, I'm
running around in baggy shorts. The rain has stopped. That helps.

The chief has sent fire trucks up one block either way to reroute
traffic. The ambulance is idling behind the wrecked car, the engine
that runs the cutting tools is wide open and sounds like a frantic ro-
totiller. The size of the crowd that has gathered suggests that over
half the town has turned out. With the exception of Travis, trapped
in the car, our so-called patients are milling about. At one point, my
mother tracks down Tricky and Elmo. She kneels in the wet grass
and attempts to interview them, and find out if they are injured.
Tricky is *motherfucker* this and *motherfucker* that, and finally I kneel
down in front of him, get right in his face, and bark, "*Hey!*" He
blinks. "This is my mom. She doesn't have to listen to that kind of
talk." I'm pissed, I'll admit. But it works, for a little while. Tricky
apologizes, and she is able to check out the cut on his nose and ask a
few more questions. Then he is off and running again, rushing over
to his car—rusty and crumpled fore-and-aft—to berate the firefighters peeling the roof. As the jaws bite into the window posts,
Tricky rushes to intervene. "What the hell!" he yells. "Don't wreck
my fuckin' car!" Tricky is irony-proof.

Irony is in part a matter of perspective. Observing a village fallen
into decay, Oliver Goldsmith was moved to compose an elegiac pastorale. Seeing his ravaged clunker under attack, Tricky Jackson ut-
tered his own sort of elegiac. Rearranging the detritus covering their
lawn, my neighbors become curators of found sculpture. Because I
am rooted in this place, it does not strike me as absurd to love the
junk. Things look different from a distance. Even your own backyards. Not so long ago, the *St. Paul Pioneer Press* sought the opinion
of expert gardener-writer C. Colston Burrell on the subject of lawn

ornaments. Mr. Burrell declared that it is time to "lighten up and fret less about being tasteful." Grab yourself a Pabst and pack of string cheese, Mr. Burrell, and welcome to our garden party. That's our dust you're tasting as you round the cultural curve. We threw off the chains of tasteful restraint the day they invented plywood. The wooden tulip, the plastic sunflower, the begonia-filled toilet? The duck with the windmill wings? Bear cubs in particle board silhouette? LP tanks as *trompe-l'oeil* corncobs? The miniature Green Bay Packer on a rope swing? Armed with jigsaws and leftover house paint, we have been expanding the boundaries—and plumbing the depths—of yard ornamentation for decades.

Mr. Burrell's quote appeared in a gardening column devoted to *Garden Whimsy*, a book celebrating the renaissance of lawn art in the new millennium. Garden whimsy, the article says, has been raised to new levels of fun and fancy, and has the gardening community "abuzz." In resounding agreement, the Garden Writers Association of America have awarded *Garden Whimsy* the coveted Quill and Trowel Award.

Good people of the Quill and Trowel, where have you been? Have you been blinded by your gazing balls? Did you miss the Golden Age of the Bent-Over Grandma? The plywood grandmas have dwindled now, but they are still to be found around these parts, their paint flaking, their plywood delaminating in the sun and rain, Grandma's exposed polka-dot bloomers leached of color.

When they first appeared on the scene, the plywood grandmas were culturally divisive. Some social critics declared them trashy and demeaning, others found them a real knee-slapper. Whatever the take, they proliferated, and soon some joker designed a companion piece: a rearview of a grandpa in overalls, a red handkerchief out his back pocket and his hand planted firmly on grandma's ample rear. Eventually, a third-generation piece appeared—a little plywood boy, taking a pee on a tree. We had achieved thematic apogee.

In New Auburn, as in any place, lawn art is a form of public display as simultaneously trite and revealing as bumper stickers and nose rings. Between the porch and the road, iconography sprouts: the bathtub Madonna, the milk-cow windmill, giant mushrooms carved from stumps, yellow Norwegian Crossing traffic signs— these images speak to who we are.

They do not always speak clearly. The most ubiquitous element of garden whimsy in western Wisconsin is the concrete deer lawn ornament. Why, in a state teeming with whitetails—in the autumn, their mangled and abraded bodies line the roads like organic brown speed bumps—we choose to buy three-quarter-sized concrete replicas by the herd and stick them in the front lawn to mow around, I do not know. I used to wonder the same thing about the proliferation of fiberglass lawn cows, but now that California has stolen our Dairyland thunder and family farms are rapidly becoming a historical footnote, the fake Holsteins have taken on a commemorative air. But the fake deer are a constant source of cultural cognitive dissonance. During hunting season, many of them are gussied up in blaze orange bunting. Real deer are not so blessed.

I admit the *Pioneer Press* piece left me dyspeptic. In celebrating garden whimsy in the form of giant steel dragonflies, gaggles of bronze crows, and faux ruins, the Quill and Trowel crowd are giving their cultural imprimatur to yard art of a gentrified sort. The inference is that our plywood and wrapped lawn mowers are tacky, but I have yet to see a teddy bear topiary in Chippewa County. Ditto "a scarecrow dressed up in bohemian duds including shawl and beret." Faux ruins? Who needs 'em, when your backyard is arranged around two rusty Pintos and a washing machine sprouting crabgrass? Lyric beauty goes only so far. I could do without whirling plastic sunflowers, but more than that, I want to be in a place I understand. Fake deer and Packer ornaments, goofy mailboxes, they tell me I am in a place where—for better or worse—I know the code. Let me be the first to say "Grandma Bending Over" is no "Nude Descending a Staircase." But when *Garden Whimsy* the book celebrates a formal Grecian statue dressed as a prom queen in tulle and chiffon, methinks a sight gag is a sight gag, marble and brass notwithstanding.

Truth be told, it was the subheadline that really hung me up: "At Last, Fertile Imaginations Are Appreciating a Little Whimsy in the Garden." Implied: Fertile imaginations are only fertile if they work in brass and marble and eschew the coarse belly laugh. It's tough to stick up for the worst of our lawn art—cartoony plastic Wal-Mart Garden Center frogs, for instance, although *Garden Whimsy* gives its seal of approval to giant frogs playing the cello (*bronze* frogs, natch)—but something about the plywood cutouts kept ringing a little bell. There was vindication in there somewhere. Then, reading the encyclopedia one day, I hit on it. The most popular tourist attraction in Belgium is a sculpture dating back to the fourteenth century. It is a bronze statuette of . . . *a little boy peeing*.

———

At first, Travis is completely unresponsive. Then he begins reacting to loud verbal stimuli. That is to say, he rouses when we yell his name. It is a diminished response, however, and he is disoriented. On the initial assessment, in which we scan the patient from head to toe, we find two lacerations on his head. After determining that they are superficial, with no underlying crepitus or depression to indicate an obvious cranial fracture, we control the bleeding by applying simple gauze squares. In the meantime, the rest of the assessment reveals no other obvious injuries. We give Travis high-flow oxygen through a non-rebreather mask, which has a little bag attached to concentrate the oxygen. Because of the severity of his injuries and his deteriorated mental status, we have already ordered the chopper. In the time it takes us to cut him free of the car, we take his vital signs three times. When we get his foot free, we take traction on his leg, holding it straight and checking for a pedal pulse to make sure blood is still being circulated throughout the length of the leg. His upper thigh looks swollen in comparison to his uninjured side, and this is a concern, as a femoral fracture can cause tremendous "invisible" bleeding in which the blood infiltrates the spaces between the muscles of the thigh. By the time we get Travis on the board and free of the car, the helicopter has arrived and landed on Pine Street, right in front of the old lumber yard. We give report to the flight nurse, help load Travis into the chopper, and away he goes.

By this time, Tricky has been handcuffed twice and released twice. He alternates between demanding treatment and refusing it. He asks us to produce a release form, then refuses to sign it. At one point Tricky puts his wrists in my face and demands that I document the red marks from the cuffs. I track down Bill, the quietest patient. He is sitting in the back of a pickup. His knee has several puncture wounds. We splint the knee, put Bill on a back board, and load him in the ambulance. On to Elmo.

Elmo has a small laceration on his chin, and my mother notices during her assessment that his left eye won't close and the pupil is non-reactive. "I was in an accident before," says Elmo. "This whole side of my body has been rebuilt. It's titanium." We urge Elmo to get checked out at the hospital, but he refuses. When we hand him a release form, he holds it but will not sign it. We summon a deputy, and with her as witness, urge Elmo several times to accept treatment or sign the release. He refuses to do either. Eventually, after the helicopter is gone and the ground ambulance is leaving with Bill, Elmo says he will sign the release. The release forms are all in the departed ambulance. The deputy chief and I write out a release on a notepad, and Elmo signs it. We begin cleaning up the accident scene and Elmo interferes. When a sheriff's deputy tells him to leave the scene, Elmo says he now wants medical attention. We radio the ambulance, and they head back to the scene. Before Elmo can change his mind, I place him in a seated position on the ground, put him in a c-collar, wrap him in a rescue blanket, and tell him not to move. I then give him a thorough head-to-toe assessment, hampered greatly by the fact that Elmo is shivering and waving his arms around. The ambulance arrives. "I'm not going to the hospital if my wife isn't here," says Elmo. The EMTs and I exchange glances—we are being pushed to the limits of professionalism. We lift Elmo to the cot. "I don't need this, guys, I don't need this." In the end, Elmo allows himself to be transported.

Later, while writing up the report I try to imagine myself in court two years from now, facing some lawyer armed with the patient assessment and scene-control portions of *Emergency Care in the Streets*. Rescue organizations devote entire four-day seminars to scene control—this particular circus would be the perfect study. The algorithm has not been designed that can cope with Tricky Jackson and his posse. The old-timers tell me that from the 1920s right up until the late 1970s the whole town used to turn out for the Free Show, a free open-air movie sponsored by the Commercial Club. The screen was set up in what is now my backyard. Videos and cable television killed the Free Show, but for a couple hours on a warm June evening, Tricky Jackson revived it. It is an accident scene, it is community theater, reality TV, and improv, all rolled into one.

By the time it is all over, Tricky may or may not have been arrested—I have seen him in and out of handcuffs twice—Elmo is on his belated way to the hospital with Bill, Travis is in the approach path to the Luther Hospital helipad thirty miles away, and Shirley was last seen north of Slinger Joe's, thumbing for a ride. We pick up the bandage wrappers, sweep up the glass, roll the hose, and engage in all the mundane little chores of denouement you rarely get to see on *Paramedics*. The crowd pretty much dispersed once the helicopter cleared the trees on Elm Street. The rain stopped a long time ago, and when I get back to my car, I find that the windshield wipers have been running dry for so long they are melting, leaving rubbery black streaks across the glass. On the drive to the fire hall, I see the townspeople filtering home, some of them visiting for a bit on the sidewalk. Their children course ahead of them, running and skipping, or pedaling furiously on colorful tricycles. The sky is gray, the night is warm. The grass in the yards is deep twilight green, and the rain seeps into the earth, draining the excitement from the air.

Oliver Goldsmith died in 1773. He had just completed the dramatic comedy *She Stoops to Conquer*, which assured him of a spot in *The Oxford Companion to English Literature*.

Cut to New York State, 1804. The citizens of Hardenburgh Corners are pleased to learn that the state commissioners intend to designate their town as the Cayuga County seat. Disquietude displaces pride, however, when certain members of the citizenry—apparently whelmed with the stately implications of this county seat business—opine that the name Hardenburgh Corners is an embarrassment of multisyllabic yokelism, a moniker neither dignified nor manageable (consider the letterhead), and wholly lacking the sense of eminence required of a county seat. It was an issue, wrote Henry Hall in an 1869 history, of propriety. "The subject," he continued, "was therefore agitated." Everyone clustered at Bostwick's tavern and began kicking names around. Quite immediately, a Dr. Crossett suggested the adoption of "Auburn," after the town in Goldsmith's "Deserted Village." Based on the lyrical implications (". . . loveliest village of the plain"), Crossett's suggestion was received with general approbation until a certain eponymic Colonel Hardenburgh pointed out that while Goldsmith's Auburn may have been lovely, it was also the most neglected—indeed, *deserted*—village on the plain, and to redub Hardenburgh Corners so would foreshadow its decay and decline. Among the alternative names subsequently proffered were the foreshortened "Hardenburgh," a stately "Mount Maria," and, plainly enough, "Centre." A roisterous debate ensued, followed by a vote, and Auburn emerged the favorite. Efforts to reverse the decision were mounted, and a second vote taken, but again, Auburn was the majority choice.

We move now to western Wisconsin, 1856. A preacher named Priddy hikes into the area and sets up shop at the confluence of a creek. The spot will become Bloomer, Wisconsin. Priddy hails from New York State and has relatives in Cayuga County. When it comes time to carve up western Wisconsin and name the chunks, the township adjacent to Priddy's settlement is christened Auburn Township in honor of Auburn, New York. Up the trail nine miles, a man named C. M. Tarr is so taken with the name, he starts a little village and names it Auburn also. Eventually, this Auburn will be subsumed into Cartwright Mills, only to resurface during the liquor license controversy of 1902. On August 3, 1904, the handwritten entry in the Village Minutes reads, "That the village of Auburn henceforth be called New Auburn." The Oliver Goldsmith loop was complete.

We wind up the Tricky Jackson call with the usual smoke-and-joke session. We talk about what went well and what didn't go so well, and how we might handle the next incident in which a carful of five people hits the laundromat—an exercise that speaks to both the importance and futility of emergency planning—but mostly we just shoot the breeze, an underrated joy. We stand among the trucks. Instead of the traditional red, they are painted bright yellow. And on the door of each truck, in reflective gold leaf, it says New Auburn Area Fire Department. It tickles me sometimes, when we're standing around the fire hall talking about coon hunting and stock cars, to look at those truck doors and think of Goldsmith, bent over his desk, composing in pentameter, crafting verse, a fragment of which would survive to be pasted on our fire trucks. It is a tangible thread to the past. Establishing a connection between the peeing plywood boy and the *Mannekin-Pis* is an exercise in corollaries, aimed at deflating pretension. Linking our fire trucks to eighteenth-century literature is an exercise in map reading. We find a trail leading back over the landscape of time, and we find ourselves bearing forward the remnants of a distant aesthetic not immediately evident in our detritus, but ours to claim, nonetheless. Whatever else he did, Goldsmith put a name on the place I have always called home, no matter where I stood at the time I invoked the name.

4

SILVER STAR

PUKE IS THE GREAT CONSTANT. Sick people puke, dying people puke, excited people puke, people puke while they're having heart attacks, they puke when their lacerated brains swell, they puke because they get carsick lying on the cot looking up at the dome lights.

I got the puke christening early. I was in training, still doing ride-alongs as the third wheel on a two-man crew. The page came during a swampy stretch of weather—humidity and temperature readings had been crowding the high nineties for a week. I pulled open the apartment door, and the stench rolled out like warm fog. The living room was packed with family. As I trotted past the kitchen table, I saw piles of trash and dishes and a capacious tureen heaped with onion skins and potato peelings. The patient, Helen, was in the bathroom. The bathroom went about five feet by eight feet, and Helen went about five feet by 350 pounds. She was on the toilet, wedged between the sink and the tub. It was upward of 90 degrees in there, and she was wrapped in a voluminous flannel nightgown. From the smell of things, there were bits of Helen that had seen neither air nor water for a long, long time. I stood in the tub. Donnie and Todd, the two veterans training me, shoved the cot in and stood watching from the door. The cot took up all the remaining floor space. I guessed I was on my own. Helen's daughter poked her head between Donnie and Todd. "She's been sick for a couple days. She had a seizure today. She can't stand up."

I tried to help Helen stand, but she just hollered. I looked to Donnie and Todd. They were giving me the rookie smirk. Behind them, I could see the faces of the family, arranged in an arc, peering at me expectantly. I began to sweat. In the end, a fireman wedged himself in the tub with me, and between the two of us, we convinced Helen to wriggle while we tugged and pushed, and after violating every safe lifting technique ever proposed, wrestled her to the cot. She immediately began to retch. Donnie slapped a towel to her chin, but only succeeded in deflecting the subsequent explosion of dark brown vomit across the wall and over the blankets. It was a copious projectile eruption that left the cot drenched. Like a flu-ridden chorus line, the arc of family bent at the waist and barfed on the carpet. We see this sometimes. It's what you call a sympathy puke.

We loaded the cot, and Donnie and Todd sprinted for the front seats. It is not standard training procedure to abandon the rookie in the back. Helen squinted her eyes shut tight, howled, and puked again. There is a little door between the front and the rear of the ambulance. It is never closed. Todd snapped it shut. Helen howled, paused again to hurl, then howled nonstop to the hospital. I never could figure out what the trouble was. She wouldn't talk. The floor was slick with soupy brown spew. The air was rank with the smell of onions and something vaguely Parmesan. The windows opened out at the bottom, only about an inch. I'd hold my breath while taking Helen's vital signs, then lurch to the base of the window to inhale. The howling was unceasing. Todd kept leering through the little communicating window in the latched door. One day he will reside in a lower circle of Hell.

The thing was, other than the soles of my boots, I had managed to stay vomitus-free. I probably tracked a little into the hospital when we got there, and I had Donnie grab an emesis basin before we took the five-floor elevator ride to the medical floor, but Helen's howling and eruptions had waned to nothing, and my uniform was still dry when we docked the cot beside her hospital bed. It took six of us to lift her across the gap. I was positioned at the head of the bed, about a foot from her face. Right mid-lift, when I had her great weight in my arms, she swiveled her head, looked me in the eye, and bound up her guts for one last mighty heave. Donnie slung the emesis basin at me, and I managed to catch the first few bursts, but she just kept puking. The basin became full. I called for another. Everyone just stared. The basin overflowed, and vomit hit the floor, splattering my pant legs and pooling on my boots. There was a slight pause, and then Helen loosed a convulsive *woof!*, launching a final horrific geyser just past my right ear. I leapt back, but I was too late. She got me in the right shoulder, across the chest, and as a sort of sloppy coup de grace, sent a few trailing dribbles down the front of my pants.

Down in the ER, I tried to clean up, but it was just silly. The boys put me in the back of the rig, shut the communicating door, and drove me home. When we stripped the cot, a glistening chunk of unchewed onion the size of a nightcrawler fell to the floor. I resolved to stay in the shower until shrunken.

But I didn't puke. And I never have.

The thing about ambulance work is, you cannot dip your toe in the pool. You don't know if you can stand the water until you dive in. When you're training, long before you answer your first page, you wonder how you'll handle the blood, you wonder how you'll react to distorted limbs and protruding bone fragments, and you wonder if dead people will make you want to turn and run. I never remember wondering how I'd handle the puking. There's no way to find out other than to get out there in it.

The first heart attack I ever worked was near suppertime, and I and my partner, Fred—a part-time hospital orderly and experienced EMT—had just picked up sub sandwiches. They slid around the console as we whistled down the highway, out to a farmstead. Following the family, we ran up a hill behind the house, where there was a man lying on his back, looking waxen in the grass. While Fred set up the defibrillator, I popped out my pocket mask and prepared to start rescue breathing. The family dog ran around and around us. I remember being wound tight inside, scared and humming like a high line, but I also remember being thrilled that I wasn't panicked, that I could remember the cardiac-arrest protocol, that I had no qualms about bringing my face near to that of a dead man. And so I gave him that big first breath—the trouble was, I forgot to attach the one-way valve to the mask, and on the exhale, the man blew a geyser of creamed corn in my face.

I didn't puke.

I called for suction, jammed the one-way valve on the mask, and gave him another breath.

Fifteen years and hundreds of patients later, I have never forgotten the one-way valve.

We worked the man all the way back to the hospital. The sweat from my brow splashed on his bare chest every time I did compressions. Once when we careened around a corner I smacked my head on the overhead cupboard. We hit the ambulance bay going full steam, and they shocked and poked a while longer in the emergency room, but the man died.

I wondered how I'd feel, but it all seemed okay. I felt we could look at the family and know we'd done what we could. What we were trained to do. I felt respectful of their grief, but I wasn't distraught myself. We shut ourselves in a little room at the back of the emergency department to review the audiocassette playback from the defib machine. As the tape rolled, I heard myself breathing and grunting, and Fred talking through the protocol, and I could hear the plasticky *tunk* of jostled equipment, and the rattle and snap of the cot straps, and through the whole thing, that dog—circling us again and again, barking and whining as we shocked, pummeled, and abducted his master. The creamed corn, the dead man, those didn't bother me. That dog set me back some.

I was introduced to the techniques and terminology of emergency medical service—EMS—through a series of night classes held in a high school library under the aegis of the Wisconsin Indianhead Technical College. After 115 hours of training, I received sanction from the National Registry of Emergency Medical Technicians by passing their written and practical examinations. The state of Wisconsin then issued me a license to practice at the EMT-Basic level. Officially prepared, I set out to learn the trade of rescue. The guts, and the art.

I entered into an apprenticeship with a passel of renegades.

The headquarters of the Silver Star Ambulance Service consisted of a ratty apartment attached to a funeral home. If this strikes you as a creepy conflict of interest, right on. Regulations now prohibit such arrangements, which were an outgrowth of the days when the local hearse did double duty as the ambulance. Existing services were grandfathered in, however, and Silver Star was one of the originals.

The proximity of the funeral home had its pros and cons. We were always being recruited to shuttle caskets and move bodies. When we washed and polished the ambulances, we were expected to do the same for the hearse. When it snowed, the funeral-home owner would summon us to his house on the hill and make us shovel the drive. I always figured that looked pretty good—an ambulance pulls up, and two uniformed medics jump out with snow shovels.

On the other hand, the presence of caskets and dead bodies kept us well stocked for pranks. Whenever new medics hired on, we took them on a tour of the funeral home and made sure to point out that the bunk room and the embalming room shared a wall. That night, we'd assign them the bunk against that wall. After lights out, the dispatcher would sneak into the embalming room and scratch on the tiles. Sometimes you'd cook up an errand that would send a rookie through the casket room. We'd plant a veteran in one of the caskets, and when the rookie got close, the veteran would moan and pound on the lid.

I used to say I would trust the Silver Star crew with my life, but not my sister. The city fire department, with its union wages and tough admission standards, tended to attract experienced career-minded individuals. Silver Star, with its low wages and cursory back-ground checks, tended to attract part-timers, novices, and talented rogues. When I signed on, I found myself part of a merry band whose personalities were as fractured as their rescue talents were solid: Jacques, the French-Canadian Sioux who cheerfully referred to him-self as a "blanket-assed wagon burner." Before turning in at night, he stripped down to his leopard-print bikini briefs and cut muscle-man poses. He and I spent a lot of time in the brush behind the ambulance garage, rigging figure-four rabbit traps and taking archery practice, city ordinances notwithstanding. Leif, who shagged anything that would stand still. Donnie, the sawed-off veteran with the most senior-ity who wore cowboy boots and refused to do anything other than drive. We used to wind him up just to watch his bald head turn red. Todd, vein-skinny, sardonic, and utterly unflappable. Baz, who lived on coffee and cigarettes and spent half the shift in the bathroom with the newspaper. Phil, the gentleman among us, with a sweet wife and little boy. And Porter, who got lit at the bar one night, tried to ride home on his bike, and ran smack into a two-story brick medical clinic.

Silver Star was managed by Arnold, the owner's son. Arnold had high blood pressure. Under stress, he tended to spring nosebleeds. He'd be in his office chair, chewing you out, and all of a sudden he'd tip back and pinch his nose, and you knew you were getting to him. The day I applied for a position at Silver Star, we were five minutes into the interview when the pager went off. Arnold tossed my résumé on the desk and jumped up. "C'mon!" We picked up a sick little old lady. She was on the floor in her nightgown, hands clenched over her belly. We carried her out on a backboard and put her on the cot. Halfway to the hospital, she relaxed a little, and a basketball-sized mass of flesh rolled out from under her nightgown and thumped to the floor. It remained attached to her abdomen by a thin, fleshy umbilicus. Arnold and I exchanged a glance across the cot. Then Arnold picked the thing up and popped it back under the nightgown like it was the most natural thing in the world. Never said a word. The lesson was twofold. Number one, failure to detect a free-floating tumorous mass the heft and circumference of a supermarket watermelon reflects a certain inattention to basic patient-assessment protocols. Number two, be cool. And if you can't be cool, act cool. The patient will draw comfort from your demeanor. *Another day*, your countenance should say, *another little old lady sprouting giant flesh balls*.

The human body is subject to an infinite number of maladies and injuries in an infinite number of combinations. This can put a little whoops in your gut if the pager on your belt designates you to sort them out on the fly. The what-ifs are daunting. The good news? It's likely you learned the most fundamental element of EMS clear back in kindergarten. In EMS, no matter what happens, no matter how tragic or banal the call, all patient treatment is predicated on an algorithm, and that algorithm begins with a three-letter mnemonic: *ABC*. A = airway, B = breathing, C = circulation. Whether grandma stubbed her toe, had a heart attack, or got hit by a Mack truck, your primary responsibility, as one of my instructors used to put it, is to make sure air goes in and out and blood goes 'round and 'round. No matter your level of practice—first responder, basic EMT, paramedic—you begin at ABC and ride the algorithm home.

So. Is your patient getting air? No? What must you do to change this? Change the position of her head? Put a tube in his throat? Blow air into his lungs? Got that taken care of? Now let's check circulation. Does your patient have a pulse? No? Has someone started chest compressions? Is it time to fire up the defibrillator? Perhaps you walked into the little old man's apartment and he said hello. You have just completed your most primary assessment. The fact that he is upright and talking tells you his ABCs are up and running. You will need to assess the *quality* of his ABCs, but at the very least they are *present*.

From ABC, the algorithm bifurcates. The bifurcations fill entire textbooks. If the patient is unconscious, you go left. If the patient is conscious, you go right. Are you dealing with a medical problem (turn left) or trauma (turn right)? You just keep working your way through the maze. At every intersection, you read the sign and turn accordingly. In general, you work from head to toe, a quick once-over the first time, to find and treat life-threatening injuries. If you find bad things of magnitude—a sucking chest wound, massive external hemorrhage—you stick your finger in the dike (cover the chest wound, control the bleeding) and get rolling. "Load and go" it's called, or "scoop 'n' scoot." If the patient is stable, or if transport time allows, you perform a secondary assessment, running head to toe again, with more attention to detail. You'll be checking for more subtle signs of trouble: the little bruises tucked behind the ears that indicate a basilar skull fracture, clear drainage from the ears that may be spinal fluid, swollen ankles indicative of congestive heart failure. Throughout the algorithm, priorities rule. See the motorcyclist with a leg like a pretzel? Ignore the leg—find out if he is breathing. Check to see that his trachea is in line, not squashed to one side by a leaking lung. The most garish problem is not always the most deadly. And through it all, remember: If at any point along the algorithm your patient crashes, you don't panic. You just move your little game piece back to square one, to ABC, and begin again. Air goes in and out, blood goes 'round and 'round.

I pulled mostly weekend shifts at Silver Star. Weekdays were covered by full-timers working in teams of two. When the full-timers rotated through weekend coverage, they split and paired up with a part-timer. One pair worked "first out" on Saturday, and the other pair worked "first out" on Sunday. Being "first out" meant you had to be at headquarters. Working "second out" meant you could go about your business in town, but you had to carry a pager and be able to make it to headquarters in under ten minutes to cover any call that might come in while the first-out team was in the field. This arrangement meant that even as a part-timer working weekends only, you were putting in a forty-eight-hour week. The calls and experience accumulated quickly.

I pulled most of my shifts with Jacques. You learned to stay on your toes with Jacques. He had a brilliant mind but was plainly bent. He used to sit around the little apartment starting intravenous lines on himself. For the practice, he said. He favored the veins in his feet. He read voraciously and was a martial arts maven. One minute he would be ruminating aloud on the restorative powers of meditation, and the next he would be doing the splits, or he'd have you facedown on the floor, rubbing carpet burns into your nose as he demonstrated some new submission hold. You learned to step through doors cautiously, because you never knew when he would have his throwing knives out. He set mousetraps in the coffee filters and rousted Baz by rolling firecrackers under the bathroom door. Returning from a call at three A.M., he wound down by hitting golf balls across the highway. Looking for a quick and easy way to gather worms for fishing, he wrapped copper rods around the defibrillator pads, then stuck the rods in the dirt. He'd charge the defibrillator to 360 joules, hit the double triggers, and shortly, nightcrawlers emerged from the earth. He rarely settled, due in no small part to the fact that he frequently worked a cigarette, a wad of chew, and a can of Mountain Dew simultaneously. He was bent, but he was fearless, and one of the best medics I've ever run with. We made call after call that first couple of years. He became my gonzo sensei.

Jacques took me to my first full-blown trauma. A woman and a man on a motorcycle lost it on a curve. The woman got flung ahead of the cycle, wound up wrapped belly-first around a pine tree. The bike followed her into the tree, crashing into her back. Her kidneys and liver were lacerated. She was in imminent danger of bleeding out. She had severe head injuries and was unconscious, but her gag reflex was still intact, and she wouldn't tolerate an oral airway. The last thing you want to do is jam an airway down someone's throat and make them puke. If they aspirate the vomit—breathe it in, literally—you suddenly have a patient with a compromised airway. The first responders already had her in a neck collar and strapped to a backboard, so we didn't linger. As Jacques hit the siren and struck out for the hospital twenty minutes away, I looked at the woman under the bright cot lights and realized I was in it for real. I taped sandbags around her head to increase the stability of her neck. Then I got busy with the secondary survey, and began accumulating follow-up vital signs, taking her pulse and blood pressure every few minutes, rechecking her breathing, looking for signs of shock. It is critical to recognize shock early, and our instructors drilled us on the signs: rapid pulse, rapid respirations, falling blood pressure. Then they added a grim little coda: by the time these signs begin to show, your patient may be past retrieving. So you do what you can. Keep the patient warm, deliver oxygen, drive fast. Start an intravenous line if your license allows—ours did not at the time. We did have the woman in a pair of military anti-shock trousers. These are essentially inflatable pants. Like much of the EMS repertoire, they were developed during the Vietnam War. Theoretically, inflation of the pants forces blood out of the legs and lower abdomen to the more vital areas of the chest and head. MAST trousers have fallen from favor in recent years. We still carry them, but we rarely receive permission to inflate them when we radio the emergency room doc for orders. I no longer recall if we received permission to inflate that evening. I just remember that about five minutes out, the woman began to seize and puke, and for the rest of the ride, I was consumed with the maintenance of our old friends, A and B.

The seizure came first. The woman's entire body stiffened, even as her eyes stared blankly at the ceiling. As soon as the seizure passed, the puking began. And for a second or two there, I was terrified. I thought surely the woman would choke and die, a pathetic irony in the face of all her other life-threatening injuries. Strapped down on her back, she was in the worst possible position. I grabbed the suction unit, but her teeth were clenched. The puke (a burgundy syrup—we later placed it as red wine and crackers) burbled up through her teeth and lips and spilled over into her open eyes. Realizing I had to act immediately, I flipped the entire backboard up on its left side. The straps and sandbags held the woman in place, and I kept one hand on the underside of her head to further support her neck. The puke rolled out of her mouth and down my arm. I got the backboard propped and swept the suction across her mouth. Using a technique we learned in class, I crossed my fingers and tried to pry her jaws apart, but it was futile. I still remember looking up through the little communicating passageway and out the windshield, dipping my head, desperate to get a glimpse of the hospital as we hammered into town and down the boulevard. I kept suctioning and trying the finger technique, and finally got the woman's teeth open just enough to admit the suction tip. When we pulled into the ambulance bay, I remember hands reaching in to help us debark, I remember being a little breathless giving report, and six months later, when I heard the woman was finally walking out of the hospital, I remember thinking that in all the madness, with all the critical things going on, the greatest lifesaving action I made on her behalf involved the diversion of throw-up using the principles of gravity. "You did well out there," said Jacques, in a rare serious moment. It was all that mattered.

From ABC on, the rescue trade is big on mnemonics. The idea, I suppose, is to help you recall assessments and procedures under pressure. Textbook authors and instructors bury you in the things: OPQRST = *Onset, Provokes, Quality, Radiates, Severity, Time*. D-CAP = *Deformities, Contusions, Abrasions, Penetrations*. SAMPLE = *Signs/Symptoms, Allergies, Medications, Past Pertinent history, Last oral intake, Events preceding*. CUPS = *Critical/CPR, Unstable, Potentially unstable, Stable*. Notice how the last two mnemonics sometimes assign the bold letter to two words simultaneously, while in other cases, the letter matches only the first word. Excusable to a point, but turn the mnemonics crowd loose, and things quickly get out of hand. ABC becomes ABCDEFGHI: *Airway; Breathing; Circulation; Deformity; Expose; Fahrenheit (temperature); EKG, pulse oximetry, vital signs; Head-to-toe exam; Interventions, Inspect back*. Okay through *E,* I guess, but the Fahrenheit thing is a little sketchy. Then, to squeeze in EKG, we completely ignore *E* and *K,* highlighting *G*. And since *P* and *V* are too far down the alphabetical line, pulse oximetry and vital signs are tacked on to EKG like a cheap porch. *H* is for head, you're on your own recalling "to toe exam." And finally, "I," presented in classic double-assignation form.

This stuff just doesn't work for me. I can never get the initials to cohere. In my head, the letters Ping-Pong off one another, triggering a parade of words and associations. *P*—was that for *Previous*, or *Potential*, or *Pills*, or *Primary complaint*? *M*—*Medications*? Or *Meals*? The letters skitter and simply won't stand still. In high school, we were required to memorize the twelve pairs of cranial nerves: olfactory, optic, oculomotor, trochlear, trigeminal, abducens, facial, vestibulocochlear, glossopharyngeal, vagus, spinal accessory, hypoglossal. Our science teacher, who favored "auditory" over "vestibulocochlear," recommended we associate them with the phrase, "*On Old Olympic Towering Tops A Finn And German Viewed Some Hops*." This phrase has worked fine for generations of students, and I encounter emergency-room physicians and physical therapists who employ it daily, but I could never summon it completely. I would try, and what I would get was the image of a guy with a big belly and knobby knees, wearing lederhosen and peering downhill at a field of barley. The Finn never made the scene. Furthermore, some instructors favor *accessory nerve* over *spinal accessory nerve*. Their Finn and German view not *Some* hops, but *A* hop. Another source disposes with the Finn altogether: "*On Old Olympus Towering Tops A Famous Vocal German Viewed Some Hops*." I see Helmut Kohl yodeling over wheat fields. And what if I *could* remember one of these phrases? How to sort those first three *O*s? And the *T*s—is it *trochlear, trigeminal* or *trigeminal, trochlear*? Kenneth

Saladin, author of *Anatomy and Physiology:The Unity of Form and Function*, proposes "**OL**d **OP**ie **OC**casionally **TR**ies **TRIG**onometry And Feels **VE**ry **GLO**omy **VAGU**e And **HYPO**active." As in, **OL**factory, **OP**tic, **OC**ulomotor, **TR**ochlear, **TRIG**eminal, **A**bducens, **F**acial, **VE**stibulocochlear, **GLO**ssopharyngeal, **VAGU**s, **A**ccessory, **HYPO**glossal.

I do believe the alphabet soup that fills my head just went bad.

The trouble is, this is one of those areas, like religion or spinach, where the folks who think you need it keep piling it on. That mnemonic didn't work? Here are sixteen more! I beg them to stop. I am, I want to say, "A Free-Associating Ruminator. Terribly Scatter-Brained. Usually, Mnemonics Bring Little Enduring Relief." A FARTS BUMBLER. Try to remember that, you mnemonics pushers.

Not all of the terminology and mnemonics I learned in those early days were officially sanctioned. A patient whose condition was deteriorating was often said to be "circling the drain." An unresponsive patient whose EKG was as flat as a certain western state was said to be exhibiting "the Nebraska sign." Sometimes you walked into a scene and declared the patient "DRT"—dead right there. DRT patients often presented with "the Q sign." You'll get the idea if you draw a smiley face, replacing the smiley mouth with a capital Q.

There was a bluffness to those early years. We were, for the most part, young men in uniform, learning to operate coolly at the nexus of dramatic events. I quickly grew to love the art of cutting through the chaos, to thrive on the idea of applying my knowledge in the field, often without the benefit of bright lights or flat surfaces. I loved stepping out of the front of the ambulance into the teeth of the wind, plunging into the deep snow on the median, the scene lights pushing my shadow ahead of me down to the upended pickup with the guy trapped inside, knowing Jacques was right behind me, and that somehow we would find a way to get to the guy, to package and remove him, to get him safely into a place with sterile sheets and delicate lifesaving tools. Our work environment ranged from dangerous to goofy—one call you are trying to figure out how to safely move a woman impaled on a fence post, the next you are jumping up on the toilet every time your partner charges the defibrillator and yells, "Clear!"

What you are given is a series of opportunities to prove your ingenuity and gumption. Rescue work is like jazz. Improvisation based on fundamentals. Protection of the cervical spine is a number-one priority, so we learn to take and maintain immediate manual stabilization, put on c-collars, and immobilize patients as completely as possible before moving them. In class, back in the high-school library, we practiced placing each other in a KED (Kendrick Extrication Device), a sort of wraparound splint designed to immobilize patients from the base of the spine to the top of the head. The protocol is very specific regarding positioning of the device, and the seven different straps are to be applied in a set order. We rehearsed over and over for the national test, in which we applied the KED to a person sitting calmly on a wooden chair in the middle of an open room. Then you're upside down in a king cab, your patient is hanging from his seat belt, his head cranked over at an impossible angle, and suddenly your usual tools are worthless. And so, using your head, your hands, and maybe some towel rolls, you find a way to pluck the guy while still adhering to the primary principles of protecting the patient from further injury. You are riffing on a basic chord structure. I was explaining this to a friend once, how the presentation of our patients often requires us to improvise in the field. I brought up the jazz allusion, and he did me one better, putting it in terms of golf. "What you're saying," he said, "is you gotta play it where it lies."

Jacques, of course, was never afraid to improvise. We went to an inservice one day in which an instructor showed us a rapid-extrication technique called a horse-collar. You take a blanket, twist it into a long roll, drape it across the back of the victim's neck, bring the ends around, and cross them in front of the neck beneath the chin, and then pass the blanket ends back under the victim's armpits, so they

stick out like wings. You grab the ends like handles. The roll is supposed to cradle the patient's neck as you lug him to safety. The instructor repeatedly stressed that this was strictly a last-resort
technique, to be used only when the patient was in imminent danger.

   Three A.M. the next morning. Jacques and I are staring at a drunk
guy in a Yugo. The wheels are down, but he has rolled the thing once
or twice. All the corners are rounded off. We are on an overpass. The
wind is cutting straight through, driving sleet into our eyes. It's a
struggle, getting the c-collar and KED on, and the guy is cussing us
the whole time. By the time we're done, my hands are numb with
cold. Finally, everything is in place. The KED comes fitted with handles, and Jacques and I each grab one. "One, two, three . . . go!" We
move the guy about six inches and can get him no further. Turns out
the Yugo has pancaked just enough so that the KED is too tall to fit
out the door frame, and it has become wedged. Now the guy is really
cussing us. We are alone. No fire trucks with equipment to cut
through the door frame. I'm standing there trying to figure out what
to do next when I hear the ambulance door slam. I look back, and
here comes Jacques. His arms are outstretched, and he is twirling a
blanket, spinning it into a long roll. "Umm, Jacques, do you
think . . . ?"

   "Get the cot," he says, leaning into the car. *Pop, pop, pop* . . . there
go the KED straps.

   I can't bear to watch. I get the cot, already rehearsing what I'll
say in the deposition. Behind me, I hear more drunken cussing, and
a *thwack!* as the discarded KED hits the concrete. I roll the cot up
just as Jacques drags the guy, cussing and gargling, from the car and
drapes him over the cot. On the way to the hospital, I quickly check
to see if the man can move his arms and feet. Everything checks out.
Up front, Jacques is whistling.

There were always the calls, though, that pulled you back. The ones
you couldn't laugh off. On a gray morning just after dawn, Phil and
I answered two consecutive pages, the first for a wounded cop, and

the second for the man who shot him. From a fundamental stand-point, everything went well. The cop had been shot through the upper chest. I got my IV lines in, and Phil controlled the sucking chest wound. The cop kept telling us how much it hurt, and when he couldn't talk, he squeezed my hand. We were deeply relieved when we delivered him alive. He was on his way to surgery when we got the page for the shooter. The shooter had tried to blow his brains out, but had succeeded only in lifting away half his skull. The right side of his brain was completely exposed and perfectly intact. His EKG squiggled out and flattened as we pulled into the ambulance garage. The ER doc stuck his head in, took one look, and shook his head. Then he told us the cop had died in surgery. We were dumbfounded. Driving back to headquarters through the morning rush, I remember irrationally wishing to flag down each and every car, to look each driver in the eye, and say, "Do you real-ize what has happened this morning?" Ten years later, I called Phil, and he says the image he retains is the cop's gun belt on the bloody ambulance floor, the buckle open, the holster empty. On a sunny af-ternoon, Jacques and I transported a one-legged, three-hundred-pound man back to his home from the hospital. He was in his seventies. He wore a trim fedora and held his head with dignity, but he was weak and pale, and said he didn't think he was ready to re-turn home. It was all Jacques and I could do to slide the man from the cot to his bed. His wife hovered in the background. She weighed maybe ninety pounds and was visibly shaken at the prospect of car-ing for him. Back in the rig, Jacques shook his head, and we talked of what it must be like to exist on such a fragile cusp. Another night, I helped a homeless alcoholic get to his feet from the doorway of the hardware store where he had collapsed. He was dirty and smelly. After I got him settled on the cot, he rummaged around in his pocket, pulled out a little black plastic comb and began combing his hair straight forward with slow, deliberate strokes. I was reminded of the way a toddler pushes a comb, trying to look grown up. It was this sad, noble little effort at tidying up. I watched, and my heart broke.

• • •

The Silver Star days were good days. There was life and death, and loose-limbed esprit de corps. I accumulated a deep base of experience. My hands still shook on the way to the worst calls, but I knew the shaking would stop as soon as I got into action. I was toughened but not hardened. The right sort of call could still put me back on my heels, and I was glad for that. But more and more, I wanted to take these things I had learned and apply them in a place where the faces were familiar. I was formulating this idea that if you took care of your neighbors, even to the point of letting them puke on you, one day someone would be there when it was you on the cot. The algorithm pointed toward home.

When the time came to move on, I was ready. The original renegades were gone. The ambulance service was sold to a large chain operation. Phil became a paramedic and took a job in Minneapolis. Leif is a paramedic in Las Vegas. Porter got a nursing degree and headed for Denver. Baz hanged himself. Donnie became a prison guard. I lost track of Todd. Fred I'm not sure about. Last I heard, Jacques was in Indiana. Recovering from surgery for a brain tumor, someone said. We e-mailed once, but lately I can't raise him.

5

STRUCTURE FIRE

THIS WAS A DANGEROUS PLACE. The low-slung cellar joists dripped with runoff from the fire hoses aimed at the outside of the burning house, attacking the fire from the exterior as we attacked from the interior. We were on a mop-up, really, trying to douse a few hot spots, those intransigent little clusters of flame that soldier on in the hidden crannies of a house afire, weakening it from within rather than devouring it from without. We arrived here by feel, knee-walking beneath the collapsed roof of the attached garage, groping through the haze, dragging a two-and-a-half-inch hose, charged and heavy with water. We advance. We're at the basement steps now. We're about to go in. I suppose the soundtrack in my head should be thundering something like, "Let's rock and roll, you smoke-eatin' sonsabitches!" but it's not. It's fretting, Will the house fall in on us? Will the water pressure fizzle right about the time the furnace explodes? Will I get my feet wet? Will I get out of here alive? For all firefighting's cinematic potential—screaming sirens, snapping flames, roiling slugs of luminous, milky orange smoke colonnading the black night sky—most firefighting deaths have very little marquee value. The firefighter who dies silhouetted in a nimbus of flame while rescuing a child is a reality, but a rarity. More likely he'll be crushed under a collapsed wall. Get hit in the head by a waterlogged beam. Touch a ladder to a power line. Run out of air in some smoky hallway. Or fall to the most common firefighter killer of all: a plain old-fashioned heart attack. The dangers linger long after you knock down the big flames.

And so I worry about the guy ahead of me in this basement. I worry about him because he is my brother. Not my brother in the universal fraternity of firefighters sense, but my brother in the we-played-in-the-doghouse-dirt sense. Jed is five years younger than I, and far more competent, but as the big brother, I feel protective. He starts down the stairs, steps off into hip-deep water, totters a bit. All that heavy gear, if he falls over, I'll have to drag him out in a hurry. I can hear a muffled exclamation from behind his SCBA mask as the water fills his boots. It's a bitterly cold night, well below zero, with a vicious west wind. He hollers that I should stay where I am. I feed him hose and aim a heavy rechargeable lantern at the darkest corners of the basement while he slops around, craning his neck to spot signs of flame above, wetting them down when he does. When he ventures farther into the dark corners, I get nervous. I holler at him to be careful. I keep checking up and behind me for signs of flame, keep patting the hose with my free hand. That hose is our lifeline. In a spot like this, you never break contact with the hose. Like Tom Sawyer's string strung through a cavern, it's your way out, should things go bad. Dance with it long enough, and fire will show you the difference between bravery and bravado. We advance, but we are equally prepared to retreat. Firefighting is often framed in terms of courage, but courage does not always carry you forward.

It is supposed that fire appeared on this planet right about the time vegetation took root. Lightning struck a patch of dry something and birthed a primeval force of nature. The term implies a certain brutishness, but fire is anything but brutish. It is lightfooted and shamanic, dancing between the visible and invisible, undoing matter one collapsed molecule at a time, wreaking utter destruction with a touch softer than breath. Its poor cousins, wind and water, are one-dimensional rubes by comparison. Wind is all push, push, push. Water is suffocating, but passively so. And even when water gets it together to be a torrent or a tsunami, it is but wet wind. Fire is at once elemental and otherworldly. Fire dances on the grave of all it destroys. Fire is serious voodoo.

How godlike, then, to strike a match. The quick rasp, the spit of the sulfur, and fire leaps to hand. We cannot summon the wind, we cannot—with any reliability—bring down rain, but we can raise fire at will. It is a mythic power: with fire in your hand, you will rule the world. Which is why, as Greek legend has it, Zeus went crazy-ape-bonkers when he learned the demigod Prometheus had stolen fire from Mount Olympus and given it to mankind. His greatest party trick revealed, angry Zeus chained Prometheus to a rock and retained a vulture to drop in daily and rip out the demigod's liver.

Nice story, but the human learning curve on fire spans epochs and is blistered with false starts. Recent reports indicate that man—or at least the *Homo ergaster* version of same—learned to control fire roughly 1.7 million years ago. *Ergaster* likely intended to do nothing grander than roast a handful of seeds or toast his tootsies, but Johan Goudsblom, writing in *Fire and Civilization*, insists the results were anthropologically profound:

> The ability to handle fire . . . is exclusively human. Rudimentary forms of language and tool use are also found among non-human primates and other animals; but only humans have learned, as part of their culture, to control fire.

But of course, we don't always control it. Goudsblom, five pages later: "The perpetual presence of fire in a human group is a complicating factor."

Ergo, firefighters are required.

• • •

I have already mentioned the favorite local joke that all you need to join the local fire department is a valid driver's license and a pulse, but the fire board does eventually require that you attend a firefighting course. The training exercises were a lark. We learned to unfurl a fifty-foot roll of hose by underhanding it like a bowling ball. We raced a stopwatch to see who could "gear up" most quickly. We practiced spraying figure-eights, the fat three-inch hose stiff and insistent, shuddering with the power of compressed water. Once, the largest student in class—well over six feet tall, 250-pound range—let his attention lapse at the nozzle. The hose tipped him over as easily as if he had been nudged by an elephant. We had a good laugh.

The instructor arranged an obstacle course. I waited my turn swaddled from helmet to steel-toed boots in heavy turnout gear, sealed in the intimate, portable environment of the SCBA mask, that transparent barrier between toxic smoke and pink lungs, able to hear little beyond the easy huff and chuff of the respirator. I felt utterly isolated and protected, the way I felt as a child curled up in the darkness beneath a cardboard box fort. We crawled around the course in pairs, the backmost partner clinging to the leader's pack strap. Always partner up, the instructor said, never become separated. Gripping the strap, facedown, unable to see, I tried to raise my head. The oxygen hose resisted, levering the mask from my face, breaking the seal. A rush of air hissed out around my ears. I realigned my face, and the hissing stopped. I still couldn't see. Scrabbling forward, I heard a clang. My oxygen bottle had struck the underside of a fire truck, wedging me against the floor. I was suddenly air-hungry. The measured huff and chuff of the respirator became more insistent. Claustrophobia pressed in. Sweat leapt to my skin. The motion sensor attached to my collar began to caw. An image flashed: Flames. Heat. Dark smoke, thick as poison pudding. Wedged against the concrete, unable to see, unable to move, I suddenly understood what panic for oxygen might drive a man to do. I sucked air out of the tank faster and faster, wasting it, trying to keep up with my heartbeat. My partner wriggled free. I lost my grip on his strap. The low-air alarm kicked in, an incongruous, flatulent ting-a-ling. A thought presented itself, unbidden: You can die doing this.

Nonetheless, fire is a tantalizing enemy. It has an undeniable pull. It lures you close, dares you inside. But as a firefighter, you must look beyond fire's hypnotic face. You see fire, you see it billow and snap, you watch it do its angry amorphous dance, and you are mesmerized into believing it has no more shape than a soul. But to a firefighter, fire is fundamentally geometric. Five minutes into our first evening class, the instructor drew a triangle on the chalkboard. Then he labeled each point: heat, fuel, and oxygen. "The fire triangle," he announced. The fire triangle isn't fire; it is only the potential for fire. For fire made manifest, you need one more ingredient: an uninhibited chemical reaction. "The fire *tetrahedron*," said the instructor, replacing the triangle. He looked around the room. "Remove any one element of the tetrahedron and you put out the fire." It's that simple.

Until you get there. The geometry of fire is one thing. The behavior of fire is another. It grows in volatile stages: The incipient phase, in which a fire is born. Rollover, in which combustible vapors accumulate at ceiling level, then explode into a rolling "fire front." The free-burning phase. Flashover, in which an entire room becomes superheated to the point of simultaneous ignition. The smoldering phase. And then the Hollywood-friendly granddaddy of them all: backdraft. If a fire in a tightly sealed house cycles through the phases and depletes the available oxygen, it will settle into a brooding stasis. The house groans for air, and if you stick your ax through the door, you'll be blown across the yard like a flaming marshmallow out a blast furnace. Should you awaken, you will likely do so in the nearest intensive-care burn unit.

Sometimes, when you're feeling reckless, you forget that. It's dangerous to get reckless, but it happens. There's an undeniable thrill in fighting fire. There are as many reasons to volunteer for this job as there are firefighters, but at some level most of us have a perverse

hunger for danger, a desire to be tested, to survive—a trial by fire, literally. I feel this recklessness sometimes, but it never lasts long. Every
month, *FireRescue Magazine* runs a column titled "In the Line of
Duty." It never lacks material. Article VI, Section 5, of our department's bylaws, a copy of which you are provided upon joining, out-
lines the procedure for draping the headquarters in mourning.

Of course, remove the danger and firefighting is just plain fun.
You get full-grown toys, you get to drive fast, and you get to spray
water. Guys who join up for these reasons roar off to their first fire,
and it's a rush, and they're all hot damn and rock-and-roll. Then the
fire's out, and we spend three hours mopping up, and then another
two hours back at the station scrubbing hoses and running check-
lists, and two or three calls later they just sort of fade away.

Many small-town volunteers feel an unclichéd sense of civic
duty. I see it as an alternative to writing a check for some bureau-
cratic megacharity. We like the idea that when there is trouble,
we're the ones sent in. But the whole "bold and brave" thing gets
overblown. I receive a catalog every few months filled with everything from shoulder holsters to disposable handcuffs. It also features
a range of popular novelty T-shirts for firefighters: WE WALK
WHERE THE DEVIL DANCES and WE GO TO HELL SO
YOU DON'T HAVE TO and I FIGHT WHAT YOU FEAR. Ash
buckets, say I. Self-aggrandizing claptrap. We study, we prepare,
but the fact remains: We are amateurs playing a game in which the
professionals regularly get their tails whipped. I fear what I fight.

In the basement, Jed is making progress, working deeper into the
structure. I track him with the lantern. The beam is solid in the
smoke. I direct it across the space between us, and when I lay it over
his shoulder it is as if I am knighting him with a light saber. I keep
twisting my neck, watching back and above for signs of flame. The
helmet and SCBA mask limit peripheral vision—if you don't keep

books and unopened music within 30 days from any Barnes & Noble store. For merchandise purchased with a check, a store credit will be issued within the first seven days. Without an original receipt, a store credit will be issued at the lowest selling price. With a receipt, returns of new and unread books and unopened music from bn.com can be made for store credit. Textbooks after 14 days or without a receipt are not returnable. Used books are not returnable.

Valid photo ID required for all returns, (except for credit card purchases) exchanges and to receive and redeem store credit. With a receipt, a full refund in the original form of payment will be issued for new and unread books and unopened music within 30 days from any Barnes & Noble store. For merchandise purchased with a check, a store credit will be issued within the first seven days. Without an original receipt, a store credit will be issued at the lowest selling price. With a receipt, returns of new and unread books and unopened music from bn.com can be made for store credit. Textbooks after 14 days or without a receipt are not returnable. Used books are not returnable.

Valid photo ID required for all returns, (except for credit card purchases) exchanges and to receive and redeem store credit. With a receipt, a full refund in the original form of payment will be issued for new and unread books and unopened music within 30 days from any Barnes & Noble store. For merchandise purchased with a check, a store credit will be issued within the first seven days. Without an original receipt, a store credit will be issued at the lowest selling price. With a receipt, returns of new and unread books and unopened music from bn.com can be made for store credit. Textbooks after 14 days or without a receipt are not returnable. Used books are not returnable.

Valid photo ID required for all returns, (except for credit card purchases) your head on a swivel, flames can sneak right over your shoulder before you see them. This is a nervous-making place, but cocoonish, too. When we jumped from the trucks tonight, we stepped into the teeth of a steadfast wind, hurling itself at us from the west, across a wide field of snow. It was a relentless blow, an icy scour. The temperature was already subzero; the wind chill was unthinkable. The wind whipped the flames, bending them out the windows, troweling the chubby rolls of smoke into a flat smear across the sky. The big flames are knocked down now, or we wouldn't be in the basement, but the battle is not won. Firefighters still hustle after equipment, punching through the snow crust like someone perpetually missing a stair step. Tankers come and go, their strobes sweeping the drifts, and the powerful halogen scene lights on the pumper illuminate the house like a monument, casting giant shadows across the siding and into the darkness. Down here in the basement, there is no light, no wind, no flashing strobes. For the moment, we are working alone. Just me and my little brother, playing with fire.

———

Once they had fire in hand, hominids faced the primary challenge of maintenance. Domestic fire required care and feeding. In this respect, the flames were a civilizing force, a catalyst nudging early man toward concepts of communication and cooperation, of unification in support of a common good. We learned to work together to keep fire alive. Subsequently, we learned to work together to put fire out. Today, with fire easily at hand, we no longer require someone to stay up all night stoking the coals. The positive capabilities of fire have been contained and subsumed in such a way that they represent rather than precipitate social cooperation, but the negative capabilities of fire still require attention at the most fundamental level, and as such, still shape the dynamics of community. Fire—dancing in the very same form as that which illumined the face of *Homo ergaster*—remains a force that compels social cooperation. And as long as it requires the formation of volunteer fire brigades, it will be so.

Our desire to court fire is balanced by our desire to keep it at bay.

While Jed and I work in the basement, our brother John is up top somewhere. He's a "red hat"—a lieutenant. I am older, but he outranks me. It is sometimes his duty to put me in harm's way. I shouldn't have teased him for not being able to draw when we were in grade school.

In some ways, fighting fire beside your brothers is the ultimate extension of play, although, for all the things I remember doing with my brothers—building cardboard ships, playing Tarzan in the haymow, crashing our Matchbox cars—I never recall playing fireman. Or even playing with matches, for that matter. There is one other set of three brothers on our department, and we joke that I joined up just to help my family pull even. What is mentioned less often is that once they were four. The fourth brother collapsed while fighting a fire outside town a few years back. He was twenty-six years old and died within the week. Our joking is tempered by a tacit acknowledgment of this history. Once, at a barn fire, deep inside the structure, I remember peering through the smoke and recognizing the two firefighters ahead of me as my brothers. We were arranged along the hose in order of birth, from youngest to oldest. Later, I joked with the chief, told him this was the equivalent of putting the president, vice president, and Speaker of the House on the same airplane.

I was once hired to write an essay about firefighting, and when the editor found out my brothers were on the department with me, he kept pressing me to expand their presence in the piece. "How do you feel, after you fight a fire together?" he'd ask on the phone. "What do you say to each other? How does it draw you closer together as brothers?" I rewrote the piece two different times, but he kept pushing for more. "I still don't quite feel like I'm getting enough about your brothers," he said. "I see this piece as being as much about your relationship with your brothers as with firefighting." I began to see what he wanted. He wanted my brothers and me standing in front of the fire hall, drenched and smoky, locking eyes like blood warriors. Or perhaps clasping each other in wordless bear hugs. The plain truth is, when we get done rolling hose and filling the tankers, we generally seek each other out just long enough for a see-ya, and we go our separate ways. We love one another deeply. I would avenge my brothers in blood if necessary. But we are stoic, and we like it that way, which seems to drive more demonstrative people batty. We are accused of repressing our emotions. In fact, I like my emotions contained. The humiliation I feel in revealing myself far outweighs the putative benefit of "letting it all out." I go for Kierkegaard, and his talk of "passionate inwardness."

So. No hugs beside the fire trucks. My brothers and I lead our separate lives. We work on fires together. We are glad to see one another. We know that. There is no need to comment. When we are done, we go back to our separate lives. It is not so different with anyone else on the department, blood or no. I told the editor this, and he killed the piece.

―――――――――

Over 1.7 million years up in smoke, and we are still beholden to fire. It may be delivered via electrical outlets, or hidden under the hoods of our cars, but it is still fire. Our control of fire has been so refined that it is possible to forget that it even is fire. But that control is hardly absolute. The idea that we have learned to "control" fire is belied by the fact that we still burn our houses down. Truth be told, things are a lot better. We've even noticed it out here—we get more people, but fewer fires. Housing codes, smoke detectors—they've all done their part. Still, fire is a primeval force, and when you bring a primeval force into the house—as we still do, in our furnaces, our cigarettes, our joss sticks, our gas ranges, our candles, our amateur wiring jobs—it doesn't always act civilized.

Fire gives little quarter, but it does play by a few rules, and that's where you must take your advantage. As soon as possible, we try to cut a hole in the roof of a burning house. Ventilation, the fire books call it. You do this to make fire dance your way, to make it rise from the hole like a cobra from a basket. This is called "drawing" the fire. If you're going to dance with fire, this is your one chance to lead. Usually, the roof is opened as directly over the flames as possible, creating a chimney effect. Hot air, smoke, and toxic gases fume out the hole, cooling and clearing the interior so that firefighters can advance and find the seat of the fire. The release of smoke improves visibility and reduces the threat of backdraft and flashover by removing combustible vapors. And in a cooler environment, firefighters are less likely to be burned by superheated steam when they open the hose line. If the hole is cut directly over the fire, the chimney effect will help stabilize it, stand it up straight, and keep it burning in one spot. If the hole is off-centered, the updraft can spread the fire by pulling it through the structure. In any case, the upside of ventilation comes with a downside kicker: If you don't get the fire out quickly after ventilation, it will feed on the increased air flow and shift to high gear. It's a scary thing to poke a hole in the roof, knowing that you are coaxing the fire into your hands by giving it exactly what it wants. It is like dangling raw meat before a lion to coax him from the den—you would be wise to consider your next move before he finishes chewing. Deal is, by the time we get on scene, the fire has often burned through the roof, effectively venting itself. It is a fact of life out here, where help is not always close at hand. Early on, one of the department veterans drew himself up proudly, looked me in the eye, and recited the unofficial department motto: "We have never lost a basement."

We make some saves. At a barn fire two years ago, we arrived quickly enough to contain the fire to one corner of the haymow. If we get a good jump on a chimney fire, we can usually shut it down before it spreads to the walls. But usually we are fighting to preserve as much of the structure as we can and protect everything surrounding it. Preservation enhances any subsequent investigation; it often also yields invaluable artifacts. After all, a house fire is a destruction of the past. The people here are losing their history. I have walked out of burning buildings carrying a charred photo album and watched a teary grandmother clutch it to her breast. I have handed over deer rifles, a child's snow boots, a soggy "Baby's First Year" calendar. These things are touchstones to the past. They have come through fire; their survival renders them totemic.

In *The Acquisition and Control of Fire*, Sigmund Freud claimed that man gained control over fire only after he gained control over his bladder. According to Freud, the first man who saw a small fire and resisted the urge to pee on it committed one of the great acts of civilization. The desire to quell fire, he posited, had to do with demonstrations of sexual potency in a homosexual competition. Furthermore, said Freud, it was no coincidence that Prometheus smuggled fire to man in a hollow fennel stalk—a symbolic penis, capable of extinguishing the very fire it carried. Sigmund would be a treat on a fire scene. The handling of hoses alone would be enough to send him into paroxysms of analytical confabulation. Every time I pull the extension ladder from the pumper and prepare to raise and extend it, I think, Here's lookin' at yer, Sigmund.

Across the majority of our culture, it is no longer necessary to teach children to gather and tend fire. But fire is still strongly associated with numerous cultural taboos and restrictions. Some of the children in this area live in homes heated by wood-burning stoves, and many learn to make campfires at a young age, but in general, their first formal introduction to fire comes in the form of what the French philosopher of science Gaston Bachelard referred to as "social interdiction." This fall, as part of Fire Safety Awareness Week, we took one of our fire trucks over to the school and performed a little social interdiction. Sixty fidgeting grade-schoolers are waiting for us in the band room. They range in age from preschool to third grade. I've been elected to do the talking, so I begin by describing the members of our department as "people just like your mom and dad," and then, looking into all those little faces from homes of every sort, wonder if the reference is universally useful. I move on to 911. "Always stay calm, and never hang up until the person on the phone tells you to." Even adults panic, and having seen people unable to give directions to their own house, we recommend that families keep a clearly written set of directions posted beside the phone. A good concept, but nowadays everyone has six phones, several of them cordless and liable to be tossed anywhere. Still, it's a good idea to know how to tell the dispatcher how to find your location, and how to call you back if you're cut off. "How many of you know your phone number?" I ask. A thicket of hands shoot up.

When I was in kindergarten, Mr. Plomber, the janitor, came to our classroom and installed a plastic phone on the wall so we could practice calling the fire department. While we gathered around to watch him drive the screws, he asked how many of us knew our phone number. Everyone raised their hand but me. "You have to know your phone number, in case you get lost," said Mr. Plomber. I ran to the coat rack and pulled my jacket from the hanger. My mother had written my name and number on the tag. I reported back to Mr. Plomber with the information. "You won't always have that coat," he said.

It was a good coat. Thick and heavy, the outer constructed of fat-ribbed brown corduroy. The snug cuffs kept the snow out, and the oversized steel zipper zipped easily, even in the coldest weather. It must have been a tiny coat; I weighed only forty-five pounds, but it felt substantial as buffalo robes. That winter, Mrs. Warren drove us home from kindergarten in a frosty blue van, and the coat kept me snug. I hated to outgrow that coat.

Without divulging his identity, I tell the children the story of the little boy who didn't know his phone number.

"Who do you think that little boy was?"

"*You!*" They laugh and laugh.

We wind up needing to know a lot in this life. Our phone number, where we live, left from right, how to make toast, how to tell the boys' bathroom from the girls' bathroom. It's daunting to look at these children and recognize how much they already know, even the dullest among them. We humans start slow, but we pick up speed fast. Your chimpanzees and elephants and dolphins and other members of the animal kingdom intelligentsia probably don't get the respect they deserve, but even the brightest lowland gorilla will be hard-pressed to match wits with *Homo sapiens,* even if the *Homo sapiens* in question is a mouth-breather crushing Schlitz cans against his forehead at a demolition derby. The faces in the band room this morning are open and bright. The eyes are a row of shiny buttons, unclouded by the opacities of irony. Attentive, joyful groups of children like this often provoke adults to say goofy things like, "The children are our future!" Of course this statement completely ignores the fact that everyone who has not stopped absorbing oxygen is our future. Children are fascinating, and surprising, and at their best, heavenly sprites, but before you go in too deeply for the idea that the world would be a better place if we were all more childlike, try sticking three kids in one room with two toys. You'll witness conflict-resolution techniques synthesizing the very worst of the Marquis de Sade and the World Wrestling Federation. The world is like it is because, on the whole, we tend to act like children.

So we give children information about fire and hope they make the best of it. I move from 911 to the old standby, "Stop, drop, and roll." Many of them know this one already, it's concise and rhythmic and sticks in your head. A child has a chance with this one, a chance that the saying will lodge in their cortex and become nearly instinctual. "What should you do if you start on fire?" I ask, realizing as I'm saying it that my poor phrasing insinuates they may spontaneously combust. "Stop, drop, and roll!" they cheer, unconcerned by the idea of fire suddenly leaping from their pockets.

"How many of you have smoke detectors in your houses?"

Hands up all over, and a babble of details: "We have one in the kitchen. . . . We have two! . . . We have *six*! . . . My grandma has a parrot . . ." I make a mental note: try to keep the open-ended questions to a minimum. We're coming up on daylight savings time. "When you change your clocks, change the batteries in your smoke detectors," I tell them. We're hoping a lot of this filters home to parents.

The rest of my talk is a miscellany of preparation. Close your bedroom door at night, it will buy you time and breathable air should a fire fill the house with undetected smoke. If you think there is a fire, stay low and find another exit. Don't hide under your bed or in a closet or in the bathtub. If you do leave the room, never open a door without feeling it first with the back of your hand. If it is warm, stay put. Practice fire drills at home just as you do at school. Have your family draw an escape map, make sure you have two escape routes from your room, and make sure the whole family has an agreed-upon meeting place once you escape the house. Never go back in the house. Not even if you have a puppy or favorite toy inside. Most of all, stay calm. We give the address of a Web site that has extensive fire-safety information geared toward children. Then we bring in a fully outfitted firefighter. When you weigh forty pounds, a fully outfitted firefighter looks like a giant swamp monster. So we bring in Tom, all six feet of him, all 230 pounds of him, and he looms even larger in his yellow helmet and sooty bunkers. He's got a tank on his back and a hose from the tank to his face, which is hidden by a mask, and the mask hisses and blows every time he takes a breath. I spin him around in front of the children, pointing out the various pieces of equipment, explaining the whole time that there's one of their neighbors in there, and that if they are in a fire and they see someone like this coming toward them, they must not hide, but instead should let themselves be carried to safety. At the end, Tom takes off his helmet and mask, and grins at the kids, and I crack a joke and stomp on his steel-toed boots to comic effect, and as the room fills with tiny giggles, we hope we have defanged the monster.

Next, the kids troop out, class by class, to a portable smoke house borrowed from the fire department up the road. Lieutenant Pam takes them into the first room. Watching on closed-circuit TV from a small room hidden in the house, Captain Matt releases peanut oil smoke into the room and triggers the fire alarms. Pam tells the children to watch how the smoke slowly descends from the ceiling to the floor, tells them this is why they must stay low, and then, reminding everyone to stay calm, Pam herself gets on all fours and leads the children on a crawl to safety. They emerge through a second-story window at the far end of the trailer, where Tom helps them to a waiting ladder. I am at the top of the ladder, and back them down, one by one, coaching them all the way. At the bottom I tell them to join their classmates at the meeting place.

Pick a meeting place. Change your clock, change your batteries. Crawl low, and go, go, go. Stop, drop, and roll. We are trying to inculcate an ordered response to disorder. Our very presence here admits the possibility of terror—we hope that the catchphrases and the fake smoke will be an inoculation against blind fear should they find themselves facing the real thing. It's a fun day for them and for us, but at the bottom of it all is a grave—to say nothing of primitive—element of any civilization daring to put reins on fire.

We got to talking at the fire meeting the other night about the fire-safety speech and how it has evolved over the years. Today we have the smoke house, bags full of stickers, activity books, and an organized presentation. Several of us remember sitting in the bleachers when we were in grade school and hearing the fire chief explain that "inflammable" was not the opposite of "flammable." He held up an aerosol can of deodorant. "See this?" he asked. "It says 'inflammable' on the label. Now watch." At which point he sprayed the can into the air, pulled out a lighter, and flicked it. The deodorant plume ignited, turning the can into a miniature flamethrower. I suspect the kids hadn't been off the bus five minutes when behind sheds all over the county you heard the roar of flaming Right Guard. I know I tried it. During this same demonstration, we noticed that the chief's hand was wrapped in thick gauze up to his forearm. He burned it while throwing gas on a training fire.

Someone else told the story of another chief who showed up with a crew and a pumper to stand guard at the homecoming bonfire back in the '70s. When the bonfire wouldn't catch, he flung a can of gas on it. The flame raced backward up the gas and leapt to his nylon jacket, whereupon the students were treated to a galvanized demonstration of the old "stop, drop, and roll" chestnut.

These forays into the community are performed to raise safety issues, but they are also intended to inspire a little comfort and confidence in the fire and rescue corps. It doesn't always turn out that way. I have yet to set myself alight during a fire-safety demonstration, but last year, while driving the rescue van in the homecoming parade, my partner, Dan, had stopped to let the rest of the parade catch up. We threw some candy to the kids, and then the parade started up again. Forgetting that the van was in gear, Dan popped the clutch and killed the engine. There had been a lot of stop-and-go during the parade, and because we hadn't kept the idle up, the strobe lights had drained the battery. The van wouldn't start. And so it was that for the last tenth of a mile of the parade route, the citizenry was treated to the sight of their very own rapid-response medical team in action: Dan fighting the dead wheel, me with my back to the rear door, sweating bullets and pushing the van to the school parking lot.

Homo ergaster decided he'd use fire for his own, and that decision shaped the world to follow. It shapes my life, it shapes my town, it forges my relationship with my brothers. Before the magazine editor pressed me on the issue, I never really thought of what role firefighting played in the context of my relationship with my brothers. I have often thought of it since, and if anything, it creates a situation of privilege. The privilege of standing shoulder to shoulder with the playmates of your childhood, sure, but that applies to more than just my brothers in this situation. Scooter Southern is on the department, and that scar on my brother's forehead is from the day I knocked him off Scooter's porch with the screen door. Firefighting isn't the only interest I share with my brothers: we grew up hunting deer together, for instance, and do to this day—but it is the closest to any shared social activity we might engage in together, say, like being on the same softball team. Our pursuits and avocations have little in common. They drive log trucks, I sit in a chair trying to herd words. Put us in a row and turn our palms up—mine are soft and clean. There's your story.

We do not, in the parlance of the day, always celebrate our differences. We're stubborn and strong-willed, and life has taken us down divergent paths of understanding. There are times when we disagree so vehemently that one of us will simply grit his teeth and leave the room. There is never any shouting or arm-waving, that is not our way. An outside observer might miss the whole thing. But disagreements with my brothers often shake me up for days, because they are a reminder of how disagreeing profoundly with someone you love in equal profundity is an intractable dilemma because you don't have the option of dismissing them out of contempt. I read volumes on the Civil War when I was a child, and was always morbidly fascinated with the idea of brother fighting brother. I could never understand how such a thing could be. Today I do. I would kill—I am not speaking figuratively—for my brothers, but I also know that if the course of civilization boiled down to a few salient points, we would be irretrievably opposed. Such a likelihood is highly fanciful, but the thought is still unsettling. There is a certain paradoxical rage weltering in us that explodes when it is nudged too closely by love. These are threads of love and hate traceable to Cain and Abel.

Fire cuts through all that. Down in the basement of that house, we are on the same side, my brother and I. Doing something we both love, fighting something we both fear, covering for each other. Fire is heat and light, able to cut through the murky complications reserved for souls born of the same womb.

Back to the basement. My low-air alarm is sounding. I still have some time, but I have a ways to backtrack before I can safely remove the SCBA. My brother, smaller and in better shape, has air remaining. He has knocked down all but a few small flames. He waves me back. I crawl back out, then immediately second-guess myself. I hear my instructor's voice. *Never become separated.* I was wrong to leave, and he was wrong to stay. Out in the driveway, in the glare of the halogen scene lights, I stare at the smoking skeleton of the house, giving no clue that someone is deep in its bowels. The cold is astounding. We are all encased in a shell of ice. Our sleeves won't bend, our gloves might as well be made of steel. Every once in a while, someone slips and falls, and he paws around on his back, helpless as a turtle, until someone helps him to his feet. I keep staring at the collapsed garage, at the spot where my brother should be reappearing. Why did I leave without him? My guts churn until a few minutes later, he crawls out safely. Anticlimax. As it usually is. What we do rarely ends in heroic conquest or tragedy. It's dangerous, and not to be taken lightly, but what we're basically doing out there, when we haul our hoses out to minivans and garages, up silos, over rooftops, and down into basements, is trying to disrupt the geometry of fire. Kick the slats out of the tetrahedron.

After the fire-safety lecture, we sent the kids on their way with a plastic bag full of goodies—pencils, a ruler, a coloring book, brochures for their parents. Thus armed with cultural interdiction, they climbed aboard their yellow buses and left for home. One of the little boys—I remember helping him down the ladder, he had a cast on his arm—went straight to his backyard and lit a fire in the leaves. Then he stomped on the fire, trying to put it out. His socks caught on fire, badly burning his legs. He stopped, dropped, and rolled, until the fire was out. It was what the firefighters had told him to do, he told the adults who came running.

6

RUNNING THE LOOP

I ONCE RAN A MILE in four minutes and forty-eight seconds. I was a high-schooler then, a New Auburn Trojan. My senior year, I was the only boy on the track team. The picture is there in the 1983 year-book—just me, up against the wall, grinning, over the caption, "Boys Track Team—Mike Perry." I trained alone, and my coach drove me to meets in his little red car. I enjoyed racing, but dreaded the gut-churning buildup to the starting gun. I spent a lot of time in the Porta-Potty. I ran solitary warm-up laps, and I was always meeting packs of grinning sprinters. I envied them the speed and brevity of their events. Win or lose, they were done in a matter of seconds. Me, on the other hand, I stood there at the start line of the two-mile with quaking bowels and the full knowledge that I was in for a minimum ten minutes of anoxia and rib stitches. The sprinters were brash and cocky. They ran their warm-up laps against the flow. In-variably one of them would leer at the emblem on my singlet: "Woo-hoo! I used *my* Trojan last night!"

I still do a little running. I have this loop, 3.9 miles, a few hills and slow rises, just enough to burn your legs and lug the engine some. I try to run it four or five times a week. The loop is laid out in a rectangle, with a bite out of one corner where Highway Q curves up and over the four-lane. To run the loop is to trace an off-kilter frame around my hometown. I think of myself taking a lap inside a living zoetrope, moving past images presented in collage and linked by constantly shifting associations, overlapping and bleeding through to form a dynamic composition of history, place and event. I run the loop, and I get perspective.

I usually lift weights first. Something to get the blood moving, prepare the lungs. I rank the joys of weight lifting somewhere between dish washing and dentistry. And lifting weights in a town where most men swing hammers or run shovels or wrassle logs feels absurd and ersatz. But a guy will not maintain tone through typing alone. So I strap in and commit myself to the process, which amounts to a series of grunts accreted in tedium. Only my compulsive counting affliction keeps me going. I am always counting: the number of twists it takes to run the can opener around a tuna tin, the number of chops it takes to dice a leek, the number of turns required to retrieve the arrow on my carp-shooting rig. Ticking off each weight-lifting repetition and arranging them in twelve-rep sets (in my head, they accumulate in neat, soothing rows) feeds the compulsion. And music helps. In particular, the group Venison and their 1996 opus *HATE!* Twelve tracks of can-do rage and post-industrial stoicism. Diesel-grade rock. Just the sort of propulsion required for pointless hoisting. "*In Wisconsin*," roars front man Rick Fuller, referencing our state motto, "*we say, 'Forward!'*"

After the last set of reps, I'm ready to run. At least when you run, you cover some ground. I leave the house and head up Main Street. Up being east. Past Tugg's Bar, past Snook's store, past the meat market, up to where Main Street forms a T with East Street, a block and a half from my front door. Fourteen addresses, counting homes and businesses and both sides of the street. Since I joined the department five years ago, I have made calls to half of them. Guy across the street hurt his back. One of the Goshen girls had a seizure in front of the store. Some kids pitched a smoke bomb in the storage shed behind the meat market and it caught fire. I nearly keeled over in the heat of that one. An old man in the little white house next to Ward Southern's was digging a pit in his yard when he began to have chest pain. When I heard the address, I just grabbed the emergency kit from the trunk of my car and ran up the street. His wife called to me through the screen. The man up at East Street and Main dials 911 when his lungs seize up. We've been there four or five times. Tuff at the bar, his heart has been kicking in and out lately, and we've given him oxygen in the back room some mornings.

If you go straight at the T, keep running east, you'll wind up in Herbie Gravunder's barn. His farm sits right off the end of Main Street. Herbie's gone now, and the real estate agents are beginning to chunk up his land, divvy it out in lots. He died a year ago, at the age of eighty-seven, after a nasty fall led to a terminal stretch in the nursing home. Herbie cussed the nursing home. Toward the end, he used to phone his cousin Delmar, try to get sprung. Delmar is seventy-nine years old now. He and Herbie used to run together. Tooled around the Mud Brook back roads on motorcycles. Delmar had a Honda 350, Herbie had a Harley Davidson Sprint. Delmar says you had to pay attention, you'd hit a patch of gravel and pack sand up your snoot. Herbie came up on a herd of cows once and had to lay the Harley down. Delmar says he shot right under a Holstein.

Herbie was stone deaf. A result, ironically or not, of the years he spent running a rock crusher for the county. And Delmar says in the old days they always pulled the mufflers off their tractors, figuring the louder the engine the more power it had. Herbie always had little tufts of cotton sticking out his ears, but then so did most of the old farmers I remember from my childhood. Anyway, what with the deafness, and the cotton, and the flannel earflapper cap he wore most of the time, Herbie lived in a muffled world. He drove this little red pickup, and sometimes he'd have his foot on the accelerator when he started it, and it would just roar. Oblivious, he'd hit the starter again, and the sound was like a sidewinder grinder chewing through sheet metal. My brother John worked behind the parts counter at the implement store for a while, and Herbie used to come in regular. He'd wander into the shop area and cuss in disbelief at the size of tractors these days. Herbie was one of your heartfelt cussers. Every other word, pretty much. He left this little trail of blue smoke, my brother used to say. Once I told Delmar, "Ol' Herbie had quite a vocabulary!" Delmar crinkled his eyes. "Yeah? Well it ain't in the dictionary."

Herbie was a worker. He'd get up at four A.M. to milk his cows, then run a school bus route, return home for chores, and reverse the process after lunch. He drove milk truck back when you slung the milk aboard in 100-pound steel cans and when there were so many farms in the country that the milk truck doubled as the snow plow. He drove the truck that oiled the country roads, and he put up light poles for the Rural Electrification Administration. In 1934, Herbie bought the local blacksmith shop. He did general repairs and welding, and sold gas until the new highway drained the traffic out of town. He went to the blacksmith shop most every morning, right up to the last. I'd see him putt down Main Street, never much over fifteen miles an hour. Herbie couldn't be rushed. I went for a bicycle ride on Highway M one afternoon, caught him on the double yellow with traffic coming, and had to dawdle behind him for a quarter mile until he turned off at Delmar's farm. Delmar says Herbie always arrived with a line of cars behind him.

Herbie wasn't always averse to speed. There were the motorcycles, and sometime in the '70s he bought a used hovercraft. He tricked it out with running lights, a sonorous Model T horn, and—in a reversal of the *noise equals power* theory—a pair of chromed motorcycle tailpipes. He replaced the steering mechanism with an airplane yoke. Delmar says the hovercraft never quite worked right because the skirt was torn and Herbie removed it, not understanding that you can't get any lift without the skirt. Herbie called Delmar one night after chores and they took the hovercraft out to Loon Lake for a test run. Without the skirt, it wouldn't do much. Delmar says they sat side by side out in the water—neither one could swim—and Herbie ginned the engine up. The hovercraft began to rise, and they had their hopes up there for a little bit, but then a giant air bubble rolled out from beneath the craft and they plopped back down. Delmar says that was about it. They just sat there and blew big ploppy bubbles. Come winter, Herbie had a brainstorm. He bolted a steel frame to the bottom of the hovercraft and welded three snowmobile skis to it. Then he called Delmar. (Delmar is spare and soft-spoken. Farmed all his life. You get the image of him as the loyal, if sometimes terrified, sidekick. He used to grumble about Herbie calling him all the time, interrupting his chores, but now he says he sure misses him.) This time Herbie and Delmar went out to Long Lake, which was a lot *longer* than Loon Lake, and took a test run. The steel skis and frame were awful heavy, and Delmar says Herbie had to flat pour the cobs to'er before they started to inch forward. Tailpipes or not, the noise was astounding. Carfuls of spectators began to accumulate on the road at the far end of the lake. Herbie kept his foot in it, and pretty soon they were shooting over the ice. The fixed skis made it almost impossible to steer, and Delmar's crow's feet wrinkle when he tells about how they fought to turn the thing as the shore approached. They had a good day, though, Delmar says, rocketing back and forth across the lake with all those people watching.

And Herbie loved airplanes. If you knew anything about flying he would talk your ear off. He used to bum flights from local pilots. He never got a license himself, but somewhere along the line he bought an airplane that had been in a crash. The wings were damaged, and it wouldn't fly, but the engine ran, and the prop was intact. Herbie used to fire it up and taxi around his hayfield, happy as a clam. If you wanted, he'd give you a ride. In the winter he outfitted it with skis. He went to visit the neighbors once, and the ski tips got caught under the snow crust. Herbie climbed out of the cockpit and was kicking the skis free when he leaned forward and the prop snicked that earflapper cap right off his head. He loved to tell that one.

We never saw them, but Herbie's hoverless hovercraft and flight-less plane were part of local legend when my brothers and I were growing up. We used to speculate on them with the fascination young boys have for things that roar and fly. Rumor had it the hov-ercraft was hidden in the blacksmith shop somewhere, buried under the heaps of junk and steel that gradually overtook the space in Her-bie's later years.

It got to where Herbie was falling a lot. I was out of town the last time Herbie fell and he had to be taken away in the ambulance. He never did make it back home. I turn right at the T and head south down East Street, along the edge of Herbie's cow pasture, now host-ing the two newest houses in town.

East Street dips at Elm Street, and drops to cross a swale. During the spring melt, water rushes through the culvert at the center of the swale, then cuts across the wide green swathe of the Lions Club Park. Last I checked, the New Auburn Lions Club consisted of five members, and they weren't getting along. After a period of neglect and decline, the park is being spruced up again. Volunteers have torn down the dilapidated old fair barn, put in new volleyball courts, upgraded the softball field, and raised money to put a foot-bridge over the spillway in the swale. A lot of the drive to improve the park is coming from my generation. They want their children to be able to play Little League ball and get a few carnival rides in dur-ing Jamboree Days. Like the old days, in 1975.

Straight across from the park is the village trailer court. The trailers are tightly packed, and arranged along a gentle up-slope. Right be-side the road, there's a rectangle of dirt where a trailer is missing. It burned last winter. We got the call at midnight. Jack Most and I were there first, with the attack pumper. Fire can shoot through a trailer in less than two minutes, and flames were already rolling out the roof on the upwind end, so I grabbed a hand line and bulled through the thigh-deep snow while Jack fired the pump. My idea was to get to the door situated roughly midway between either end of the trailer and try to cut the fire off, keep it contained to one end. Time and the wind were against me. By the time I hit the flimsy steel steps, Jack had fed me water, so I got low, and forearmed the door open. Peering through my face shield, I could see the interior was filled with smoke, and the flames were already past the doorway. The water punched a hole in the flames, but I was overmatched. I heard the sirens of Pumper One and the other trucks arriving. Someone ran up and said the residents were unaccounted for. We huddled quickly and figured if someone was still in the trailer—someone of whom there was any hope at all of saving—he or she would be in the bedroom, which was on the downwind end. The chief sent someone around the exterior of the trailer to scout for a second point of entry. A couple of us slung on air packs and tugged our masks on. "Packing up," we call it. You practice over and over so you can pack up without a hitch in moments just like these, but the cold and the snow and the darkness and spinning lights make it tough. Sometime your hands go numb and stiffen with cold. Sometimes you get it all on and then you're hung up with something silly, like maybe you can't find a glove. You bend at the waist and peer around at the ground like a myopic robot. When the tank is on my back and the straps are all tight and the mask is sealed and locked, I wave at Brianna, the firefighter who is lining up the extra air tanks. She gives me a quick once-over. She checks for any gaps between the fireproof Nomex hood and my mask, adjusts and refastens the Velcro collar tab that forms a protective wrap around my throat. It's critical, what she's doing. Leave any skin exposed and at some point it will be fried or frozen.

The scout is back. He has located a small porch attached to the rear of the trailer, alongside the bedroom area. We'll make an attack from there. A new guy drove Pumper One, and he missed the drive and backed into the ditch. There'll be an award in that. The headlights are pointing at the stars, but the crew has still managed to lay and charge the two-and-a-halfs and set up gated wyes (devices that split one large hose into two smaller hoses), so we've got plenty of water and hose. Armed with a charged line and a heavy flashlight, three of us head in through the porch. Two other firefighters stay just outside the door to feed and retrieve hose. I'm on the nozzle. Lisa, a firefighter who got her training in the military, is right behind me, one hand gripping the cuff of my bunkers, the way we practiced in class. They used to teach us to hang on to each other's boots, but this often results in getting your boot yanked off. Actually, our instructor told us it was safest to hang on to the strap of your partner's air pack, but then you wind up right on top of him. The cuff is a compromise.

We crawl through the porch, and off to the right I can feel a door. *Try before you pry*, our instructor used to say, and so I turn the knob and sure enough the aluminum storm door swings out and the interior door swings in. I can tell we are in a hallway, but that's it. The flashlight is no help. As soon as it hits the smoke, the light turns into a white pillar. We've only just received our thermal imager, and someone back at the truck is still setting it up. Flames are advancing down the hallway. I sweep the nozzle back and forth across the ceiling, pushing the fire back. The flames disappear, and we can feel the heat of the steam through our Nomex hoods. We advance a little more. Muffled behind her mask, Lisa hollers at me to check for heat on the floor. If the fire is working underneath, we could break through and become trapped. Good point. I pull off a glove and feel the floor. It's an inch deep with warm water, but isn't hot. Later I wonder how smart it was to pull off a glove in there.

Four feet inside the door, we're at a dead end. As good as blind in the smoke, we can't find a way into the bedroom. And the flames keep coming back, flashing down the hallway and over our heads. We repel them, and they return. We're still fighting time and wind. I keep having this vision of a body in the bedroom. Once, the fire drives us back out to the little porch, and the storm door latches. Flames shimmy behind the glass. I twist the nozzle to fog stream, swing it like a baseball bat, smash the glass, then stuff the nozzle inside and whirl it around and around until we can fight our way back in. We gain, and get the door open again, and make another charge. I knee-walk up the hallway, holding the hose waist-high, like an Uzi, and blast away. We knock the fire clear back to the living room. I get caught up in the battle, and like some *Backdraft!* wannabe, give out with a "*Wooo-hooo!*" Smoke and steam close in all around us.

Someone finally hands up the thermal imager, and when I swing it around, I see I might have spared myself the woo-hoos. There are flames above me. There are flames to the right of me. The black-and-white screen reveals the outline of the bedroom door—behind us, it turns out, our access blocked by the porch door—and it frames a dancing shock of flames. None of this was visible without the imager. The smoke and steam obscure everything. I scan as much of the bedroom as I can, looking for a body, which should show on the screen as a glowing white lump. Nothing. We have to retreat again. This time, while we're kneeling on the porch steps, regrouping, someone hollers into my mask. They've located the family. Someone has them on the phone, they're out of town. The battle plan is re-drawn. The vinyl siding on the adjacent trailer has begun to ruffle in the heat. We go from trying to save lives to saving property. I'm glad we went in, though. It's good to look at Lisa or Matt or Jack, or any of the others who took their turns, and know they've proven themselves. If they had made it in, and pulled someone out, they would be heroes. I don't care to think of myself in terms of hero-ism—it's distasteful and presumptuous (previous performance does not guarantee future results), and frankly, you do a lot of this stuff without thinking and against training and better judgment—but I am intrigued by the idea that the recognition of heroism requires your being caught at it. Under the supposition that someone is trapped in the bedroom, fighting your way into what turns out to be an empty house is no more or less heroic than fighting your way into one harboring a victim. The difference is one of result, not intent. But until courage meets circumstance, there are no heroes.

· · ·

Up the street from the trailer park, I jog past the Seventh Day Baptist parsonage. The pastor's car caught fire once. Total loss, but we kept the fire out of an overhanging pine tree. Next door to the parsonage, a small green house. We've been there several times to treat a toddler having seizures. Two doors farther down, the house where I fought my first chimney fire. I'd been in town only a few weeks, and when the siren went off, I ran to the hall, thinking, Please let me not do anything stupid. I've always been one for setting the bar low. I was an awful basketball player in high school, and was flooded with relief when I went to the foul line during a game and missed the shot, but hit the rim. Anything but an air ball, I remember thinking. I jumped in the brush rig with Mack Most, a department veteran, and, bless his heart, he popped the clutch and blasted out the garage door, forgetting the battery charger hooked to the on-board pump. The charger hit the floor with a screech and a clank, and I felt the same craven relief as I had on the free-throw line. Veteran screwed up, pressure's off. Once we got to the fire I mostly hauled buckets of ash and cinder. Tony Barker reminded me to leave the hose nozzles cracked on nights this cold so the water didn't freeze, and he showed me the trick to popping the heavy lantern out of the charger rack on the pumper. Little bits of knowledge to be squirreled away. Last month we responded to an alarm at the new high school and I found one of the new guys fighting to get the lantern loose. I reached over his shoulder and popped it right out. Now he knows. Off to the right I see the banker's house. Never been there on a call, but in grade school, his daughter hit me with a dodge ball and chipped my two front teeth. I never got them fixed. When I muse, I mouth-breathe and poke at the divots with my tongue.

To the stop sign now, the one marking the end of East Street where it tees with County Road AA. There's a little house out here, stuck out away from the rest of the town. Used to be yellow, and one night we went there because a woman thought she was having a heart attack. I believe what she was having was her seventeenth beer. I gave her a sternal rub, this thing they teach you that is the equivalent of giving someone a chest noogie, and she didn't even flinch. At some point, that family moved on, and now Lisa (the fire-fighter who went into the trailer with me) lives there with her boyfriend. He's a master electrician. They've fixed the place up nice—new siding, sturdy garage. They've got a nifty kennel setup on the back of the garage, where they keep half a dozen coon dogs. When I turn right at the stop sign and head west past the house, the dogs howl and bay. I haven't been coon hunting since high school. It's a pleasure listening to the dogs work, to hear the change in their tune when they switch to barking *tree*, and I liked stumbling through the woods and swamps after dark—so familiar by day, so foreign at night—but I never quite got used to the part where the treed coon was transfixed in the light and shot. When the coon hit the ground, the dogs set upon it in a fury. A coon will rip a dog up good, and given water enough, will drown a dog by dunking its head, but I was never comfortable with the coon hunt denouement. These days, a coon skin isn't worth much, and you can't run the land the way you used to, what with all the newcomers and smaller properties, so coon hunting is on the fade. Lisa and her boyfriend have taken to running bear. Another stop sign. I look left, right, left, and head across old Highway 53.

I try to stay in shape for the usual reasons, but also because it makes me feel better on fire and ambulance runs. You'll notice your aver-age volunteer firefighter isn't always in fighting trim. If my heart has to pound—and it does, every time—I'd like it to pound strong. Although I do fear the Jim Fixx curse. Fixx was one of the forefa-thers of the jogging movement. Kept himself in tip-top shape. And keeled over dead at the age of fifty-two, while running. The come-dian Denis Leary speculates he was discovered by a pair of smokers on their way to the 7-Eleven for a pack of Lucky's. It will be a mat-ter of no small irony if my beer-bellied brethren drag my carcass off someday, thanks to some anomalous disruption in my QRS com-plex. Or thanks to my getting smacked by a turkey truck while taking my aerobic constitutional. I feel good when I'm in shape, though, and so I put down the Ho-Hos, drag myself out of the chair, and run the loop.

I am across the old highway now, across the railroad tracks, and leaning into the easy uphill curve of County Q. I was chugging along here last fall when I was forced to the shoulder by a pack of Amish youths cruising down the hill on RollerBlades. There is really no way to prepare for that sort of thing.

I'm a little loath to write about the Amish, because I am not an expert on their culture and beliefs, and it seems that most folks are. You'll notice that people who wouldn't know the Pope from the Reverend Sun-Myung Moon will jump to set you straight on the Amish creed, rattling on at great length and detail about what it is exactly that the Amish will not eat, snort, wear, do, or drive. I have a friend who has researched, lived with, and written about the Amish for years. When she lived with an Amish family for a week and wrote about the experience for a popular magazine, it seemed that half of her mail was written by hair-triggered autodidacts questioning her authority because they had spied a telephone wire in one of the accompanying photos. The truth is that the Amish spin off splinter sects as prolifically as every other group organized around religion and lifestyle. "Our" Amish, apparently, are OK with the in-line skating.

I worked on a building crew with a local Amish fellow one summer. His name was Levi, and I gave him a ride to the job site every day. He tended to hog the power tools, but other than that we got along fine. I once interviewed a man who drove the Budweiser Clydesdales at the World Series, and it turned out that he was lapsed Amish. As lapses go, that's world class. He said several of the drivers were lapsed Amish, a fact he attributed to the diminishing number of young people in America raised to drive horses. One of the Amish neighbor boys used to go deer hunting with us. He wore a red satin ribbon around his neck to ward off nosebleeds. Today my mother and his trade food and baby-sitting tips.

There have been Amish families in the area for years, but lately the influx has increased. Most are not your postcard Amish. In addition to the skating, they cuss and smoke cheroots. Several of them live in slapdash trailer houses. I have hung with them at auctions and they say rude things about particular women. One night when I was on my way to take the night shift on the Chetek ambulance, a horse and carriage pulled out from the convenience store parking lot ahead of me. We were only about 300 yards from the Highway 53 on-ramp, so rather than pass, I just settled in behind. I was kind of relishing the cross-cultural moment when my Amish brother leaned out and slung a Popsicle wrapper into my headlights. An Amish litterbug. It was like seeing Santa Claus hawk a loogie in the mall.

It would appear that what we have here—and appropriately so— are your redneck Amish. I'm all for it. The friend who wrote the magazine piece tells of how a loud bejeweled woman in a Lincoln once reported a picturesque Amish man to the local tourism board because he wouldn't stop plowing and pose for a snapshot. I'd like to think that if she'd tried that with our Amish, they'd have skated her down, made rude comments about her pantsuit, and stubbed out their Swisher Sweets on her Valino-grain Landau vinyl roof.

At the crest of the rise in Highway Q, I cross the Highway 53 overpass. If it's daylight, a trucker might blow his horn or a motorist might wave, but mostly everyone is preoccupied with pell-melling one place or the other, bound for home or the cabin up north, or hammering off to Wal-Mart to buy yet another plastic storage bin. In the summer, you'll see a lot of Illinois plates. Saturday afternoons you'll see battered stock cars on trailers being towed to the dirt track races up north. There are times—the Friday night before opening day of deer season, for one—when the northbound flow will be steady late into the night, a river of taillights. The whole works reverses itself late Sunday afternoon. Mostly, though, traffic is spotty. From up here along the bridge rail, you hear the hiss of the tires more than the engines.

Sometimes condensation will form up beneath the overpass, and if it's cold enough, an ice slick forms. One night, a van pulling a horse trailer hit the ice and flipped. When the page came in, I was setting up a tent in my living room and eating venison jerky. I was leaving for Central America the next day. When I ran out of the house, I had a piece of the jerky stuck in my teeth. I sucked and probed at that thing throughout the whole call. Drove me nuts until I got back to the fire hall and flossed it loose with a piece of paper torn from an envelope. It was face-numbing cold and snowing out there. We were dispersing to check for victims when we heard this buzzing sound, so low it didn't register at first, and when we turned, a car was pinwheeling toward us. The buzz was emanating from the snow tire treads as they slid across the ice. The car whizzed right through our little group. It was one of those moments where you just exchange glances knowing you are alive only by luck and by inches, shake your head, and go back to work. Twenty-four hours later, I was in Belize City, sweating under my backpack and fending off a street hustler. We function under cosmic whims.

By the time I make the overpass, I can tell what sort of run it's going to be. My heart rate is up, the sweat is flowing, my breathing has settled on an in-and-out groove. Lately I've been able to push the pace below seven minutes per mile, but I reckon my days as a sub-five miler are gone for good. Advancing age, for one thing. A maturing aversion to elective suffering, for another. A stretch of several years spent racing bicycles left me with the heavy quads and glutes of a sprinter, *sans* the speed. And any runner will tell you there are times when you feel like your feet are set in concrete, no matter what shape you're in. But some nights—through the aggregate voodoo of biorhythm, the alignment of the Crab Nebula, and the angle of approaching weather fronts—I feel as if I am in my little Trojan top, heading into the last turn, trim and kicking it a little, with no one between me and the finish line.

Almost immediately after the overpass, I turn right, heading due west again, down Tarr Road, named after Charles Tarr, the man who surveyed and platted our village in 1883. There is a machine shed and a set of grain bins on the corner here, always kept neat as a pin by the farmer who owns them. He was transferring some liquid fertilizer last spring when a coupler broke, and he took a pretty good dose to the face. I drove the ambulance so that the two Bloomer EMTs could work together in the back, flushing his eyes and keeping close watch on his respiratory status. We got him to the hospital in a hurry, and it was good to see him back on his tractor later that week.

Just past the grain bins, the land opens and falls away north in a gentle, expansive draw. A good chunk of the village is visible from here, and you can form a picture of how the area looked when David Cartwright arrived to set up his sawmill in 1875. I enjoy erasing the buildings, trying to imagine the view as it was in the days of the Sioux and Ojibwa, the timber so thick snow clung to the north side of hills through the end of summer. When the logging crews stripped the trees, sunlight went straight to the earth, and the growing season expanded by ten days, or so a local history book claims.

From this perspective you can understand what the state highway designers saw on their topographical maps, how they designed the four lanes to sweep up the draw, skirting the south and west sides of the village in a wide curve. Old Highway 53 ran right up the gut of the village, and when the highway moved out of town, it stripped those guts out. Like countless other villages in similar circumstances, New Auburn is creeping out toward the newer interchange, but progress has been slow. We don't get enough traffic to keep the Gas-N-Go open after midnight.

Onward now, past Dave David's dairy farm and his archetypical red barn full of archetypical Holstein milk cows. Through the 1970s, this country was studded with one-man operations like Dave's. Today his setup is rapidly approaching museum status. During the holiday season, he strings the tall face of the barn with blue Christmas lights in the shape of a giant Star of Bethlehem, visible to all the southbound cars on the freeway. When I run past it at night, it makes me feel small and steady.

I tend to run at night. The idea of running in the morning is repulsive, and I retain strong reservations about anyone who launches their day with briskness of any sort, let alone an alacritous jog. I'll run before dinner sometimes. That seems civilized, and the metabolic boost is a friend to digestion. But the best running is after midnight. Especially in the frozen heart of winter. The earth is still, and the air is liquid ice. Every breath is a purification. I'll have been writing, I'll be all tanked up and humming on black coffee, but by the time I hit Tarr Road, everything is recalibrated. The ratio of breaths to footfalls fixes itself in my head (again, the compulsive counting) and becomes a mantra. Four footfalls in, four footfalls out, usually. Down a stride or two on hills. When I reach this state, the running becomes autonomic. Mind and body separate. The bone-and-muscle machine churns along, all kinetics and mechanics, literally a body in motion. The mind, focused by rhythm, settles into a placid state of cogitation. It is fascinating to contemplate the unspooling of thought amid all the corporeal overrevving. I have unstuck many an essay while running Tarr Road. The tangential associations that lead from one thing to another seem to reveal themselves, flushed from cover by the hydraulics of pumping blood. Sometimes the sorting is personal—I have arrived at signal decisions (re-finance the house; tell her we need to see other people; paint the old International dark green and the rims black) on that little westbound stretch.

If the night is particularly black, the road will be indiscernible at my feet, and despite that fact that I am bundled and bulky, the invisibility of the blacktop heightens the sensation that I am running lightly. I trust my feet to find their way, to read the road as they hit it, to share the information with my gyroscope head and make the perpetual split-second adjustments required to keep the body upright. One deep-freeze night, I ran the loop at about two A.M., under weak moonlight. The road was patchy with pack snow and exposed blacktop. White patches and black patches. I stepped on the black patches wherever possible. Just past the barn and the Star of Bethlehem, the black patch in front of me—not six feet away—exploded with a *whuff!* and went gallumphing away, now a black spot receding across an open field. My heart was going like a trip-hammer. The black spot was a black bear. Another two yards and I'd have been astride the beast. Although I was running into a slight headwind, I can't understand how I got so close before he bolted. Or why that bear wasn't hibernating. I navigated the remainder of the course at premium velocity.

By the time I descend Rogge Hill—a meteor once slid from the black sky here at such a vertiginous angle it threw me off stride—and make the right turn onto County M, I am into oxygen debt. Most of the clear thinking is finished. The body reclaims my attention. I have to focus on my legs to keep them driving, focus on the counting to keep the ratios tuned. This is the stretch for mind over matter.

Last spring I spotted the first flowers of the year here. When the snow recedes, it leaves the ditch grass flat, and you'll spy a lot of little treasures. Lots of trash, sure—your beer cans, your IGA broasted chicken boxes, your foam coffee cups, a bundle of discarded deer legs—but some unexpected goodies now and then. I found a nine-inch adjustable jaw wrench once, and a magnetic door sign from an electric company truck. I switched the wrench from hand to hand the rest of the way home, thrilled to chalk a twelve-dollar victory into the sparse little "things that went my way" column we all keep in our head. The door sign I stuck on my fridge. The electric company had changed names, so I figured they wouldn't miss it. At one foot by three feet, it is the mother of all refrigerator magnets.

The flowers were in the left-hand ditch, right at the base of the final hill. I'm not a big flower guy—I prefer green to gaudy—but their vivid magenta stood out so against the muddy tailings of the ditch that I was compelled to stop. I bent to look them over and was struck by their delicacy. They had the shape of tiny daisies. Each flower was about the size of a dime, and they were arranged in a piquant little clump. "Yay, life!" they seemed to say. You couldn't help but get a little boost. I started running again, and sixty yards down the road, spotted another flash of color. A mint copy of *Bizarre Letters*. Red-letter headlines: "NASTY NIPPLES," "DIRTY LITTLE PANTIES," "I WATCH MY WIFE GET BANGED!"

Up the last hill now, a long climb up and around the last curve into town. To my left, a cornfield that caught fire the first year I was with the department. Got it shut down before it made the buildings. To my right, a handful of horses that have a habit of crowding the fence and pacing me up the hill. I look at them rippling and snorting and figure they must take me for a halting toad. The dog at the top of the hill will bark and chase, but he never bites. Around the curve then, and crest the rise to the overpass that takes me back over the four-lane. The town opens up to me here, straight through to Main Street, and once again I can superimpose history. I have seen the photos from the turn of the century—the buildings arranged in a sparse huddle, the long-gone clapboard schoolhouse, the vanished United Brethren Church, the false-front buildings and plank sidewalks, Mr. Tarr's farm right on Main Street, his rectangular white beehives scattered across a field where the fire hall stands today. If I study the pictures for too long, I am swept with that futile longing we humans seem to have for irrecoverable days. I ache to step into the photo, just have a look around. The best I can do is ignore the asphalt and conjure up the dirt track I see in the old pictures, soft and ribboned with buggy tracks. Two blocks and I am recrossing the railroad. Half a block more, and I am at my porch. If it's summer, and the sun is still up, I'll take off my shoes and socks and sit on the stoop with something cold to drink. My body feels flush and my heart feels strong. I rest my back against the storm door, wiggle my toes some, and when someone drives by, I give that little hometown nod.

• • •

Life is not a perfect little loop. I talked to Delmar Gravunder the other day, and he said Herbie always swore he'd never have an auction. "He ended up having one, all right," said Delmar. Delmar was there, and I was there, and so were a lot of the old-timers and locals. Herbie's seven tractors were there, all in a row. "None of those things ever started," chuckled Delmar. "He'd pick one and call me, and I'd have to drag him around the field until it fired." Hundreds of hand tools, some of them dating back to the 1800s, were leaned all around the base of the barn. There were wagonloads of junk and treasure, and you could tell whenever something was treasure, because people none of us recognized would slip to the front of the crowd and start running the prices up. "Herbie gave me an old flat-iron one day," said Delmar. "He said, 'Here, you take this.' I figured I'd pick it up some other time. Well, that thing went for eighty or ninety dollars." He doesn't care about the money, he just can't imagine.

I hung around the edges, bidding now and then. Got a stack of old ledgers dating back to the days when New Auburn was called Cartwright. They were from the livery stables that used to stand where Herbie had his blacksmith shop, and I felt like I was being allowed just a taste of coveted time travel when I leafed through and recognized some of the names. I bought Herbie's old ice-fishing sled, some fishing gaffs he had rigged up, and a carp spear he hammered out on his forge.

In the face of Herbie's vast and eclectic accumulations, the auctioneers split the sale after lunch. Delmar stayed at the farm, and I followed the second auctioneer over to the blacksmith shop. I had never been in there. I had heard it was crammed with junk, but the auction crew had cleaned and swept and arranged everything neatly for sale, and there—*glory be!*—was the legendary hovercraft. A 410 Air Cycle. It looked straight out of the Jetsons, light blue, with a low-slung seat and a gaping maw, covered with chicken wire, that housed a beautiful three-bladed aluminum prop. I was circling it when my brother John

pulled up in his old dump truck. I waved him over and pointed at the
hovercraft. He grinned, big. I had no idea what the thing might go
for, and I was pretty much tapped, but I figured I'd go two hundred
dollars. I looked at my brother. "Think we could get two hundred
dollars' worth of fun out of that thing?" He grinned bigger. "A-yep."

They fired it up before the bidding began, and it filled the shop
with wind and thunder. Herbie's customized steel frame and snowmobile skis were still attached, so it wouldn't float, but you could see it
straining to lift. The auctioneer started the bidding, and for a while no
one bit, but then some guy went thirty-five bucks. I got in, and from
then on it was just me and him. Turns out when they split the auction,
most people didn't realize it. There were only about ten of us in the
dark little building. We bounced it back and forth between us, Mr.
Thirty-Five Dollars and I, cueing the auctioneer with just the slightest little tilt of an eyebrow. You're playing a sort of poker here, and I
was stone-faced, but my arms were crossed over my chest and I could
feel my heart going like mad. We cleared $100 and worked our way
up to my limit, and then the other guy bid $210, but it seemed to me
that he was starting to grind his gears, so I hung in and went $220,
and then the auctioneer was pointing at the other guy, and pointing
again, and then the guy shook his head and turned away, and I owned
myself a hovercraft. The minute we got it to his farm, my brother Jed
put it on his shop hoist and pulled off all the extra steel.

We convened that evening in Jed's yard, a little knot of us: me, Jed,
John, Mom (the home farm is adjacent—she cruised up in her bat-
tleship Lincoln), and Cerise, a friend of the family who was accompanied by her daughter Brandy and son Adam. Jed is the smallest
and lightest of us brothers, and was thus elected to make the inau-
gural flight. He switched the key to on, and Herbie's running lights
glowed up red and green. Then he twisted the key to start, and the
engine caught as if it had never been parked. The propeller became
an invisible blur, but you could hear the vicious buzz as it sucked
down air and blew it out the base of the craft. The grass flattened

ten feet in every direction. Jed punched the accelerator, the engine noise rose to an astounding howl, and then he was floating, down the length of the yard, gathering speed, headed for the barn. He cranked the airplane yoke to the left when he hit the gravel driveway, and as he spun and headed back for us, a great cyclone of dust rose as high as the cupolas. We were grinning like gap-toothed hillbillies.

Pieces started coming off the thing almost immediately. It was shaking itself apart. But we had agreed we would get our joy, and so we kept it going. Jed put Adam on the seat and trotted beside him, running the throttle. At nine, Adam was just old enough to want to be a little bit cool, but he was chewing gum, and the more throttle Jed gave him, the faster he chewed that gum. Then he found the horn pull, and now you had that Model T *blaaagh!* added to the mix. The noise was abusive, and apparently carried, because the neighbors started showing up. Scooter Southern, with his two little girls. Big Ed, from his trailer a mile down the road. All that noise and dust, that horn a-blowing, the hovercraft slowly self-destructing, everybody gathered 'round gawking, I looked around at us and flashed on *Tobacco Road*, the scenes where all the Lesters congregate to watch the newlyweds Bessie and Dude thrash the tarnation out of their brand-new Ford.

We did quit before we ruined the thing. We'll rig up a skirt one of these days and see if she'll go. But it'll be tough to match the goofy joy of that summer night in Jed's yard.

The thing is, when I head out to run the loop these days, I feel better when I jog past Herbie's place. Life can't always be counted off and neatly arranged. You don't close the loops, you keep spinning them. And maybe, if you're lucky, someone will spin one for you when you're gone. The deafening, dusty hoo-rah in Jed's yard was a celebration drawing on the legacy of a man who never let a lack of wings keep him from flying. We are pleased to take up a remnant of his goofiness and march on. In Wisconsin, we say, *Forward!*

MY PEOPLE

WHEN THE LADY FROM THE BANK called one summer day and asked me to be in the Jamboree Days parade, I figured I'd pitch in. "You want me to drive a tractor, pull a float?" I asked. "Oh, no," she said. "We want you to be *on* a float."

"Huh?"

"Yes," she said, brightly. "*On* a float. We'll put a sign on there that says Writer."

Were I not frozen with horror, I might have dropped the phone. A video-clip vision assembled itself, of my townspeople—these loggers, these butchers, these farmers, nurses, carpenters, gas station cashiers, concrete trowelers, and truckers—looking on from the sidewalks as I was towed up Main Street on a hay wagon, decked out maybe with some spangles and crêpe-paper streamers, cradling an oversize papier-mâché pencil and scrubbing the air like a dairy princess.

I said I would be out of town.

How does one negotiate the terms of belonging? Speaking perhaps too broadly, I consider my loyalties divided between the Gun Rack

Crowd and the Pale and Tortured Contingent. Commonalities of spirit and pretension abound. The man in the Hooters cap and the woman with the NPR tote bag are not promoting restaurants and radio. NRA decals and Free Tibet bumper stickers are tools of the proselyte pushing orthodoxy via aphorism. The poet who takes his poems to the coffee shop and the hunter who takes his buck to the bar are both hoping for approbation and maybe a girl. Crying in your beer is just gazing at your navel, only louder.

There are men in this village who will scrub the floor with you. The Most twins work all day—Mack is a butcher (his brother Bob the One-Eyed Beagle is not the only butcher in the Most family), Jack runs a feed mill—and cut firewood nights and weekends. They don't stand much over five foot ten, but they are equipped with arms like hydraulic rams. Jack was at the Tugg's Bar with a beer and Mack had stepped into the rest room when a Bloomer slattern pushed through the door, reached behind the bar, and pegged the volume on the jukebox. The music was painfully loud. "Turn it down!" said Jack.

"Fuck you," said the woman. "It ain't your jukebox."

"No," said Jack, "but I was in here first. I walk into a bar and the music's too loud, I walk out. You walk in here and turn it up, that's a different story."

Two men had accompanied the woman into the bar. Ratty fellows. They moved in on Jack, too close. The tall one leaned in threateningly. "Looks to me like it's two on one," he said. A hand shot out over Jack's shoulder, grabbed the tall man by the neck. Mack was back from the bathroom. He slammed the tall man backward over the pool table, got right down in his face, and laughed happily. "Looks like one on one to me!" Think of your windpipe, clamped in the hand of a man who butchers for a living and splits wood for sport. Given the option, the two men and the woman departed in expeditious order.

I want, sometimes, to be that brand of badass. To reach out, grab the neck of some egregious nitwit, and stick him to the wall. But I don't, because—no more, no less—I don't want to wind up in a courtroom. Weak reasoning, really. I think I might be missing out. A while back in these parts, a man was accused of molesting a child. One day after he had been charged, he was sitting in his truck when the child's mother approached, toting her purse and a Bible. "Stick out your hand," she said. He did, and she quoted him some scripture: "If thy hand offend thee, cut it off," she said. Then she reached into her purse, drew out a pistol, and blew a slug through his palm.

I am impeded by restraint. I avoid bar brawls. Heck, I avoid bars. I don't bowl. I can't polka. In New Auburn, this last is bigger than you think. The standards against which you are measured are dependent on the milieu. Go to the café for meatloaf, or watch the old men roll dice at the implement store, and listen:

"He's quite a worker."

"That boy can knock the stuffing out of a softball."

"The man can flat run a wrench."

"His checks are good."

"She's a helluva shot."

Not frequently overheard: "He crafts a lovely metaphor."

I speak to writing clubs sometimes. Someone with a notebook always puts their hand up: "What's the secret to making a living as a writer?" Stubbornness and blind luck, I want to say, but they're looking for something tangible, so I tell them I discovered the secret years ago while cleaning my father's calf pens. That is, you just keep shoveling until you've got a pile so big, *someone* has to notice. A childhood spent slinging manure—the metaphorical basis for a writing career. I have used the same illustration to explain myself to butchers, truckers, and turkey pluckers. Believe me, they get it.

I admit there are times vanity gets the better of me and I entertain visions of myself as the Bohemian Farmboy. The Arty Redneck. I imagine myself bridging two cultures. Truth is, I am a dilettante in either camp. I own a rusty old pickup truck, but it's not running right now, and I don't know how to fix it. I can run a welder, but I lay a keloid bead. I'm a fair shot with my 30-06, but don't ask me to recite muzzle velocity and ballistics. I have read great works of literature, but recall only the grossest details. I can no more diagram a sentence than rewire an alternator. I enjoy classical music, but nothing moves me like a Telecaster tuned to a drop-D twang. I marvel at the grace and anger in a single line of a Sharon Olds poem, but the audacious awfulness of a Confederate Railroad lyric—"Life's a picture that you paint/with blues and grays, cans and cain'ts"—leaves me gleeful.

Lowbrow, highbrow, I do fine in either scene if I just hang out and play by ear. When I try too hard, when I am too overt, that's when I get my comeuppance. I once composed an essay, and it had this aw-shucks feel, which I maintained right up to the third paragraph break, only to resume the narrative with the words, "Heraclitus said . . ." I read the essay aloud at a bookstore engagement, and when I invoked Heraclitus, a large man in the back of the room snorted like an ox. In a fit of acculturation triggered by a *New Yorker* essay on the Ring Cycle, I went online and ordered a Wagner CD, then felt like a goober when it arrived in the mail and I discovered I had selected the collection decorated with images of the choppers from *Apocalypse Now*. Involved with a French farm girl, I resolved to learn the language. We dated for two years. The most complicated phrase I can muster: *Est-que les vaches sont dans l'étable?* Are the cows in the barn?

Twelve years I lived away from here, and what I missed—what I craved—was the lay of the land. A familiar corner, a particular hill, certain patches of trees. Somewhere along the line, my soul imprinted on topography. I returned, and the land felt right. The land takes you back. All you have to do is show up. Finding your place among the *people*, now, that is a different proposition. A community is a conglomeration of characters, and you can't force your way in. Your place in the cast evolves over time. In my case, the fire department provided a point of access. The minute I joined up I began to accrete history and acquaintance. I began to meet my neighbors at the invitation of the fire siren.

A man is having a heart attack in the middle of nowhere. Bob the One-Eyed Beagle is at the wheel of the rescue van, foot to the floor. Lieutenant Pam, a mother of four, and the Beagle's brother Jack are with us. We're a good twelve miles out of town, on a dark road that twists through trees and swampland, when we spot a rust-pocked car with its hazard flashers lit. When our headlights pick up the car, a man hangs out the window and waves us on. The car surges forward, then careens off the paved road down a snaky dirt trail covered with glazed snowpack. We drop Jack at the turnoff with a flashlight to flag down the ambulance in case we lose radio contact. The road is slick, and we have a hard time keeping up with the car. Keying the radio mic, I relay turn-by-turn directions back to the ambulance, several minutes behind us. Beagle has his eye on the road, and isn't saying much. We get a glimpse of taillights now and then, and suddenly the road peters out and we're fishtailing up a twin-track logging trail. We are traveling deeper and deeper into the forest. The van spins and slides, but somehow Beagle keeps it out of the brush, and suddenly our lights break out across a clearing. A leery knot of men peers back at us. Some are dressed in camouflage, the others in greasy coveralls. One man detaches from the group, meets me halfway across the clearing. He puts his rawhide face to mine, and I smell bacon grease. With a boozy, baccy-stained gust, he announces, "He coded three times. I did mouth-to-mouth." It's a little strange, out here in the moonless boonies and snot-freezing blackness at the tail end of some logging trail, to be informed by an alcoholic apparition wearing stained Carhartts that someone has "coded." I reckon he picked up the term from TV, and suspect that after a long day of whiskey-stoked ice fishing, his buddy hadn't coded, but simply passed out. I don't doubt for a moment, however, that he revived whenever Doctor Deliverance laid on the lip-lock. The very thought purses my lips.

The patient is big and bearded. I try to give him oxygen, but he won't have it. He acts woozy, but his eyes are fierce. The ambulance struggles into the clearing. As the lead EMT approaches, I try to give report. "This is your cardiac arrest," I say, pointing to the patient. A big rangy guy hears the word *arrest* and dives between me and the patient. The other men form a protective circle, stomping in the snow like musk oxen. "You ain't takin' him to jail, fucker!" blusters the one leaning over me like some loony muleskinner. A brief course in remedial medical terminology seems in order. I talk fast. Apparently my explanation penetrates the fog of ethanol and paranoia and is deemed satisfactory. The patient is released back into our care—although not until he whispered something into the ear of his chief defender, who then clasped him by the head, looked deep into his eyes and declared, with great solemnity, "I promise, man, I *promise*." Once on the cot, the patient commences to thrashing and cursing and tearing his shirt to reveal slack tattoos of an unprofessional sort. The trip back to the county road is a trial and a test of our goodwill, although the patient's determined efforts to wrassle do provide us the opportunity to surreptitiously pat him down for weapons. When we finally emerge from the trees and reach blacktop, we transfer him to a waiting chopper and gratefully release him to the sky.

———

You belong to the land first. From there, your allegiances grow more fluid. I assemble anecdotes in the hope that I might wave my hand over the characters and say, *These are my people*. This is specious yap. One can hardly lay claim to one person, let alone an entire community. To say *my people* is to imply *my people* will be grateful for the dispensation, when in fact they might be wishing you'd just mow your lawn and get the rusty truck out of your driveway before it sinks through the blacktop completely. The term is presumptive, simultaneously implying ownership and membership. And how to establish standards of inclusion? Geography? And if so: one city block, the county, the northwestern portion of the state? Occupation? Avocation? Hobbies? Favorite beer? Loyalties wax and wane on a sliding scale. From noon 'til three on Sunday, Packer fans are of one accord; by evening they are flipping each other off in the Wal-Mart parking lot.

Unity delineates in a thousand ways. Red-blooded American conservative vs. red-blooded American liberal. Country vs. rock. Ford vs. Chevy. When the fire siren wails, two dozen of my neighbors and I act as one, on behalf of the community—*my people* acting on behalf of *our people*—but once the trucks are parked and the reports are filed, we diverge, filtering back to our personal tics and politics. Under the yellow helmets, we quite literally put our life on the line for each other. Out of uniform, we cancel each other's vote on the new school referendum, question each other's taste, engage in activities that would get us kicked out of each other's respective homes. At some point, unity becomes utterly dependent on civility.

While living in Eau Claire, I was cast in a community theater play directed by a man named Laurent. Laurent grew up in a small rural town. He was gay and part Indian. Recess was a gauntlet of grim taunting. We often discussed the milieu of our childhood— battered pickups, bass fishing, guys bragging up their tractors—and at some point Laurent would puff up his chest, affect a hilarious heterosexual swagger, and declare, "Them's m'people!" It was an entertaining bit. But it raises the question: If your people exclude you, are they still your people? What if they ignore you? In the wake of the controversy involving Indian spear-fishing rights in northern Wisconsin, a fellow over on Pine Street slapped a bumper sticker on his truck that said, You Spear Walleye, We Boycott Casinos. I guess we all know how that worked out. Take a run on up to Turtle Lake, or the Lac Courte Oreilles reservation, and check out the casino parking lots. Packed. The call to abstain has not been heeded. In fact, it is unlikely it can be heard over the ringy-ding of the slots. I should mention that the man with the bumper sticker is part Ojibwa. The singer John Prine has stated publicly that it's a big ol' goofy world.

———

With all due respect to the lady who wanted to put me on a float, I have a pretty good sense of the scope of my renown. I get some after-dinner laughs at the annual firefighters dinner, I make the odd regional public radio appearance, and though I blush to say it, my recent reading of an essay on the joys of spring was quite a hit with the Bloomer Women's Club. I am a tiny fish in a puddle of a pond. In short, I am not float-worthy.

Still, I am as susceptible to ego as the next self-absorbed noodler, and honesty compels me to cop to the fact that there have been times—after, say, a particularly successful appearance on the Moose Country 106.7 FM morning show—when I posit myself as the most accomplished writer this village has ever produced. My ego was in need of a little tuning then, the day I stopped at a local yard sale, bought a New Auburn commemorative centennial plate for two bucks, flipped it over, and while reading the little mini-history printed on the reverse, discovered I was about 125 years behind the curve. In 1875, the same year he founded this village, David W. Cartwright also found time to complete the 280-page best-seller *Western Wild Animals*. Or, more completely, a:

Natural History
of
Western Wild Animals
and Guide for Hunters, Trappers, and Sportsmen;
Embracing
Observations on the Art of Hunting and Trapping,
a description of the physical structure, homes, and habits

of Fur-bearing Animals and others of North America,
with general and specific rules for their capture; also,
narratives of personal adventure.

According to the back of the plate, the book enjoyed "a considerable reputation." Life has delightful ways of keeping us humble.

Humility in this case being a moot point, I can tell you I have written nothing of "considerable reputation." I did slap together a booklet of otiose homilies entitled *How to Hypnotize a Chicken (Plus 30 Other Ways to Liven Up Your Life)* in 1991, and, sadly, it sold well enough on the greater Chippewa County arts-and-craft fair circuit that it still pops up now and again to haunt me at local readings, but there is little danger of your running across it in the stacks, of say, the Hancock Natural History Collection at the University of Southern California. *Western Wild Animals* you'll find in the SK41.C33s.

Overtly and covertly, we stake out our persona. The Most twins load their pickups down with firewood, then park in front of Tugg's Bar so everyone knows they've been hard at it. Some locals advertise their virility on bug deflectors. Once I saw a grim-faced man in a greasy ball cap hunched over the wheel of a four-door rust bomb with a bumper sticker that said, I Like My Whiskey on Ice and My Women on Fire. This is evidence of profound self-knowledge and deranged optimism. And not so far removed from the practice of strewing back issues of *Harper's* across the coffee table. Guilty, by the way. The spring issue of *Varmint Hunter Magazine* provides the necessary balance and cultural ass-covering.

Here, there is always the danger that you will lose control of your persona. To pass the time during the drudgery of housecleaning, I am in the habit of playing old country music albums and singing along at volume. Once, while dusting the living room and singing along to *The Best of Donna Fargo*, I got the feeling someone was watching me. I turned, yellow feather duster in hand, and found the town maintenance man peering through the front door. He had come to fix my water meter and had been banging on the door for some time. I felt a little silly. Then the music registered, and a chill went down my spine. What does the maintenance man think of this fellow, new to town, armed with a feather duster, and singing, at the top of his lungs, "I'm the hap-pi-est girl in the whole U.S.A.!"?

I am thinking maybe I should make a preemptive bug deflector move.

I tracked down a copy of the Cartwright book. A rare book dealer in Cleveland charged me an even hundred dollars for it. I have no idea if I got gouged. I claimed it as a business expense. I have never seen any photographs of Cartwright, but the title page of *Western Wild Animals* is faced by an engraving tagged with the caption, "David's Return to Camp." He wears a white beard and a flat cap, and he is striding down a wooded trail, a rifle in his right hand and a dead deer balanced over his left shoulder. In short, he looks like a forbidding version of the Quaker Oats man. A selection from the preface seems a continuation of the furrow in his brow:

> *He is . . . not a professional book maker, and he knows that it is only by practice that there comes any great degree of perfection in any art or trade. What he gives you, he puts upon the basis of an experience of forty years, and gives it with that assurance that he believes should come of practical knowledge, as opposed to any hypothetical and visionary trash.*

No dancing 'round the campfire with patchouli and rain sticks, then. All well and good. But here's where my ears really pricked:

> *Since the author of this book claims for himself an incompetency to the task of putting it into shape, and the more exact wording of its pages, and has placed that part of the work into the hands of another, it is due to him to say that . . .*

Just a cotton-pickin' minute. Back to the title page. *Western Wild Animals,* etc., and etc. *By* David W. Cartwright. In much smaller print: *Written by* Mary F. Bailey. Turns out David W. had a ghost writer. Who did not live in New Auburn.

Perhaps I have a shot at reclaiming the Village Writer crown. On a technicality, but still.

I'm thinking maybe we'll trim the float with some of that nifty silver foil.

The writer Thomas McGuane has said he worries about becoming "some horrid nancy with pink palms." Growing up on the farm, I spent enough time on the wooden end of a pitchfork to keep my palms decently callused. The five summers I worked as a ranch hand in Wyoming, when I was at the peak of my limited mechanical powers, when I could swap out a spun bearing, or weld up my own sickle bar, I had laborer's hands. Scabbed knuckles, thickened fingers, the palm-side nicks and whorls stained an indelible black. Your hands feel good like that. Sturdy and durable. Like you can handle things. I stop typing and rotate my hands outward. The dreaded pink palms. McGuane is grateful that years of cattle roping have given him a crooked thumb, enlarged knuckles and rope burns. I need to fight a fire. The water and soot and the canvas hoses leave my hands roughened and swollen. My fingernails become outlined in black. For a few days, I can put my hand out for change at the Gas-N-Go without shame.

Rough hands are a comfort. Like jeans and old boots. I love to attend poetry readings, to skulk in the dark, skimming words from the smoke. (Riffing on a line by Jim Harrison, I find smoke-free poetry readings the moral equivalent of chamomile near beer.) The right little conglomeration of words makes my heart pop open like a tulip, and no matter the venue or talent, you're almost always going to get the gift of a good line in there somewhere. The whole scene makes me peaceful, although I throw a systolic spike whenever someone introduces a piece "given to me this afternoon." As if poems drop from the sky pre-formed, like sparrow turds. In my experience, art is not to be awaited; it is to be chased down, cornered, and beaten into submission with a stick. This belief correlates to Tom McGuane's and my worrying about our hands. Working-class prejudice never quite shakes the idea of art as frivolity, and frivolity has pink palms.

When Barry Lynn was a boy, he racked tobacco in North Carolina. The fieldwork made him hardy, and gave him a man's hands, but he was never like the other boys, and childhood was not easy for a boy with no appetite for mud or baseball. He speaks fondly of an aunt, who even then, even in Carolina before the First World War, understood the boy was different. She'd sneak him bits of lace and ribbon: "pretties," he called them. Like a scattering of bright feathers left by a flown bird, the pretties implied other worlds.

Barry is eighty-nine years old now. For the last two decades, he and his younger partner, Michael Doran, have been teaching and performing modern dance in a weathered schoolhouse up a dead-end road just off Highway 27, south of Ladysmith, Wisconsin. The area runs heavy to fishing, hunting, and logging, and the surrounding townships are salted with poverty and backwoods scrabblers. The studio sits at the edge of an abandoned farmstead, a lily amid a stand of pulp. It is an anomaly only if you think art belongs somewhere else.

The first time I met Barry, he was eating salad at the Old Country Buffet. With his velour top and sandals, his longish snowy locks, his shoulder bag, and his eyeliner, he was an octogenarian sprite among a herd of all-you-can-eat size XXXL roughnecks sausaged into size XL NASCAR T-shirts. Michael was wearing a blousy, tie-dyed purple pirate shirt with matching long-tailed bandana and tasseled neck pendant. The NASCAR crowd didn't pay much attention. Disinterest is a form of tolerance.

I go see Barry and Michael dance sometimes. It isn't far. Over the river and through the woods, basically. My knowledge of dance doesn't extend much beyond what I can find in my copy of Microsoft Bookshelf '95 and a *New Yorker* profile of Merce Cunningham, but sometimes, when Barry is moving to the rhythm of his breath or Michael arcs a finger just so, I want to run down to the local tavern league softball field and say, drop your gloves, your bats, your beer, and come and see this astounding, delicate thing! There are times in that studio when I feel the husk fall right off my soul.

When you come from rural stock, there is this tendency to overplay the rube. To swipe your toe in the dirt and reckon, well, shoot-fire, I don't know nothin' 'bout birthin' no babies. Or shake your head in wonderment at the fripperies of city life. It's a knee-jerk thing. I catch myself doing it all the time. It's also a cop-out. Goodness knows, the worlds of politics, art, and intellect provide targets so obese you can nail 'em in the ass with aspersions cast from clear back here in the Chippewa Valley, but any behavior that excuses us from acknowledging the complexity of human experience resides one slim remove from smug disdain.

A little while back, I happened to be passing through Appleton, Wisconsin, on the same day the philosopher Martha Nussbaum was at Lawrence University to deliver the lecture "Global Duties: Cicero's Problematic Legacy." What the heck. A guy finds himself a block and a half from a woman described as the nation's preeminent classicist, feminist, multiculturalist, and humanist, he figures he can stop to listen for an hour. I am not overplaying the rube when I say I understood only about 20 percent of what Ms. Nussbaum said. I felt more than 20 percent edified, however, and resumed the drive home with a sense of intellectual invigoration, which lasted maybe six miles, whereupon I began to mope over the idea of the rubber meeting the road as it relates to the gulf between theory and application. Part of the blame lies with intellectuals who are unable or unwilling to convey their ideas in terms that will play down to the café. But anyone who sits in that café and dismisses complexity by reveling in their own simplicity is no less pretentious. Civilization itself depends on complication. As a dyed-in-the-slop farm boy, I find I have an almost atavistic urge to poor-mouth anything more theoretical than a bag of feed. I have come to realize this is not always attractive.

It's tempting to wear backwardness like a chrome-plated crown of thorns. The first time I went to New York City (well, the second time, but the first time was in my uncle Stanley's eighteen-wheeler, by gum), an agent representing a prodigious literary firm quite kindly treated me to lunch at a desperately happening restaurant on West Fifty-sixth Street. I had the wood-roasted sea bass. The bill cleared three figures, easy. There was this part of me, the part whose Billy Bob's Texas—World's Largest Honky-Tonk jacket was hanging in coat check amongst the minks, that wanted to say, Well, dang, down to the Legion Hall, five bucks will get you all the smelt you can eat. My gullet countered by reporting that this particular filet of sea bass—brushed with an herb vinaigrette and arriving in repose on a mattress of blanched spinach—was a trip to the Louvre, and furthermore, the honey-lemon custard that followed was composed using eggs evidently cracked by cherubs and whisked by angels. I fixed my internal hick with a severe glare and dispatched a memo reminding him that smelt is essentially deep-fried bait, and he should cut it out with the disingenuous yokelism.

We are not just a bunch of jolly Norwegians bowling, *yah hey*. Right up the road, there is a graffito spray-painted on the bricks of an old garage and partially obscured by weeds: Fuck the System! I had to grin. What you have here is evidence that a few of our young folk are reading something other than the *Chetek Alert*. At certain speaking engagements I say we are twenty years behind schedule here " . . . but that's the way we like it." We're not, of course. These days, all the little gray satellite dishes keep everyone smack in the present. The sepia tones of place are outshone by the flashing image of whatever you wish. Cultural anomaly becomes de rigueur. The local boys cruise up and down Main Street as you might expect, in their pickups with their gun racks and hot rod decals and their lips slugged with chew, but they are wearing skater pants, suckling Mountain Dew, and booming hip-hop out the windows. Loafing around the Gas-N-Go, they affect gangsta poses. The temptation is to round up these bad boys and provide them a taste of the genuine Compton, but insight and understanding can rarely be forced. Last year the county judge sentenced a nineteen-year-old New Auburn man convicted of thieving money from his grandparents to read and deliver a report on Thornton Wilder's *Our Town*. Can't hurt, I guess, but tearful epiphanies are a long shot and in any case rarely possess staying power.

In 1975, the New Auburn Centennial Committee produced a commemorative album. It contains a number of historical (that is to say *old*) photos of townspeople, and sometimes I study those photos and try to draw contemporary parallels, try to figure out where or how I might have fit in. Or tougher still, try to bring these characters into the present. I find it impossible to put any of these faces in a minivan, or imagine the fellow running the cream separator slouched in a recliner with a bag of chips and the remote. Why do the faces in old photos look so out of time? So *historical*? Not the clothes, or the haircuts—the *faces*. The eyes, the noses, the ears, the components are standard, but the countenance as a whole seems dated. Perhaps it has something to do with the ongoing recession of innocence as a general concept. At this point, the historical evidence accumulated on behalf of the perpetuity of change is overwhelming. The point is not to fight it, but to negotiate it. I don't wanna die before I grow old, but I do hope I can keep the By-God-in-*my*-day grousing to a minimum. The two most ludicrous words in the English language are *I wish*.

There is no television in my house. It is my contention that cable and little gray satellite dishes have contributed more to the intellectual torpor of the nation than groundwater contamination, smog, and Twinkies combined. I make this assertion, and yet harbor the hope that Oprah might have me on to talk about the book. And two or three of my friends will report that I tend to visit a lot on Sundays and Monday nights during football season. And I rarely get decent sleep in motels, because I click back and forth through the basic cable channels like a junkie scrounging a thirty-two-room apartment for loose change. The lowest common denominator is indefatigable and frequently delicious.

Having done my grumping, it seems to me that the globalization of human experience via everything from satellite feeds to online kipper boutiques is good news to the extent that even the most reclusive among us receive daily updates on the complications of the human condition. There was a time when ignorance—and the prejudice it fostered—could be grossly excused as a result of cultural or geographical isolation. Nowadays, ignorance must be willfully tended, like a stumpy mushroom under a bucket. Light is hitting more and more of the earth. Trouble thrives, but more and more humans share a general sense of life as it is on this spinning rock, and that is due, in part, to war correspondents in Kabul, *The Food Network*, and lesbian chat rooms.

The trouble is—and this is not a complaint, but a report—the world has our attention in a million ways it never did before, and we find it tougher and tougher to focus our loyalties. Tougher to know how to belong, or to *want* to belong. Individual freedom is essential to the human spirit, and a theoretical individualism makes for cool Nike (or Army, for that matter!) commercials, but sometimes you have to team up. To fight a fire, for instance. I love—the word is not too strong—the idea of neighbors coming together to put out fires, and I am thrilled to be a part of that effort when I am called. It feels good. It feels right. It feels like I belong. Sometimes you find yourself looking for little commonalities. Go Packers.

What you hope for, I think, is to reconcile the dichotomies and negotiate a position of comfort. This is mostly a passive process. Which is not to infer limp acquiescence. In a town founded by a successful author who set up his own sawmill but didn't write his own book, I make a living writing, but some of my credibility is maintained by the fact that my helmet is hanging on the wall over at the fire hall right now, and while no one on the department has any idea what goes on at these poetry readings, or what I could possibly get from watching an eighty-nine-year-old man dancing *Ulysses and the Sirens* in a headdress and gold lamé g-string, they do know that when there is smoke in the sky, I will pull hose and roll.

Exclude issues of culinary excellence, and there is no question I am more comfortable attending the smelt feed at the Legion Hall than I am choosing from six forks on the five-star mezzanine. I love cycling through the line with my neighbors, loading my plastic foam plate with smelt and cole slaw and beans. There's buttered bread, a cooler of Kool-Aid, and a couple coffee percolators. If you want a beer, you give your money to the lady at the card table. She makes change for your fiver with singles drawn from a tin box and you grab a can from the tub. We sit at folding tables under pictures of departed local veterans and a framed version of the Preamble to the Constitution. The smelt are flat and lightly breaded, about the size of a pocket comb. The tails are on. Some people strip the bones out. Me, I eat the bones. Calcium, I figure. If you like, the members of the Fish and Game Club put shrimp sauce out. Shrimp sauce being IGA ketchup and Silver Springs horseradish mixed in a bowl. You spear the smelt with a plastic fork, swab it through the sauce, and fork it in. Repeat until full, or a little beyond, which is the way around here. Whatever table you land at, you're going to know someone. Conversation runs to weather and catch-up. Last year I sat next to the school shop teacher. He married a girl up the road from our farm. He wants to know what my brothers are up to. Making wood and hauling logs, I tell him. He says he's going to build a house in town, might get my brother John to dig the basement with his big backhoe. We get back in line for seconds.

Last time I was in the Legion Hall, it was to perform. A seed-corn representative hosting a customer-appreciation luncheon hired me to read some of my work for a group of local farmers. That was daunting. I stood there with my essays in my hands, looked at their red faces and thick fingers, and remembered the old "football builds character" speech my high school football coach used to deliver on parents' night. I was always embarrassed for him, knowing half his audience had been up and grinding since five A.M., milking cows, bucking hay bales, lugging feed, wondering if the bank might cut them some slack. Football? Standing inside a manure spreader chipping frozen cow manure off the beater bars when it's ten below, that builds character. So I led off my reading with the thing about learning to write by cleaning calf pens. That eased things quite a bit. Physical labor is not in and of itself virtuous, but when you can carry your work around on 8 1/2-by-11 sheets of paper, you stand before a group like this with your metaphorical hat in your pink-palmed hands.

There are those who say he chokes up on it a little more than he should, but Ross Johnson's hand is formed to grab a hammer handle. If you get up early, you can catch him at the Gas-N-Go most mornings, with his van and his crew, the coffee drinkers getting their fix before the ride to the latest project, a house, a pole shed, a cow barn. Ross has been building things for forty years now, and last summer he donated his time to help the fire department put up rain shelters down at the softball field. Most of the time, his head was three steps ahead of his troops. It's an art, keeping a work crew busy. The overbearing ramrod triggers their resentment; an indecisive ramrod loses their respect. Ross kept us all busy, and was quick up the ladder with his own hammer when necessary.

Like most of us around here, Ross takes off work for deer hunting, and last year he shot a legendary local buck. Twenty-six points. A monster. He made the television news and all the local papers. He was pretty low-key about the whole thing, but if you wanted to sum up our local ethos, you'd be hard pressed to do better than Ross, quoted in the *Eau Claire Leader-Telegram*. "I got a new pickup last week, shot that buck, and yesterday the Packers won . . . so it was a pretty good weekend."

What we like, we like. We are happy when we are happy. We identify with some people, not others. That guy the Beagle and I wrassled out on the logging trail, I hope I never see him again, but I sure am glad we have history. We're on the same team, he and I, even if we don't play well together, and even if he'll never remember me through the whiskey haze he wore that night. Ross Johnson found satisfaction in the Packers, a truck, and a deer. The things that bring you joy tell you a lot about who you are. The reading is not always definitive.

I am in a motel. Running the basic cable. This video comes on. "Home," by Sheryl Crow. Everything is shot in black and white, that lustrous black and white with the silvery spray-paint sheen. Sheryl is singing at a demolition derby. The possibilities of heaven expand. The derby cars are jouncy and sprung, tagged with ads for pressure washers and muffler shops. The drivers careen with earnest idiocy. Heads bobbling, radiators fuming, they smack each other tremendously, in stark contrast to the wistful adagio of the music. The camera cuts from the cars to the grandstand, dwelling on faces. Every face is different, but they share the patina of hard living. Wrinkles and wind scour. Pale brows and burnt napes. A woman's skin, jerked and cured by a lifetime of cigarettes. A thin-nosed child with bad teeth. A stiff-backed man with guarded eyes. A girl, maybe out of high school, pregnant and beaming, the old lady she will become already evident in her uncomplicated face. The boyfriend's hand, meaty and tan, cupping her belly. This is a powerful human study. Every countenance is proof of a common verity. Proof of how station, time, and circumstance shape our visage. Every day I see these faces.

Sheryl, of course, is beautiful. She is exempt from our verity. She is standing amid the sheet metal and the dust and the hardscrabble rednecks and she is singing her soft, sad song, and—in a juxtaposition perhaps confirming the existence of God—she is wearing leather knee-boots and an abbreviated nightie. Between her hemline and her boot tops there is such an equine stretch of thigh as to imply a lifetime of mystery and wonder. The song is ending. Cut to Sheryl standing atop a hay bale—O ineffable image!—at the lip of the mud boggers' racing pit. A beastly four-wheel-drive slams into the slurry. It screams through the frame, lifting a vast, chocolaty curtain of ooze, which obscures, then breaks (in delicious slow motion) over Sheryl, legs a tad astraddle, head tipped back, arms held wide.

Awards should be arranged.

Behind her, my people rise to their feet and cheer.

Gawping at the TV, I make a noise. Sounds a little like a walrus.

8

DEATH

I CAN TURN YOU INTO A CORPSE. I can look at you and know exactly what you would look like dead. It is a disquieting ability, one I must frequently suppress. I will be seated across a table from someone, they can be talking, eating, laughing, and I will see them stiff on the floor, skin drained, mouth gapped, teeth dry, eyes staring. For fourteen years now I've had occasion to observe the recently deceased in a variety of presentations, and as a result, I have developed the ability—similar, in a macabre way, to those computer programs used to create age progression in pictures of missing children—to look at the living and see them dead. Frankly, it is a talent I could do without.

The dead and their faces have never haunted me. I can conjure them up, but they never come unbidden. There has been only one exception, from a call I made back in the early days. I recall a hot summer afternoon, and I remember Jacques and myself banging out the door even as the page was still transmitting, the dispatcher saying only that a state trooper had been struck by a vehicle on the interstate. We knew it wouldn't be good. At interstate speeds, a car-versus-pedestrian strike is apocalyptic. Jacques drove, and I trembled in the passenger seat, all the while constructing a vision of some burly trooper lying twisted and silent in the ditch weeds. When we rounded the sweeping curve, I saw a blanket-draped lump on the concrete. Someone waved me in, and I ran to the lump. As I bent to the blanket, the first thing I saw was a hand extended from beneath the cloth, the white fingers set in a curl, the palm cupped. I remember a fleeting impression, something about that hand being not quite right, and when I stripped back the blanket, there, like a rumpled child, was a tiny uniformed woman, her face framed in a thick splash of long blond hair. The hand . . . it was too small. I was ready for the violence, prepared to view a blunt, wide-shouldered busted-up man; I was unprepared for beauty, for the color and abundance of that hair, for those delicately drawn fingers. We tried, but there was nothing to be done. The damage was overwhelming. I recall listening overlong for a heartbeat, then looking at Jacques. We quietly replaced the blanket and stood down until we were cleared to transport the body.

Now and then I have occasion to run that section of interstate. When I pass the white cross planted in the grass and hung with the dark blue Smokey the Bear hat favored by the Wisconsin State Patrol, I feel the stillness of the cross. I usually think about the guy who hit her. He claimed he was digging under the passenger seat for some jewelry, didn't see her, despite the long, flat curve, the flashing lights, the stationary vehicles. The day he was acquitted of manslaughter charges, the local television station ran footage from the courtroom. When the jury announced its verdict, he made this little move that seemed celebratory. Jacques and I had lifted her so gently from the concrete—when I saw his reaction, I felt a flare of rage. Still do. Knowing that such a thing might happen, that a fellow can be pleased to have things go his way in the wake of such mortal carelessness, I want to know how one attains the peace implied by that quiet roadside cross.

Time passed, and one night, in a dream, I was climbing, burrowing through dead weeds, and I pulled myself up to a high spot, and there, down below, nesting in dead grass, was the hand. Even in the dream, I recognized it immediately. It happened again, off and on over time. I have never seen her face, or her hair, or her body—just the hand. It is always the same; palm up and cupped, fingers curled. It would be overdramatic to say the image haunts me. I have gone for long stretches without seeing it. But every once in a while, I'll be flowing through a dream, and there it will be. And despite all the years, I recognize it immediately. When I awaken, my gut is laced with ice.

It is a given in the fire and rescue business: Sooner or later, you will handle a corpse. Unprettied and unposed, the bodies allow death no romance. Heeding Dylan Thomas, we generally do not go gentle into that good night. We go hacking and drooling, lurching and puking, darkening and purpling. Someone who has flown through the windshield of a Pontiac at seventy-five miles per hour to ricochet off a white pine and land in the brush like a bag of wet gravel does not look as if he is sleeping. People who shoot themselves, people who hang themselves—even people who quietly overdose or suffocate themselves—may find peace beyond the vale, but they leave a blotchy, seeping mess back on this side. At best, a corpse looks worn out.

Worn out, and yet, powerful. I once bought a used book called *Celebrations of Death*, in which authors Richard Huntington and Peter Metcalf wrote, "The vitality of a culture or ideology depends upon its ability to channel the power of such mordant symbols as the corpse." We honor the dead, but we are speaking to ourselves.

Tracy Rimes was seventeen years old when she rolled her car on Jabowski's Corner. A little less than a year later, her classmates graduated. A folding chair on the front row of the dais was left empty, save for a white rose placed across the seat. The next morning, in the local café, a group of women were discussing the girl's death, describing in turn how upset they had been, laying out their ties to the girl and her family. One remembered her as a child. One had just spoken with her parents. One said, "Those kids shouldn't have put that rose out. . . . I was fine until I saw that rose . . . then I just lost it." There was a certain tension to the conversation. While the women waited to speak, they nodded, but they nodded as if they were marking time, waiting for their own opportunity to stake claim to a piece of the grief. Given the slightest space between syllables, they interrupted—often by agreeing: "Yeah, I . . ."—and pinched the end of the previous speaker's sentence, gently pirating the conversation, steering it back to their own waters. The subject was always the girl, but the object shifted from person to person. *Celebrations of Death* includes the following passage regarding the French sociologist Emile Durkheim:

> *What Durkheim finds important . . . is the way that other members of society feel moral pressure to put their behavior in harmony with the feelings of the truly bereaved. Those who feel no direct sorrow themselves will nonetheless weep and inflict suffering and inconvenience upon themselves. How can it be other than a positive affirmation of their commitment to an abstract value of neighborliness, of society?*

So on the one hand, we're a little selfish. On the other hand, it's nice to suppose that the conversation in the café was driven at least in part by an innate desire to find common ground, to knit individual experiences into a cloak of mourning wide enough to drape across our neighbor's shoulders.

If nothing else, bless that girl for bringing us a little more together.

Names sand-blasted into the polished Bangalore marble of the Vietnam Memorial, notes left at Ground Zero in New York, the white rose on the folding chair, these are commemorations, but they are also attempts by the living to draw conclusions from the dead. A lot of it, I'm sure, comes from years of being steeped in Christianity, of being told Christ died for our sins. *For* something. Surely, we tell ourselves, we can't die just because we hit a patch of pebbles on a curve. Surely there is preordination in the pea gravel. We are creatures of myth, hungry for metaphor and allegory, but most of all, hungry for *sense*. Death—a stillness within the chaos, after all—serves these cravings. Death provides us the pretext and the context within which we may arrange and participate in our own symbolic mythology, to establish significance and import, to reassure ourselves that it all *means* something. Death is the ultimate passion play, and we want to be on the bill, if only as a member of the chorus.

A man drove up to the café while the women were talking. He parked his pickup across the street, crossed over, and took a seat at the counter, and ordered the pork chop special. He wore a seed-corn cap at a tilt, and left it in place as he ate, elbows splayed over the counter to either side of his meal. His face was weathered and creased. One of the women wondered aloud how the girl's parents would get over her death. The man turned to look at her, a spoonful of corn niblets hovering halfway between his plate and his mouth.

"You talkin' about somebody losin' a child?"

"Yes," said the woman.

The man's gaze drifted down and away from the woman, to a space just above the floor in front of him. Then he rolled out the words flat and cold as a length of strap iron:

"You *never* get over it."

He pronounced *never* as quietly as the rest of the sentence, but both syllables were laced with a poisonous certainty. He returned to his food, and didn't speak again. After a few looks, the locals went back to talking. When the man paid his bill and left, no one seemed to notice. But I watched him, and halfway across the street, he stopped, and right there on the centerline, with first one and then the other sleeve of his rough coat, he wiped his eyes. Then he was in his truck, and gone.

I think of that guy whenever a celebrity dies and I hear some talking head in the media say we have lost a part of ourselves. You have to figure that's a little tough for him to swallow, when he knows what it is to grieve a child, all alone in the middle of a highway. This is a grief neither assuaged nor exalted by the attention of a nation. This is a grief that refuses to arrange itself around prime time.

"Get out of bed!" my high school science teacher used to say. "People die in bed!" Truth be told, ambulance calls have taught me otherwise. People tend to die in the bathroom. They tip over while groping in the medicine cabinet for Maalox, or straining on the pot just enough to blow a leaking abdominal aneurysm. Rare is the EMT who hasn't performed CPR between the tub and the toilet. I have found people dead in bed, but I have found more of them in the bathroom. I have also found them in the brush, in snowbanks, in cars, on the road, sitting upright in chairs, draped over the kitchen table. My brother once drove his ambulance to a corn field and got stuck with an abiding vision of the pulverized remains of a farmer still spinning on a power shaft. I had a partner who once found a man hanging from the ceiling with alligator clips on his nipples. Another partner, responding to a call on an empty stomach, relished the smell of turkey when he entered the house until he walked into the living room and found an old man, dead for days, his forearm slow-roasting at the foot of a space heater. Last winter, a fisherman collapsed and died on Lake Tres Verde. He must have been catching fish pretty regular, because when the ambulance crew arrived, another fisherman was standing over the body, with his line down the hole previously manned by the deceased. We enter this world in generally uniform fashion; the means of egress, on the other hand, are infinite.

On a cold night in early autumn, a universe of stars pinpricked across the black sky, we round a sweeping bend of the interstate and the usual burst of state trooper lights directs us to an accident scene. I am still in training, back in the Silver Star days, riding with Leif and Todd. Leif pulls the rig past the farthest patrol car and parks on the rumble strip beside the guardrail. Looking over the edge of a sloping embankment, I can see the sweep and wink of flashlights forty feet below.

Following the wobbly lead of my own light, I make my way down the steep slope. Something crunches beneath my feet. Then it happens again. As I go lower, the crunching increases. I direct the light at my feet and tiny points of light wink back, reflected off scattered shards of black fiberglass. A group of officers are standing at the woven wire fence running parallel to the interstate, searching the brush with their flashlights. Suddenly one of the officers makes an exclamation, and the beams converge in a shifting blob of light. The lights focus on a body.

He is a young man, maybe eighteen. Barefoot. He is lying at an impossible angle, and steam is rising from his torso. His upper body is facedown, but his midsection is so severely twisted that his buttocks rest flat on the ground. One leg is extended naturally. The other is flexed at the knee and then, midway up the thigh, is bent again at a ninety-degree angle. His hair is curly, brown, and tousled.

Leif checks for a pulse and I check for another passenger. There is no pulse, and one of the officers tells me the boy was alone in the car. The officer seems a little dazed, keeps shaking his head. "It was a routine traffic stop. Kid was speeding. He pulled over, no problem, he was real cooperative. Showed me his license, answered all my questions, no sign of trouble." The plates hadn't checked out, however, and the officer asked the boy to follow him to the patrol headquarters one exit back.

"He said fine, no problem. When I pulled into the turnaround, he just disappeared. Killed the lights and split. I knew I'd never catch him, so I just followed slowly. Got to this curve, could see a vehicle had left the roadway. No skid marks, the kid never touched the brakes."

The car was a Corvette. Later, the reconstruction experts will calculate that the vehicle was moving at well over 100 miles per hour when it launched from the embankment. After casting around a bit, I find the bulk of the car far below, leaning against a sturdy tree. It looks a foil gum wrapper that has been rolled between a giant pair of palms. The two bucket seats are wrapped tightly around the engine. The rear axle is bent at a severe angle, one tireless chrome rim sticking straight up in the air. Backtracking, I can see that the vehicle began snapping off trees about twenty feet up. One large pine has a two-foot-square gash of bark ripped away. I bump into the battery. I find a shoe. The gas tank, separated from the frame, is resting in some weeds. I sweep my light through the treetops, and see a flash of white. A sweat sock, hanging from a branch. Then I see another flash of color, and another. It takes me a minute, but then I recognize them. Comic books. They're everywhere, as far as the light can reach, the brightly colored sheaves of paper draping the branches like unfallen leaves, or Christmas tree trimmings. There is no wind; they do not stir.

The boy landed forty feet beyond the bulk of the car. We crunch back up the hillside to fetch a longboard, some straps, and a body bag, and return to the body with the coroner. An officer is taking pictures of the scene. The white flash fires sporadically, painting the whole scene white for fractions of a second. The coroner bends down, inspects the body. It still steams, but not so vigorously. Leif looks at the coroner. "Wanna mark his position before we move him?"

"Yeah," grunts the coroner, a fat man wearing a loose tie. "Anybody got paint?"

We stand there then, silent, while the trooper hikes to his car for spray paint. This is how it goes when you die this way, people stand around your body, poke it and prod it, turn it over to look at your wounds, conjecture about how it might have gone. One minute you're alive and flying, the next you're cooling in the leaves. You drop to the temperature of the dirt, and it's all over.

The coroner digs out the kid's wallet. He's carrying five hundred bucks and a picture of his girlfriend. She lives in Minneapolis, and he was on his way to meet her. Minneapolis is just over an hour away. She's probably putting on her makeup. The kid is seventeen.

He's three states away from home. The trooper returns with the paint and says the license check is back; the car belongs to the boy's dad, and it's been reported stolen. That explains the kid bolting.

The coroner shakes the aerosol paint can. The glass mixing ball rattles noisily in the woods. Then, bracing one hand on his pudgy knee, he bends over and laboriously traces a fluorescent orange line around the boy. The paint sticks to the brown leaves. Some of it spatters on the boy's jeans. The coroner straightens, nods at Leif and Todd. "All yours."

We move him to the body bag, every move accompanied by the gentle grating of pulverized bone. We wrap the bag in a white sheet, strap it to the longboard, lug the whole works up the hill and stow it in the rig.

The ride to the morgue is a quiet one. Whenever we turn or hit a bump, the body rocks gently beneath the sheet. Leif and Todd are in the front. I ride in the back with the boy. I think of the father, probably still angry about his car, and the girlfriend, checking herself in the mirror, making herself special. It is eerie to know someone is dead while their loved ones are oblivious. We sit with the bodies and wonder about the family, a mother, a father, a lover, someone occupied with the mundane business of living, and here we are, in possession of information that will shatter their life.

It is the darkest secret you can hold.

Do you know how to tell if someone is dead for good? The distinction, if I may understate, is critical. And yet isn't always easy to tell. Sometimes you bust through a door at four in the morning and find someone who might be dead, or might not. Do you start CPR? Or do you comfort the family and call the coroner? The text used in my first EMT class, the fourth edition of *Emergency Care and Transportation of the Sick and Injured*, decrees, "CPR and appropriate treatment must be instituted unless there are obvious signs of death, such as rigor mortis, decapitation, or other massive injuries not compatible with life." Another passage excused us from heroic interven-

tion if the body was consumed by fire, or exhibited signs of "putre-
faction." We were also directed by the authors to roll the body and
check for *dependent lividity*, a condition in which noncirculating
blood pools, causing dark discoloration of the dependent portions of
the body. In contrast, areas of the body in contact with a hard surface—the scapulae and buttocks, for instance, if the victim is
supine—are blanched, the blood pressed from the skin. Dependent
lividity sets in fifteen to thirty minutes after death; if you see it, you
can put your pocket mask back in its case and turn the defibrillator
off. Rigor mortis kicks in several hours later. If a patient is stiff and
cool, you have nothing to do. An excerpt from chapter 6 of *Emergency Care and Transportation* reads, "CPR should not be adminis-
tered if obvious signs of irreversible death are present," a directive
that seemed to support the concept of *reversible* death. A little glim-
mer of hope amongst the rigor mortis.

So. We are given the responsibility of calling death by name.
With our own hearts in our throat, we look for the signs, make the
call. But here's the kicker: Despite the training, despite the onus of
the decision, we are not granted the authority to pronounce an individual dead. As soon as we decide someone is irreversibly dead, we
have to summon the coroner to make it official.

It can be a nervous-making wait. On a muggy summer evening
around midnight, Jack the feed mill guy and I find a woman sitting
upright in a chair. She has no heartbeat, and blood has already pooled
in her feet and lower back. But every once in a while she seems to
breathe. Heartbeat without breath, that I've seen. But breath without
heartbeat, that shouldn't be. The woman's seventeen-year-old daughter is right there. Looking at me. Waiting for a decision. The woman
is hooked up to an oxygen system, a big hose running to a little mask
over her nose. We're told she has amyotrophic lateral sclerosis, and
was expected to die in three months. I listen again, hard, for a heartbeat. Nothing. But every now and then, she seems to breathe. I'm just
about to pull her from the chair when Don, one of the Bloomer
medics, appears. Speaking low, I tell him what I've seen. He pulls the

little mask away, switches off the machine. It's an external respirator. She wasn't breathing, it was the machine.

We call the coroner and gather on the porch. I go back in, ask the daughter how she is doing, if we can help with anything, or call anyone. She is phoning relatives. I sneak back in to the body, feel for a pulse once more. I've done this before. I have a terror of being wrong about this. We are so primed, so *taught*, to fight for revival, that when we decide not to intervene, it takes a long time for the doubt to dissipate. I'll find myself riding home in the dark van, and suddenly I'll shudder at the idea of the body in the bag, the hearse pulling away from the house, the heart squeezing and pitching, a muscly gray metronome . . . *thup . . . thup . . . thup . . . oops . . . oops . . . oops . . .*

Sometimes I go to the forest and prepare to die. So far, I've simply fallen asleep, but it strikes me that sleeping directly on the dirt is good practice for the Big Nap. I usually conduct these rehearsals while hunting. I'll put my rifle down and curl up on a patch of leaves, or settle against the base of a solid white pine—if the air is crisp and I can cop a patch of sun, *c'est magnifique*. Jack, my brother's beefy half-Labrador mongrel dog, often tags along on these walkabouts, and if I stop to sleep, he drops to his haunches at my side, bull-chested and alert, sniffing and cocking his ears, seated but still on the hunt. As I drift off, I can feel him glancing down, impatient to move on. Eventually, he slides to the ground, drapes his jowls across his forepaws, heaves a deep sigh, and settles to his own rabbity dreams.

I've had the bug to sleep in the woods ever since I was a child. My brothers and sisters and I—five of us, at the time—rarely slept in the house during the summer. We would gather at bedtime and traipse off to the woods, trailing our sleeping bags and dragging our pillows in the dirt. Out beneath the trees in the Breeds Woods forty, we'd lie on our backs and pick out stars, and speculate on the nature of the satellites that moved through the branches on their slow, straight line. I don't remember ever being caught in the rain, or worrying about bears or hydrophobic skunks. I also don't recall the mornings . . . whether or not we trooped home en masse, or just straggled home as we woke. We didn't always sleep in the forest. I can remember sleeping in the yard, although not often, because in the morning everything would be chilled and soggy with dew. I recall sleeping in the smooth concrete mangers of the cow barn, and we spent many nights atop the hay stacks of the pole barn, burrowed into the bales twenty feet off the ground. Our sleeping bags were lousy with chaff.

But back to the woods. To sleep in the presence of trees and in the proximity of the earth is to get a sense of what it is to be holy. They say when Christ needed to get his head together, he did forty days in the wilderness. I stop at forty winks, but I believe I get a taste of what he was after. When I sleep on the forest floor, I never feel as if I'm simply taking a nap. I feel as if I'm performing some sort of embryonic ritual. When I awaken, I feel as if some important work has been done. This is not rest—this is ablution. By placing myself on the altar of the earth and retiring all my defenses, I am receding within myself, plucking a little transcendence from the perpetually gnashing jaws of time.

I am on the verge of rhapsodizing, so let me reframe: I'm no tree-hugger. I'm a tree-leaner, and a tree-sitter, and a tree-seeker, but I also have the ability to appreciate a tree in the form of a straight set of two-by-fours. I do not believe the trees are sentient beings, nor do I believe they have a spirit of their own. The trees do not speak to me. But I am pleased to take their shelter, pleased when they reinforce my smallness, pleased when they give me separation from the everyday static jamming my head. There is a big old white pine I like, deep within in the same forty where we slept when we were kids. It is ringed with a blanket of shed needles, rusty orange and springy. They make a fine mat, and while the tree towers above me, I am equally humbled by the idea of the tremendous roots threading the soil beneath me, knitted to the earth, clasping the soil in a way we surface-running humans never do. Such gravity. I rest above them, and they feed me as surely as if they were joined to my own veins. I absorb their ballast, resetting my keel for the journey back into a spinning world.

You have to get right down there. Don't mind the dirt—we need more of that, anyway. Our society has gone bonkers for cleanliness, but I fear—and research biologists are beginning to confirm—that all of this compulsive disinfecting will ultimately leave us vulnerable. I'm all for a little dirt in the gut, if only to hatch some resistance to a broad spectrum of microbaddies. So. Catch the scent of the earth. Smell that vital decay. Put your cheek to the rough skin of the planet. What you feel is time settling constantly into itself, and this is deeply reassuring. You belong here, you see. This is where your cells, your minerals, all the microscopic bits of you can best blend into the cosmos. To seep gently through the leaves in a graceful descent back to the beginning of things. I have come to think of my sleeps in the forest as a rehearsal for burial, and I have come to wonder why anyone would want to be sequestered in a casket, sealed away from the embrace of all this peaceful dirt.

The earth is a fine cradle. We are all bound to sleep there.

A regular contemplation of death seems a worthy exercise. There's no need for a morbid obsession—death will find you in its own time, regardless—it just seems worthwhile to give it the odd ponder. Not its form, or nature, or significance. Based on what I've seen, the forms of death are infinitely variable; and its nature is—for corporeal purposes—quite simply final. And as to the significance of death—as a portal, for instance—I am resigned to discovering that one in transit. The contemplation of death may or may not lead to any sort of explication, but it does provide a preemptive psychological advantage, in much the same way you might nod to a policeman when you know he just clocked you a few miles per hour over the limit: If he pulls you over, it seems less ignominious to have met his gaze prior, to be able to say, "Well, I figured you had me," than to have averted your eyes, pretending not to see him framing you in the radar gun. Death is coming. Why not give it a nod now and then?

•   •   •

As an EMT, you are at war with death. Collateral damage is inevitable. And sometimes, in the middle of the battle, you wonder why we fight at all. On a sweet spring morning, I am struggling to push a Combitube down the throat of an elderly woman when I glance up to see her husband, silent and teary-eyed in the corner, and I wish we hadn't been called at all. I wish he had simply put the phone down and held her hand as she died. Instead we push back the little wooden table where their coffee cups still rest, and we tear at her clothes, poke and prod her, shock her weary heart, strap her to a plastic board and scream away, and she will die anyway. The first time you press on the chest of an elderly person, the ribs separate from the sternum, popping like a string of soggy firecrackers. There are times when rescue is nothing more than organized physical assault. Sometimes I wish we would just leave people be, let them slip quietly over the vale. Sometimes life is not ours to save. Driving east one day, I passed an abandoned farmstead glittering in the winter sun, and thinking of the hands that built the tumbled wooden buildings, I suddenly saw death as a peaceful thing, an opportunity to check out of the game, to dispense with toil and trouble, an inky comfort in the unknown. No more appointments, no more petty recriminations, no phones, no more hurry or worry. Gonna be easy from now on, as the song goes.

When my brother Eric died, we had a parade. First came the hearse, Eric's little casket curtained within, then a heat-skewed line of cars that stretched the length of Main Street, headlights switched on and sapped by the midday sun. We drove from the city of Bloomer—population 3,085, Jump Rope Capital of the World—and rolled slow and easy up and over the middling hills of County Highway F, northbound.

It was June. Hot, and the corn was coming on. Twin Lakes Cemetery lay fourteen miles up-country, notched from a farmer's field half a forty shy of the Rusk County Line. Ten miles into the trip, we

banked through the cambered sweep of Morley's Corner and strung
out along the straight stretch running past the old Alan North place.
The North place, with its patchwork pines and long dirt drive, was
long ago flattened by a turkey farming conglomerate. My brothers
and I always resented the giant irrigation circles that had replaced the
tuckaway meadows, and by virtue of association, the men in the behe-
moth articulated tractors churning to and fro across the fertile dirt.
Omnivorous dusty green bullies, they didn't so much till the land as
rough it up and leave it humbled. But today, as we filed down the
two-lane beside the factory fields, the man in the monstrous John
Deere, its eight-row cultivator tailed by a scudding dust bank, drew
his rig to a stop smack in the middle of the field. The dust bank converged on the cab and rolled beyond, and still he held his place, the
tractor idling, until the whole quarter-mile-long run of cars passed. I
thought of the missing-man formation, in which a squadron of fighter
planes performs a fly-over and one craft separates, veering to the
heavens. Howling ballet, starring killing machines. But it tightens my
throat every time. The figure in the air-conditioned tractor cab was
indistinct, but I wondered who he was and what was in his heart as he
held the clutch down, his steady foot restraining the diesel while it
knocked and grumbled, raring to plow to the end of the row.

All around these townships, I see the dead. It is landscape as sepul-
cher. There's the school sign erected in memory of Tummer Olson;
there's the ski hill where Lisa Stansky died; in that house we found
an old woman gone in her bed; here is where Harry lay; there is the
house from which they ran with the Jensen baby, too late. Bob shot
himself in that cabin, the train hit Jake right at that bend. How important this is, this constant remembering, these unremarkable me-
morials. Every death is a memory that ends *here*. These are stakes to
peg your history on. Be grateful for death, the one great certainty in
an uncertain world. Be thankful for the spirit smoke that lingers for
every candle gone out.

9

CALL

THE PAGER IS A PICKAX hurled through the window of dreams. The signature *deedley-deedley-deedley-deedley* tones are a sonic cleaver, splitting the night wide open, driving straight to the base of my brain. I lurch in the sheets, heart drumming. The dispatcher's voice blasts from the dark three feet from my head and I jump to the light and grab my pants.

"New Auburn first responders needed at the northbound rest area on Highway 53 for a person having difficulty breathing."

The northbound rest area is eight miles away. By the time the second page bounces off the repeater, I'm sprinting across my backyard.

This kick-start thing worries me a little. When you get paged out from a deep sleep, somnolence disintegrates like a crystal vase dropped on a parking lot. One minute your heart is idling in a nocturnal *lup-dup* groove, the next second it's bucking beneath your sternum like a startled carp. Adrenaline floods your system like white-hot light. Usually you wake on reflex, ready to roll. But if the page comes while you're swimming a particularly murky section of the sleep cycle, you'll be utterly fuddled. There are times I hear the tones and burrow deeper in the sheets, thinking it's too bad for the poor slob who's gotta answer that, then they hit the tones a second time and I jackknife out of bed, panicky, realizing that slob is me. There are times my head crackles and buzzes, as if my cerebrum is wreathed in static, waiting to discharge. I hear buzzing when my eyes move. I feel that if I roll them too quickly, I'll have a seizure.

I should probably get that checked.

Folks who have tracked these things tell us that a firefighter's heart rate increases by over sixty beats per minute in the first fifteen seconds after an alarm sounds. The blood pressure spike created by this instantaneous, thundering tachycardia is profound. Long-term, this isn't good for you. Think of how you ease and creak around for those first few waking moments in the morning. Now imagine beginning the day at the arbitrary crack of a starting pistol, followed by a quick wrestle with your clothes, capped by a lung-busting 100-yard dash to the breakfast nook. Within five minutes of sweet dreamless slumber, I find myself hammering down the highway, lights flashing, siren whooping, and an update blaring out the radio:

"Further information, patient is a twenty-four-year-old male, bystanders are now performing CPR."

Our guts tighten and sink a notch. Pam unzips the oxygen bag, checks for oral airways. "Might as well use the Ambu bag," says Jack, referring to a simple device that we use to pump air and extra oxygen into the patient's lungs. You squeeze it like a soft rubber ball. Beagle is in the passenger seat describing—as he always does—where he was when the pager went off, and I'm at the wheel, hammer down, head rapidly clearing. Some departments have taken to softening their pages, starting quietly and gaining volume gradually. Others have taken to using a soft female voice to announce calls. This will help, I suspect. But no matter how gently you are wakened, you still have to find a way to pass the news to your heart: *Eight miles from here, someone has stopped breathing. They need you, now.* Boom. Right back to startled-carp mode.

You can't buffer yourself against the page. You never know when the call will come. Somewhere out of sight someone is blowing up a balloon, and you will be alerted only when it explodes. There are times late at night, when I'm one of two people on ambulance duty, that I am haunted by a vision of the thousands of hearts beating out there in our assigned patch of darkness. The county plat book hovers in my head, a tangled maze of dead-end roads and out-of-sequence fire numbers. I get spooked by the responsibility. The idea that if one of those hearts fails, someone will call for help— even this instant a finger might be punching out 9-1-1—and out of all those hearts, and all those twisted addresses, we will have to narrow it down, get there as fast as we can, and put our hands to the very chest that holds that heart.

They call at night, they call during the day. They call on sunny June Saturdays, holy holidays, run-of-the-mill Tuesdays. Usually they call on the phone. I have had people run up my sidewalk and pound on the door. I was jogging up Main Street one day when someone called out through a screen window, "In here! In here!" There is no way to know who will call, or why they will call, or when they will call. But they will call, and they will trump everything on your agenda, whether it is supper, the football game, a good novel, or your matrimonial duties. You'll be in a rush, but you have to keep your head. Once, when a fire call came at three A.M., we all showed up red-eyed and rumpled, and charged off to do our thing, and it wasn't until we were on scene that I realized my helmet was still hanging in the rack at the hall.

I remember thinking *too young* when the page came in tonight, and it turns out the man at the rest area has a history of heart trouble. We find him on the sidewalk, where his friends have pulled him from the car. He collapsed two exits ago. It is unclear why they continued driving. This does not bode well. The American Heart Association preaches a thing called the Chain of Survival. The Chain of Survival consists of four links: early access; early CPR; early defibrillation; and, early advanced care. You try to shrink the links, keep the chain as short as possible. In this case, access was delayed until someone at the rest area dialed 911. In the meantime, the car drove fifteen miles past the hospital back in Bloomer. It's not clear when CPR began, but even if the man's friends were doing their best, it's likely that his position—sitting upright in the back of a crowded compact car—affected the efficiency of their efforts. Frankly, early defibrillation is unlikely in these parts, as "early" is defined as occurring within minutes—for every minute that goes by without defibrillation, the chances of survival decrease by 10 percent; after ten minutes, the chances of survival are practically nil. The last link—early advanced care—we address by driving as fast as conditions and prudence allow.

The ambulance arrives. It is the volunteer service from Chetek, nine miles to the north. I cover several shifts a month for the Chetek service, and so I am familiar with the EMTs and their rig. While the others continue CPR and prepare the cot, one of the Chetek EMTs is applying the defibrillator. I pull the airway kit from the side door of the ambulance and prepare to insert a Combitube.

In simple terms, the Combitube is a breathing tube. Actually, it is two tubes in one. If you have surgery in a hospital, you will be intubated with an endotracheal tube. That is, the anesthesiologist will place a tube down your throat and into your trachea, which leads to your lungs. If the tube goes down the wrong "pipe"—the esophagus, the tube that delivers food to your stomach—the patient will suffocate. As such, proper placement of the endotracheal tube is critical. Endotracheal tube placement is a delicate procedure under any circumstance; in the field, everything from vomitus to blood can make the procedure extremely difficult, and its use has generally been limited to paramedics. The Combitube is designed so that no matter which "pipe" you stick the tube down—the esophagus or the trachea—you can still get air into the patient's lungs. It is essentially a tube within a tube. You grab the patient's lower jaw, lift, and push the device down the throat. Once it has reached the proper depth (you try to position the patient's teeth or gum line between two black lines inscribed on the tube), you inflate two balloons. The larger balloon fills and blocks off the nasopharynx—the space in the back of the throat. The second, smaller balloon, located at the tip of the tube, presses against the walls of the passage into which it is inserted, creating the seal necessary for effective air flow. Once the tube is inserted to the proper depth and the balloons inflated, you attach the Ambu bag to the blue-coded tube and try to push air in while listening under the arms and over the stomach with a stethoscope. If the chest rises and you can hear air going in the lungs beneath each arm, the tube is placed in the esophagus and you can continue to give the patient air through the blue tube. If there are no lung sounds, but you can hear a gurgling sound in the stomach, the device is placed in the trachea, and you have to switch to the white tube. Either way, you can get air into the lungs.

Sometimes you can hear air going into one lung but not the other. In this case, you've pushed the tube in a little too far, past the spot where the trachea forks into bronchi—a place called the carina (long *I*). I have long felt some car maker should produce a mid-size four-door and dub it the Carina. If you push the tube past the carina, you need simply deflate the small balloon and retract the Combitube back past the carina so that air can pass down both bronchi and thus to both lungs. Basic plumbing. It is amazing sometimes, how a patient will pink up when you get the tube placed. Even patients who are PNB—pulseless nonbreathers—will take on a healthier hue.

That doesn't mean they are fixed.

I get the Combitube in without much difficulty. The readout on the defibrillator screen indicates that we don't have a shockable rhythm. In other words, shocking the patient will help nothing. And so we are on our way. Out the easy downsloping curve of the rest area exit and into a merge with the four-lane, our little cube of light flying through the darkness. From the scene to the hospital, there is a lot of time to focus. We check and recheck to be sure we have our equipment in optimum position. We recheck lung sounds, recheck the position of the Combitube. We cycle through our defibrillation protocols, hoping for a shockable rhythm. We continue with chest compressions, switching off if we get winded. But at some point, all the drama simply settles into a groove, and can become downright conversational. Utterly calm. We know the odds are stacked against us, or rather more specifically, against our patient. He has been PNB for too long. He has a history of heart disease and cardiac surgery. Our resources are limited. The hospital is fifteen minutes away. But we will give him what we can . . . we will deliver oxygen to his bloodstream, and do our best to keep that blood circulating with our chest compressions. It's a primitive process, and dubiously effective. In fact, some studies have suggested a need to reexamine the efficacy of CPR. But there is always an outside chance, and that is what we are working for. The patient is absent, acquiescent, pliant, letting us do what we will do. You are pushing on a body. Out in the darkness, the night is flipping past, one delineator at a time. Mostly people are sleeping. I think of a man who used to pick up girls in local bars by telling them he was the guy in charge of polishing all the delineators.

Rick is driving, and he runs as fast as safety will allow. At the hospital, the sick bay lights are bright, and the patient's skin appears pale purple. The doctor makes the call quickly: "Stop CPR." Vicki pulls her hands from the man's chest. A nurse writes the time on a chart. The Ambu bag is detached from the Combitube. We put clean linen on the cot, and retrace the route home. Out on the highway, we pass through strands of fog. This night is no spookier than any other, but the three of us ride quietly. You have this sense, after calls like this, that something is amiss. As if the earth, lighter by one life, is spinning just a fraction faster. On any other night, fog is fog—tonight, it suggests there are souls about, newly wandering. These feelings fade, but for a while you carry a sensation in your gut like a wheel in the air, slowly spinning down.

• • •

We nearly made the millennium without 911. Until 1999, whether for a grass fire or a heart attack, you dialed a seven-digit number that rang in the homes of everyone on the department. A "phone bar," it was called. Now we're summoned by pager, but some tradition survives: The old-timers still call the old number, and the first person to the fire hall still triggers the water-tower siren. We all come running. Someone is calling for help. It's that simple, really, and that profound.

On a frozen December night, the pager goes off when I am on the edge of my bed, having just killed the light. A woman stopped to visit her grandfather and found him flat on the bedroom floor. In the parlance of the dispatcher, he is unresponsive. In the parlance of mechanics, his heart has stalled. Mine, on the other hand, is now pumping blood enough for two men. Light switch, pants, shirt, boots, I'm on my way. Grab a jacket on the porch, and thump down the backyard footpath.

On a dead run, it takes me roughly thirty seconds to get from my house to the fire hall. A little longer, if I have to punch through frozen crust and hurdle the snow bank at the Legion Hall. Once, on a warm summer night, I cut across the neighboring lot on the dead run at two A.M., tripped, and was airborne before I remembered the concrete foundation of the abandoned filling station. I experienced one of those extruded moments produced when startle precedes impact—when your car is skidding toward another car, for instance, or when a flowerpot is headed for the tiles—and time hypertrophies. Nanoseconds become roomy and habitable. The forces of physics continue apace, but our synapses fire with such stroboscopic precision that afterward we can't believe we thought all we thought. I recall gliding in the pitch-dark night, recognizing what had just happened, considering the history of the long-gone building, the smell of the grass, the pleasant feeling of suspension and motion, the push of the air on my face, the arc of descent, the palpable bulk of the giant sugar maple I knew stood to my left. I visualized my hand, cocked at the wrist, reaching out for the ground. I entertained a series of omniscient stop-motion views revealing the orientation of my body in space. In free-fall, I calculated the likely angle of impact and prepared to roll with it. I thought of my father, telling me that a bullet shot from a perfectly level gun would hit the ground at the same time as a bullet simply dropped from the same height as the barrel. It's a mind-twister, accepting that horizontal motion doesn't extend hang time. And then I hit, tucked, rolled, and was just as quickly on my feet, running again, remembering to duck the neighbor's clothesline.

That old foundation is gone now, replaced by a yellow prefab, and so tonight I run straight out my backyard, through eight inches of snow. The temperature stands at dead zero. I feel as if I'm pushing my face through rubbing alcohol. My cheeks stiffen, have the feel of butter hardening. With every inhalation, the hair in my nostrils freezes. The village is still, the stillness intensified by the cold. Christmas is a few weeks away. Here and there the neighborhood glows with illuminated plastic snowmen, electrified garlands, and strings of icicle lights. At the house across the street, a four-foot glowing Santa slumps against the door in a nimbus of red. From here he looks drunk.

I clear the snowbank at a good clip, cross Elm Street, and punch the combination into the fire door. In the summer, it's *click, click, click,* and you're in. Tonight the works are seized with cold. It feels as if I am pushing the buttons through taffy. I expect to see Pam or Jack or the Beagle, but no one is around. I'm pretty sure the address is just west of town, but the rule is, you don't go anywhere before you find it on the map, so I run to the meeting room and check the wall to be sure. Yep. There it is. I spin on my heel, flick the garage door opener, start the van, and, hoping someone else is going to show up, let it idle while I pull on a pair of rubber gloves. Nobody shows. I'm going solo. I hit the lights and hit the road.

The calls blindside you, always. You will prepare and prepare, and you will never be prepared. We are never ready, and our patients are never ready. Over the years, I have developed a visceral reaction to families and victims expressing surprise at tragedy. Why are we surprised? Why do we forget we are mortal? Bad, bad things happen everywhere, every day. Humans, for better or worse, harbor this feeling that we—individually—are special. A patch of ice or a pea-sized blood clot makes a mockery of that illusion in a heartbeat. We are not special at all. I hear people on scene saying, "Why? Why?" and the answer is, there is no why. Ambulance work will exacerbate your inner existentialist.

My brother John made a call, he came busting in the kitchen, and the first thing that hit him was a palpable wave of cigarette smoke and bacon grease. A man was spilled backward on the floor, his chair upended. His plate was mounded with half-finished eggs and sausage links. His cigarettes had slipped from his shirt pocket. His white belly protruded like risen dough. And his wife looked at my brother, and she said, "I don't understand . . . he's never been sick a day in his life."

And John says he remembers his first thought was, Well, he's sick now.

Alone in the van, I have a ball in my gut. I can already feel the eyes that will turn to me as I step through the door. The eyes will be stricken and hopeful, and I will throw myself into doing what I've been trained to do, not so much out of hope as a means of avoiding those eyes, because I know the man who lives here, and I know his health is poor, and I have a terribly accurate idea of the likelihood of my doing him any good. I step through the patio doors and one woman is tearful in the kitchen, pointing down to the end of the trailer, and in the bedroom, the man is flat on the floor and another woman is doing CPR, and as soon as I enter the bedroom she stands, backs away from the man, and bursts into tears. The bed has been pushed aside. A half-eaten muffin rests on the windowsill.

• • •

I strip my stethoscope out of the pack now and listen for a heartbeat. In the midst of the mess and panic, you plug the earpieces in, press the bell against the still chest, and listen. You are hoping to hear audible hydraulics from a fist's worth of muscle. You are scanning for life's backbeat. The *lup-dup* groove. A little heavier on the *dup*. That most ineffable iamb.

Nothing. I place an oral airway. It is a simple plastic device that keeps the tongue from the back of the throat, allows air to pass through the mouth. I resume CPR. Headlights sweep the window, and shortly my mother is kneeling beside me. She has a defibrillator and a Combitube. We attach the defib pads and fire up the machine. The line that should be bouncing across the screen is flat, flat, flat. Doing chest compressions with one hand, I grab my radio from the floor and call Chetek 245, to give them an update. When they answer, I can hear their siren in the background.

"This is two-forty-five, go ahead, New Auburn first responders." I recognize the voice as Karen, an EMT I've taken shifts with for years.

"Two-forty-five, be advised we have an elderly adult male patient who suffered an unwitnessed cardiac arrest. . . . CPR was in progress . . . at this time the patient is . . . is . . ." And then I lock up. For some reason, when I try to come up with the term we use in these situations—PNB, for "pulseless nonbreather"—I draw a complete blank. The only term I can summon is "Nebraska sign," the old EMS chestnut equating the patient's EKG tracing to the topography of the Cornhusker state. Not the sort of line you want to use over the airwaves or in front of family. I blurt out the next thing that comes to mind.

". . . ahh . . . this patient is a *flat-liner*."

After a little pause, Karen 10-4s me. There is a grin in her voice. It seems inappropriate, and unlike her. Later, she says when they heard that "flat-liner" business, they got the giggles in spite of the situation, because they wanted to know exactly what TV show was it I thought I was on?

Back in the trailer, my mother and I are working on the man, and I can feel the family behind me, watching. When the ambulance arrives, we hustle equipment in and out, get the man loaded on the cot and on the way. I have a moment then to speak with the family, and I tell them gently that it doesn't look good. It is the only way, I think. I don't go for false hope. I ask if there is anything I can do, or if they need someone to lock the place up. It is one more poignant facet of small-town volunteering. Someone calls for help, and it turns out the best you can do is make sure their windows are all shut, or that they get a ride to the hospital.

What a profound thing it is to call for help. How astounding, the number of people fate allows to float through this life never once confronting their own mortality. One of the benefits of the fire and rescue business, if you will have it, is a near-constant sense of vulnerability. A recognition that at the cellular level, or the speeding freight train level, we are but a particle removed from chaos. I have carried my kit in to find tattooed tavern-clearing monsters weeping in bed, hairless from radiation, leaking soupy feces from a colostomy, skin like mottled paté, and on the walls beer mirrors and bellicose biker tchotchkes, and I think, how do we ever forget this sort of possibility? How do we lapse into what you might call *ignortality*? In part, I guess, because you simply can't function if you are always feeling the scythe pressed to your neck. I have knelt beside a wrecked car, seen a burly forty-year-old shaking with pain and fear, and realized the last time I saw him he was steaming under the bright lights of the hometown football field, running his body like a weapon. I superimpose the image in my head over the image before me, and try to keep the new one from displacing the old one, so that later I can ponder the contrast and see what it might teach me. The lesson never concludes, but I'm getting parts of it. I understand that what you're doing when you dial 911—it sounds so perfunctory—is announcing to strangers that you are losing the battle. I no longer have the strength, I no longer have the answer, the trouble is winning, and won't you please come help?

We have our frequent flyers. People only too willing to dial us up. The little old lady with heart trouble who meets us on the porch, all buttoned up and smiling, suitcase packed and set beside her. The woman with the flu who makes us wait until she gets her makeup right. The round man on the floor who calls because he has fallen and can't get up, and as soon as we hoist him to his feet, he says thanks and toddles off to watch TV. "Tip-ups," we call those.

One day, back before the 911 system, back in the phone-bar days, I was pulling weeds when I heard the steady jangle of the fire phone beside my bed. I banged through the doors, thundered up the stairs, vaulted the bed, and yanked the receiver from its cradle. "Fire department!" I said, heart pounding, chest heaving. An elderly man was on the other end, his voice placid. "Just checking my automatic dial," he said, and hung up.

When our victims can't call for help, others do it for them. "In here! In here!" screams a wife through the screen window, her husband pale and sweating on the floor. "She's on the couch," rasps an old man, waving the cherry of his cigarette in the direction of the living room. "There's some guy bleeding on the road in front of the café," says the farmer on my porch. We are hailed by relatives waving their arms at the end of driveways, or neighbors swinging a flashlight beside the mailbox. An old man whose wife was having trouble with her blood sugar flicked his porch lights when we rounded the corner. "It's my mother again," says a woman who has called many times before. In the middle of an all-night writing jag, I come downstairs to boil water for tea. I am capping the thermos when I hear noise in the street. I kill the lights and peer out through the porch. A van careens to the curb. A man leaps out, runs up the sidewalk, and pounds on my door. I let him knock a while, until I've had chance to study him in the streetlight glow. When I do step out on the porch, I keep the heavy steel thermos in hand and keep the door closed between us. A little paranoia, for safety's sake. He hollers at me through the glass. "Is there a cop in this town?"

"Not tonight."

"There's a car in the ditch out on SS! With a guy in it! The car's still runnin' and he don't answer! We seen your light on, so we thought we'd try to get help."

"I'll call," I say. He runs back to the van, and the tires spit snow as it peels away from the curb. I write the license number in the window frost, in case this turns into something weird. Then I call the fire number and dispatch myself.

We find the car just beyond the village limits, eased nose first into the ditch, deep in the snow. A car idling in snow is potentially lethal. Back in the late '60s, a couple went parking on Springer Lane and were overcome when they backed their tailpipe into the snow and the car filled with carbon monoxide. I remember my mother telling this story when I was a child, and I'm sure it was on her mind the night of my first date. She stopped me on my way out the door. "If you decide to go parking," she said, "please come home and do it in the yard. We won't bother you, and otherwise, I'll just worry." I knew her too well to think this implied carnal carte blanche, but to hear such straight talk from this churchly woman with her hair up in a meek bun—you could have knocked me over with a peck on the cheek. As it turned out, the girl in question only kissed me twice, both times under a pine tree in the open air, and she dropped me in less than two weeks. But the image of that young couple—I always imagine them in a '50s vintage car—stuck in my head. Even after studying the effects of carbon monoxide poisoning, about how the carbon monoxide sucks up oxygen's spot on hemoglobin and lulls you to sleep before it chokes you, even after studying the chemistry and the symptoms, the first thing I always think of when I see a car stuck in the snow and running, is my mother's story. And so it is tonight when I see the body slumped in the front seat of the little red car.

It's a young man. He's pink-faced and unresponsive. Pink skin is a classic—but not so reliable—sign of carbon monoxide poisoning. I see his chest rise, feel for a pulse. Rapid. Ninety-six beats per minute. Feeling my hand on his wrist, the man rouses. His eyes peel open, slowly, and turn toward me. His sclera are bloodshot, and I can smell alcohol. I try to give him oxygen, try to take his blood pressure, all without luck. He pushes me away, slowly. Occasionally he raises his head and fixes me with a stare—a stare I've seen before on the psych ward and on detox calls, the one you get right before a previously complacent patient suddenly decides to go off at you. When I try to pull the keys from the ignition, he tugs them from my hand and stuffs them in his pocket. He gives me the glare again. "I think," he says, slowly, ponderously, as if with great thought, "I'm gonna do something stupid."

I back out of the car just as he takes a poke at me and lurches from his seat. He stands on the roadside for a moment, listing from side to side. Then, at a slow walk, he begins to leave the scene. He walks south, out of the headlights, following the centerline. It isn't our responsibility to physically confront or restrain a guy like this, but it's vicious cold out. If we lose track of him and he freezes in a snowbank, or he gets hit walking on the road, it won't look good. We are hung up between the very real legal issues of assault and abandonment. Jack and I follow him. He looks back, starts to run. We fall in behind him, staying about five yards back. "Man, don't do this," I plead. "You can run from here to Bloomer and every time you look back, I'm gonna be right over your shoulder." I run five or six times a week, and I'm in pretty good shape. Better shape than a drunk man at three A.M., I figure. Even in my fireman suit. He cuts to the right, heading for the ditch, which is filled in level with snow. He steps off into it and pitches face-first, punching through the crust with his bare hands. He flails around, gets his feet, half-swims, half-crawls to the other side, and takes off south again, into a patch of trees. Jack and I get across the ditch and fall back in stride. It's a clear night, and there is enough moonlight to keep track of the guy, but not enough to see all the face-slapping underbrush, so I tuck right in behind him, like I've got the ball and he's my lead blocker. We keep zigzagging through the brush, and I'm on the handheld, radioing a sort of directional play-by-play so that when the cops get here they can maybe cut us off somewhere. It had to be entertaining, listening to me trying to talk on the run, puffing and stumbling through the snow. Later my mom told me she was in bed following the whole thing on the scanner. Worrying, of course, because after all, her boy was chasing some drunk through the woods in the dark.

He stops finally, and starts fiddling with his pants. "Gotta pee," he says. He looks over his shoulder. "S'pose yer gonna jump me now."

"Nope," I say. "We don't get paid to fight." It's quiet out there in the woods. Still and cold. Just the sound of one man tinkling. Jack and I stand by. The man finishes, puts himself away, zips, turns, and stares at us. Then he shrugs, and takes off again. I radio our new direction of travel and resume the jog. It must have been a sight, the three of us in a line, one barehanded guy in a light coat and street shoes, dogged by two fully turned-out firefighters. I was fine with the running but I was wearing rubber gloves, and my hands were going numb. Rubber gloves have a built-in wind-chill factor. It was all I could do to key the radio mic. It looked like we were headed for a clearing over behind the natural gas station, so I updated the chief. We could see blue lights through the trees. Cops. We broke into the moonlit clearing and the man stopped. There were flashlights bobbing toward us, about seventy-five yards out. The three of us stood in a cluster, our breath steam-puffing across the moon. My hands were dead numb. Jack handed me his helmet. During the last leg of the run, he ran a stick in his eye. Messed it up for a week. When the guy was cuffed and in the squad, I asked Jack what the deal was with handing me his helmet. "When I got stuck in the eye, I had it," he said. "If he'd of took off again, I'da coldcocked that sonofabitch."

There is no standard call. The second you get your dispatch information, you commence to forming this picture in your head, drawing on all the calls you've made before, and when you get there, the picture never really matches up. "Person having difficulty breathing," says the dispatcher, you get to the northbound rest area and the guy is a full-blown code. Not four hours later, I get dispatched again. "Difficulty breathing," says the dispatcher, and this time it's a cheerleader with a mild case of hyperventilation. Dispatchers have a tough gig. They function as interlocutor between two parties occupying various states of panic. They sort it out the best they can. It's fascinating to think of them wherever they are, with their phone, their microphone, their maps, playing such a critical role in a drama where they never meet the other players. The dispatcher is hip-deep and detached, all at once. Think of a football coach locked in an office during the game, calling plays and relaying them to the quarterback based on reports given to him by a fan on a cell phone. The dispatchers gather what they can get and pass it on. Their voices float to us over the air, and we try to act accordingly. "This would be a larger male person," says the dispatcher one night, and I figure, Well, that's something to go on.

The most important information the dispatcher can convey, far more important than *what*, is *where*. Get us there. Get us there, and we can figure out what needs to be done. It is gut-wrenching to be lost when you know someone needs you. The new road numbering system has helped a lot—this is hard for me to admit, having written dyspeptic essays griping about Beaver Slide Lane becoming 270th Street, and the Dirt Road becoming 3 1/2 Avenue—but you still run into trouble with transposed numbers or missing signs or the mad twists up around all the lakes, where north/south reckoning goes right out the window. I still get lost now and then, but with each year, the map in my head gets larger and clearer. It's a comfort to feel that, to feel the landmarks assembling in my brain, more and more available, more and more a part of me.

And then about the time you think you've got it pegged, you find yourself stumped at an intersection, lights blazing, siren wailing, the fleet rescue rig suddenly a very gaudy, public and *stationary* monument to your befuddlement. With capable pride I once led the troops to a barn fire out by the Dovre church—me out front in the rapid-attack truck, with a loyal parade of tankers bringing up the rear. I was on the radio, directing the stragglers, and the directions I gave them were spot on, which lent greater irony to my inexplicably exiting the main road a quarter-mile early. All the other rigs charged right in behind me, of course, and it was quite a sight, all of us executing frantic Y-turns there in the wide open. It's like the Blue Angels—if the lead guy dives into the desert, everyone else follows.

Sometimes when you get close, you get help—people on porches, or out at the mailbox, or even out at the nearest intersection, crisscrossing their arms in the air, waving us in. We had a fire call last winter and there was some confusion about the address. We knew only that it was a chimney fire, and that an Amish family owned the house. I was out front with the pumper, and we knew we were getting close when the tanker driver behind me called on the radio. "Any idea which house?" And right then I saw all I needed to see. I got back on the radio. "Maybe the one with the Amish guy on the roof, waving?"

And then I kicked the radio over to the local government channel. "New Auburn Pumper One to dispatch, we are ten–twenty-three." Ten–twenty-three is ten-code for "we're there." Now you have to fight your fire or do your CPR, but the tricky bit is over. You found the place. You are where you are supposed to be.

"Call," we call it. You *take* call, you're *on* call, you *have* a call. "Are you on call today?" people ask. In New Auburn, we are on call twenty-four hours a day. We are not scheduled, we are simply assumed to be available. We carry our pagers everywhere we go, we sleep with them beside the bed. You get so you jump at anything that beeps or jingles. I stayed with a friend over the holidays, and she had this Christmas clock with a little Dickens scene, and every hour on the hour, it played a wheezy electronic carol, the first note of which matched the tone of the fire page. Every hour on the hour, that clock would fire up, and I'd jerk as if I'd been goosed.

I was paged one hundred and six times last year. Fires, drunks, babies, grandmothers. Injured farmers, frightened salesmen, old fishermen. The pager is on my hip right now, even as I type. It will go off, perhaps in the next five minutes, perhaps next Tuesday when I am in the bathroom. My heart will jump. If I'm getting something from under the sink, I may crack my head on the grease trap. I'll listen for the details, find out *where*, begin forming a half-baked picture in my head. I'll run across the backyard, headed for the hall. Whoever's out there needing help, they're getting me, for better or worse. Me, and a handful of my neighbors. We'll do what we can. There was this old man, we used to get called to his apartment almost on a weekly basis. He had a heartbeat like a broke-down roller coaster, and every once in a while he'd just check out, and his wife would dial 911. He was usually mildly dazed but smiling and conscious by the time we got there. We answered call after call until finally his old heart cashed in. But I remember walking in his bedroom at two A.M. toward the end there, and seeing this little man looking up at us with such trust, and I thought one day I will be the little old man on the bed. And I hope my neighbors come when I call.

When I take call for the Chetek service, things are a little more formal. The day is split into three standard eight-hour shifts, with two EMTs on duty around the clock. It's still a volunteer service, and you are free to go about your day, but you have to wear your uniform, and you have to be able to make it to the ambulance within five minutes of being paged. That means I have to drive up there for the duration of my shift. I take some writing and stay with friends. It's a lake community, and in the summer, I'll sneak out with my fishing pole. Sit under the long bridge and try to fill a pail with bluegills. Simple bobber fishing, a worm on a hook. Watch the fluorescent orange bobber ride the wavelets, wait for the *bump-bump* of the nibble, and then the *shloop!* when the fish gets serious and lugs the bobber under. The thing about bobber fishing is it's always charged with potential. No matter how bad or good the fishing has been, the idea that at any given moment the bobber will go *bump-*

bump, shloop! keeps you focused as a dog eyeballing a biscuit. On a good day, I catch supper. If I catch only one or two, I clean them and take them to my grandmother.

It's peaceful under the bridge. Traffic is light, just an off-and-on thump and rumble through the concrete overhead. The girders are studded with swallow nests. The adults swoop in and out, fluttering to the lip of the nest mouth, where the young ones lean greedily, their sharp, flat beaks open wide, their *griiitch-griiitch* calls echoing amongst the pilings. Emerging from a relationship that ended in a way that simply brings to mind the word *abattoir*, I once spent a day on call under the bridge, fishing and willing the waves to wash up something I could use. Late in the day, a speedboat carved a wide arc far across the water. A young boy leaned over the prow, cambered against the wind, chinning the spray like a spaniel. I tracked the boat, straining to hear the engine, thought of the way we strain at love when we sense it fading. When I did isolate the sound, it was keening and hollow and lagging well behind, never catching the craft. Somehow this reinforced my belief that the important lessons we learn one remove too late.

There are times, when the black dog has me backed deep in the cave, that I hope—this is ignoble—the pager will go off. Like the bobber on the water, the call gives you something to focus on. It is a mind-altering excuse to dismiss everything but the emergency at hand. Vindictive or weepy lovers, divorce lawyers, credit card balances, the ghosts slow-dancing with the skeletons in your closet, they all disappear at the sound of the tones. I have driven to fires with guys whose wives are leaving them, wives whose husbands are leaving them, guys who are facing liver surgery, guys who are facing bankruptcy, and the fire sets it all aside. A man is trapped in his car after a head-on with a semi, and when I run toward the vehicle, the halogen scene lights have created a magical tunnel in the falling snow. I run down the tunnel and am surprised how peaceful it feels in that car. I spent the week caught in the crossfire of a friend's child-custody case, for which I am a witness. My guts are tattered. It is searingly cold, and we have to slide the man out over the waist-deep snow on an inflatable sled. We are struggling with straps and cutting tools and keeping track of the man's vital signs, and I find myself perversely grateful to him, because he has given my sour guts a reprieve.

My brother John is a bearded, backwoods-looking fellow. Lives in a log cabin, owns his own dump truck. He was on call up in Chetek last summer when he got paged out on a LifeLine call. The Life-Line is a big button attached to a bracelet or necklace and worn by elderly or infirm patients. In an emergency, they just punch the button, and their address pops up with an alarm at the dispatch center. Then we get paged out. Even more than your average call, you don't know what you're getting into with LifeLine pages—all you know is someone has pressed the alarm. The call was out in the country, and John and his partner, Sharon, made good time, lights and sirens all the way. It was a hot day. When they arrived at the address, a lady was sitting in the yard on an electric scooter. Beside her was a prostrate goose, covered with Frisbees. It seems the goose had passed out in the heat. The frisbees were for shade. "I can't pick him up," said the lady. "And I need to get him in the shed, where it's cool." Moving carefully, my brother picked up the goose and placed it in the shed. He says it didn't look good for the goose. In the meantime, the deputy sheriff who had responded tried as gently as he could to explain to the lady that this was not appropriate use of the LifeLine. John and Sharon drove back to the hall and entered the run in the logbook. Under "Nature of Call" John wrote "goose weakness."

Over the years, your calls tend to conflate. Time presses singular events into the thin strata of history. We accumulate a body of calls like an artist accumulates a body of work. It becomes difficult to recall specific works. Some, like the goose weakness, stand out; most recede to latent memory. You have to remind yourself sometimes, then, that with the exception of a few frequent flyers, your arrival at the end of the driveway is a significant event in the lives of those who call for help. It is not just another call. It is a moment likely to be incorporated into family lore as "the day the ambulance came."

You try to act accordingly. To meet the expectations. To—simply—*help*. You won't always live up to the hype. "What we're going to do . . . ," I was saying, when the woman on the couch interrupted me. "Oh, I know," she said, "I've seen *Paramedics*." This is like telling your Little Leaguer you expect him to yank a Randy Johnson fastball over the left-field wall. We are basic-level emergency medical technicians. We have skills, but they are *basic*. We can't always match what you see on TV. But people are generally kind. A week after John carried the goose to the shed, a painstakingly scribed note arrived in the mail:

Dear Abalane Driver with Beard

   I am sorry I just wanted you to help my goose. Thank you for your help putting him barn She was in 30's year's. She died at 1 pm That day. On E.R. they fix animls. The policeman made me Feel Bad I will not wear LifeLine any more. I did not call Police Man.

   Thank you For helping

                                           Ramona

   He died
   with his wings out
   He went
   to heaven.

10

CAT

EARLY LAST SPRING, my neighbor called and asked if I had ever killed a cat.

I had not.

But I had heard stories, and was inclined to believe they took some killing.

Trygve Nelson owns a computer company. We have an arrangement, heavily weighted in my favor, in which he provides various services, including virtual handholding, hard-drive voodoo, digital exorcisms, and extended sessions of commiserative tut-tutting. I, in turn, proofread his business cards. To hear Trygve talk me through computer trouble is to hear an indulgent father reassuring his blubbering, dimwitted toddler that the ankle-biting monsters under the bed are gone bye-bye. I fear the effects our long-term relationship may have on his mental health. Every time I solicit his advice on a new program or piece of hardware, the poor man is forced to execute a reverse drop-shift to dumb-down gear so violent it smokes his intellectual clutch plates. Imagine Einstein forced to explain the theory of relativity to a classroom of second-graders using only a Ping-Pong ball, a spoonful of custard, and a bag of lint. Without Trygve, I would be scribing in the dirt with a stick. He is my technosavior.

But when it's time to get fundamental, guess who he calls?

"This stray cat's been hanging around, and it's getting sicker. It's coughing. Hacking up stuff. Sandy's in her rescue mode, but this cat is miserable."

Sandy is Mrs. Nelson. She spotted the cat moping in the hostas a day earlier, but today it had collapsed on the deck and was too weak to meow. Its eyes were crusted and pus oozed from each nostril. Its coat was matted and foul. She helped it lap at some water and called the vet. The vet was out, so she left a message and called the humane society. The woman there told her to call the local constable. She dialed the number and explained the situation to the man who answered. His reply was gruff.

"You got a gun?" The constable didn't sound as if he intended to leave the recliner.

"Well . . . yesss . . . but is it legal to shoot something in your backyard when you live in town?"

The constable remained focused on the cat.

"It might," he rasped, "have the rabies." He pronounced it *rabbies*, as in *tabbies with rabbies*, that sinister, prefatory *the* insinuating certain ominous eventualities.

"It's awfully sick," said Sandy.

"Just have your husband shoot it."

There is a way of thinking out here—it has its roots in farming—that when an animal is past the point of recovery, you put it out of its misery. I came home from school one day to find that my father's little flock of sheep had been savaged by two neighborhood dogs. Several ewes were dead. Others were horribly wounded, wool dangling at their necks in bloody fluffs, the meat ripped from their haunches. In a blood frenzy, the dogs tore at the sheep even as they dragged themselves forward. My father went to the house for his deer rifle and then, alone in the pasture, walked among the fallen sheep, shooting them one by one. Unable to amend the suffering, he ended it.

"Well, not everyone can just shoot an animal," said the vet, returning Sandy's call. "But there are so many feral animals . . . you really shouldn't expose them to your own cats." She's all but saying the cat should be euthanized. Still, taking the cat to the vet for euthanasia, *the blue juice*, as we call it 'round here, isn't free. And so now I have Trygve on the phone.

"I know a place," I say. "I'll be over in a little bit." Hanging up, I already feel a little light in the gut, a little tight around the mouth, the way I always get when I figure I'm about to see something nasty. I've seen so much blood and mess up to this point, why would the death of a bedraggled cat bother me?

Because I know exactly what we're in for.

Trygve and I are driving north. In the trunk we have a cat in a box, a shovel, and a rifle. When I got to Trygve's house, the cat was so far gone it was tipping over. It opened its mouth to meow, but raised no sound. I took a pair of bright blue latex gloves from my medical kit and slipped them on, what with all the pus, and wrapped the cat in an old towel. I volunteered at the animal shelter for a week every summer when I was a child, and one of my jobs was to retrieve the cats and dogs whose numbers came up on the euthanasia list. A dog might sit still for the needle, but the cats you had to roll in a towel or you'd get slashed. I remember speaking gently and petting each animal until the air eased from its lungs.

We are driving to the hidden patch of land where my brother lives. A dirt track leads off the main road through a stand of jack pines to his cabin. Trygve turns up the track and drives until we reach a swale that opens into the creek bottom below. I carry the box down the swale and set it on last year's marsh grass, pressed and brown after a winter beneath snow. Trygve follows with the shovel and rifle. There is some sun, but the sky is pale, and the air is cold. Trygve digs a small hole. I take the cat from the box.

The spade cleaves a neat wedge from the peat, and the cat sways on the flat grass. In an empty trailer house at the foot of a Wyoming mountain many years ago, I was thumbing through a discarded *Newsweek* and came across a series of photos in which a man in South America dug a shallow grave, lay in it, and was bayoneted. The trailer tin ticked in the high-noon sun, and I went cold. I was queasy for a week. I get the same sickly flush whenever I see the horrific black-and-white footage of Nazis shooting Jews in trenches. And now, there was that cat, waiting by the hole.

What a warm fuzzy story this would be if we had taken the cat in, plied it with eyedroppers of warm milk and medicine, spent the next few weeks nursing it back to health. I tended my share of shoebox hospitals as a child, standing vigil over limp baby birds, or baby rabbits dragged into the yard by our old calico cat. When one of our sheep refused a lamb, my father would swaddle the lamb in rags and place it on the heat register, and we would take turns coaxing it to suckle milk from an old ketchup bottle capped with a rubber nipple. I once watched my mother resuscitate a newborn calf, blowing air down its throat and pressing on its ribs until it shook its head and opened its eyes. But this cat we have decided to kill.

We are not making the decision lightly. There are people in this world who quite happily stuff healthy cats in a bag with a rock and toss the whole works in a lake. There are people who will swerve across the road in order to pin a cat's spine to the centerline. Trygve and I, on the other hand, have given consideration to the cat's condition and decided it would be better off out of its misery. To say the least, this is a judgment call, based on cloudy anthropomorphism. The responsibilities of being human are various. We were not feeling good about it out there on the dead grass. I'll say this for Trygve. He was quick, and he was true. He put down the shovel, took up the rifle, a walloping *Blap!*, and it was done.

Trygve looked at me. "Well, he didn't feel that."

The rifle was loaded with 240-grain .44-caliber hollow-points. Shooting a cat with armaments like that is roughly equivalent to swatting a mosquito with a spade. I was standing just off his left shoulder, and at the sound of the report, a clutch of white fur flew past my head. A peanut-sized wad of phlegm hit me in the leg and clung to my jeans. There was blood on my shirt. Trygve toed the remains of the cat into the hole. We tipped the peat wedge back in place, tamped it down with the shovel, and drove home. I went straight to the basement. Standing beside the washing machine, I removed all my clothes and started them immediately on the heavy cycle.

Humans possess no monopoly on the powers of preservation and destruction. Our ability to wield these powers with sustained intent, however, is unmatched on this earth. Nature can trump us in an instance or over millennia, but in the day-to-day main, humankind has developed a preponderant ability to fiddle with destiny. More than any other natural force or creature, we decide what will go and what will stay: the rainforest, an old building, a sickly cat . . . ourselves.

When they tore down the old Farmers Store, I swore I wouldn't write about it. Last thing the world needs, really, another elegy on a pile of bricks. But then the first wall tumbled, and the vibration transmitted itself through the dirt, resonating in the foundation of my house half a block away. Upstairs, my writing desk trembled and shook the lamps. The electric letters on my computer monitor went jittery, and concentric ripples flared in and out of phase inside my coffee cup. The destruction became difficult to ignore. I made some notes. As I typed, the shudder of falling bricks was perceptible through the keys.

The Farmers Store building went up in 1905. The concept behind the store originated in 1891, when a small group of locals pooled their resources to buy goods in quantity at wholesale prices. Their initial order consisted of a barrel of sugar, a barrel of molasses, a barrel of crackers, some vinegar and seasonings, and a bolt of calico. A year later, the venture had become so popular that the group incorporated, and commenced to building community stores. The New Auburn store was outfitted with plank floors and pressed-tin ceilings. Hand-sawn oak stairs led to the second floor, and the building was fronted with a bank of plate-glass windows. In vintage photographs, the wooden sales counters are glassed in and ponderous, docked against the wall like barges. The men behind them are kitted out in ties and aprons; the women wear their hair in a bob. Behind them, dry goods are packed to the ceiling on shelves running the length of the store and accessible by a rolling library ladder. Out on the main floor, vast wooden tables are stacked with hats and lace-up shoes. Another photograph, taken from the center of Main Street in 1908, shows a cluster of locals standing on the plank sidewalk beneath a pinked canvas banner that reads FARMERS STORE COMPANY. The planks shine with rain, and a man with an umbrella blocks the doorway. A padded wooden rocker and a dining room table with slim Chippendale-style legs are visible in the display windows. A buggy is parked front and center, with a steer hooked in the traces. Along the lower left-hand margin of the photograph, some wag has written *Quadrapedmobile*.

The New Auburn Farmers Store ceased operations in 1966, the year my family began farming north of town. I was in the building a handful of times. I remember the creak of the wooden floors, the polished dark rail along the stairway, and warm summer air coming through the open twin doors where the man with the umbrella stood. A series of enterprises sprang up and died in the old building over the years. About the time I was in eighth grade, the store was known as Don's Discount, and was filled with day-old bakery and crates of castoff merchandise. I riffled through boxes of vinyl records, and bought the only song I recognized, a 45 of Supertramp's "The Logical Song."

Sixteen years later, I returned to town and found the plate-glass windows blocked with plywood. The double doors were enclosed by a cobbled-up wooden vestibule that had begun to shed pieces of siding. The day before they knocked the whole works flat, I wandered up and took some pictures. A homemade sign hung from a pipe extended over the entryway. The Farmers Store's latest incarnation was posted in hand-painted letters:

MAIN STREET
STORE

The script was cramped and thin. Below, in a willy-nilly arrangement of stenciled letters so small as to be indecipherable from Tugg's Bar across the street, the scope of the final venture was defined:

GROCERIES
DISCOUNT ITEMS
BAITS
CLOTHING
ICE CREAM
PIZZA
BOLTS
KNICK KNACKS
COLD POP
CRAFTS
HARDWARE
WORM'S
MINNOW'S
SNACK'S
BEST B.S. IN TOWN

"I hate to see it go," I said to one of the old-timers who watched the excavator push the store down.

"Well, it served its purpose," he said.

Hugh Ruud was born on May 1, 1922, in the second story of a house overlooking Main Street, across from the Farmers Store. The house still stands—I can turn in my desk chair and see the upstairs windows. Little Hugh hit the air bawling, and squalled all night long. His father took him in his arms and paced the floor. "Snookie," he murmured, "what am I gonna do with you?" Eighty years on, and Hugh Ruud won't even turn his head at "Hugh." He is Snook around town, he is Snook in the phone book, and if I turn my desk chair again, I can see a yellow sign hanging over the door of a little brick building kitty-corner from where the Farmers Store stood, and the black letters say, SNOOK'S STORE—HOMEMADE SAUSAGE & BACON.

"That sign come all the way from California," says Snook. I have gone to his house to visit. To try to sort out some local history. We are at his kitchen table, having coffee. His wife, Betty Lou, has cinnamon rolls in the oven. Snook sold the store in 1988, but that name was too good to let go, and so the new owners kept the sign up. "We paid five hundred dollars for that thing," says Snook. "But it was a nice sign. Lit up nice."

Snook's health has been a little hit-and-miss lately. For a while last summer, his heart got so bad his daughter was certain they were going to lose him. He got pretty down, and there was a stretch in July when he really didn't care if he lived or died. But today he's all grins and stories. I'm just basking in his rambling. He cusses delightfully, and the village he describes is magical. When he talks, the blacktop and aluminum siding and satellite dishes evaporate, the streets fill with storybook folk, and the old buildings resurrect. I just let him go.

"Up there by the railroad tracks, they had a hobo jungle up in there. Right where all them damn cars are." He's describing Slinger Joe's, a junkyard at the north end of the village. "Them guys would come in on the train, and they'd go around the gardens and pick a few carrots and some cabbage and cook it. There were two big pickle vats in there, up higher than this ceiling. They had a salt brine in there, just to keep them from spoiling. They used a real coarse salt. We used to jump up there, go up, and get one of them pickles. Geez, they was sourer than hell!"

Betty Lou breaks in, points at Snook. "The Tom Sawyer of New Auburn!"

"You live in the old Gravunder house?" Snook asks me. I nod. "There used to be a free show right behind your house. And a popcorn stand. During the Depression, they had free shows every Saturday night. Christ, everybody in the country came. Hell, they'd park a hundred cars in there."

Snook takes me through all the buildings that are gone—the brick factory, the creamery, the band shell, the potato warehouses, the railroad depot, the old charcoal kilns, the old wooden schoolhouse and fire hall, the old brick schoolhouse, the old jail, the old bank, the old post office, the old three-corner gas station at the corner of Main and Old Highway 53. And now the Farmers Store.

"When I was a kid, you know, we used to go up at Christmastime down to the Farmers Store," says Snook. "Those big bay windows, they'd have that lined with toys. Geez, I remember after supper in the wintertime around Christmastime I'd go down there and look through that glass, look at all them toys and you'd know goddamn well you wasn't going to get any because things were so damn tough. But I liked that old Farmers Store. I hated to see that building tore down."

Talk turns back to Snook's store. Snook says it was built around the time of the Depression. Back in those days, it was a Red & White store. According to Snook, there were Red & White stores in nearly every town in those days. Chain stores before chain stores were evil. The original owner spent most of his time across the street at Blaisdell's Tavern—in business today as Tugg's Bar. "He'd sit at the end of the bar by the window," says Snook. "If somebody went in the store, he'd come over." In the mid-1930s, Harry Jacobson bought the store and ran it for the next forty years. I can remember walking in the door sometime around 1970, standing beside my mother and staring up at Harry in his white apron. He kept a giant candy jar on the long wooden counter, and sold cookies out of a barrel. You gave him your grocery list, and he gathered it from the shelves. Even in

1970, it was like walking into a western. Snook bought the store in 1974. He had served in World War II, worked on the railroad, and had training as a butcher. He turned the butchering experience to his advantage.

"Six head a week we ran through there, just over-the-counter beef quarters. Maybe down to around four in the wintertime. And we always made at least four to five hundred pounds of sausage a week. Bratwurst, bologna, garlic stick, head cheese, roast beef, all that stuff. We worked hard. That's where I made my money. I couldn't make no money on groceries, because we couldn't compete with nobody. But the meat business, hell, we could skin the hell out of them on the meat. But I took a lower price on my meat than most, you know. That's what I used more for a drawing card. On Friday nights, all these lake people would come up to my store and buy their meats. They were good customers."

"The first ten years were great," says Betty Lou. "We made a little bit of money, and we were busy. And then the supermarkets came in at Chetek and Bloomer . . ."

"They were cutting prices to beat hell," says Snook. "Made it tough. Our distributors started going out of business. . . . Christ, you'd get bananas on Monday, and you wouldn't get another delivery the rest of the week." Still, they stayed at it.

"We worked seven to six, every day except Sunday," says Snook. "Sundays we'd try to get out before noon, but we never got out before one. It got too much for me after I had my heart trouble. I'd lift the quarters of beef out on the meat block and would purt' near black out." So Snook and Betty Lou sold out. "Betty Lou worked awful hard in that store," says Snook. "She was glad to get rid of it. But I loved that store. I *still* love that store." He takes a pull at his coffee. Puts the cup down. Smooths the tablecloth. "But I just couldn't do it anymore."

We stop for a while. Work on the cinnamon rolls. Then Snook gets going again. Tells how they built their house in segments, as money allowed, and how shortly after declaring they couldn't yet afford an indoor toilet, he spent $500 on a motor for a speedboat someone gave him in a trade. Betty Lou went out and stenciled JOHN across the bow of the boat. "It was a *john* boat!" he says, slapping his leg. When he finally walks me to the door, his eyes are twinkling.

Like a million other nostalgia-addled fools, I want to bottle time. It's part of the reason I love to shoot the breeze with the old-timers. It's why I stare longingly at old pictures and flip through the records of the former livery stable. It's why I called the man who owned the Farmers Store the night before the excavator was due and asked if I could have the Sherwin-Williams paint sign attached to the side of the store overlooking Spruce Street. My buddy Frank and I spent half the day getting the bloody thing detached. The weather was ten degrees and windy, and the sign was so far up we had to park a half-ton truck beneath it and prop a thirty-foot extension ladder in the bed. From the ground, the sign looked like a little tin deal, maybe a foot square. Up close, it was two feet by three feet and made out of enameled steel. Must have weighed forty pounds. It was bolted to the bricks, and I almost gave up, especially when I chiseled the first bracket loose and the sign swung out and nearly knocked me into the freezing wind. I could see Frank down there, shrugged deep into his sheepskin coat and bracing the ladder, as if that would help. I was ready to give up when the second bracket gave way and dumped the whole works in my arms. Once I got my heart rate back to where it didn't vibrate the ladder, I inched my way down to the truck. I have the sign downstairs now. I like to look at it, feel it radiate the years. But I'm glad I talked to Snook. Glad he recited that litany of places that no longer exist in this place. There was a lot there to remind me about the constancy of change. How much it means to carry those things with us. And how to know when it is time to let go. As it is with buildings, it is with ourselves.

● ● ●

There is a big swamp just north of town. We call it the Keesey, after a long-gone settler who farmed the flats before the government stuck a little box dam around one end of the Beaver Creek culvert and backed the water up over the hay fields. In spring, the trail to Keesey's abandoned homestead reemerges as a narrow trace of canary grass running due west into the wetlands, a palimpsest revealing that the swamp is not entirely primordial. And yet on certain autumn evenings, if you tromp far enough out there, if you plant your butt in the muck and get your head below the cattail tops and wait, you will shortly hear the clotted bugling of sandhill cranes, and when they circle and descend in their lanky echelons, you will feel you are living in the time of pterodactyls. I seek the swamp because, unlike me, it is a patient servant of time. The swamp is all percolation and decay. It is the perfect place to make yourself small in the face of the earth.

I will go to the swamp in my camo cap and waders, toting my shotgun and four cheapo plastic decoys, hoping maybe to bring home a duck for supper, but I also take a little notepad and something to read. The local duck population benefits from my literary pretensions. At the whistle of wings, I frequently look up from my book to see a mallard pair flaring out of range. There are times, in the early fall, when much of the swamp is still green, that the sun will warm the air to the point where spiders and tiny winged insects reemerge. The spiders climb to the reed tips, spin out a little silk, and sail away, while the insects flutter over the water, apparently aimlessly, but who am I to say. By morning the water is skimmed with ice, and I wonder where the bugs wound up.

It's a powerful thing, to sit low in the swamp as the sun goes down. You can feel the heat leach out and the cold press in, and it feels irrevocable. Last year's reeds are broken, brown, and half-rotted, this year's reeds will be there soon. A methane bubble pops the still water now and then, the message being, this is what it all boils down to. I get bleak and overwhelmed. In the west, the sky goes pale red and brassy. I feel the spreading color more than I see it. In 1970, the Berlin Philharmonic made a recording of Wagner's *Götterdäm-*

merung. At about 3:05 into Siegfried's Funeral March, a solitary trumpet peal rises over the strings and fades. I find it to be unbearably plangent. That note captures exactly what it is to watch the sun set from the Keesey. Sometimes nature is a comfort. Sometimes it presses down on you like cold steel.

I set out wandering one morning, with my shotgun and my waders. The reeds were furred with frost, and I was well bundled up. The day before, several ducks had overflown me, only to drop from sight into some invisible pothole halfway across the marsh. I was on a mission to locate and hunt the pothole.

From a distance, the swamp appears as a grassy plain, but when you get out on it, you realize it is actually a floating mat of plants and muck. With each step, I sent out bulky ripples. It seemed as if I might break through. I probably should have turned back, but I have stomped all over the swamp, and never came across a spot deeper than waist level. By the time I spied the pothole, I was pretty warm from all the awkward tramping. The water was scattered with lily stems and bits of tuber—a sign of heavy feeding by ducks and geese. Looking for a spot to hide with my shotgun, I stepped to the edge and the earth opened up and swallowed me. In the split second it took for me to realize I was dropping, I threw out my arms. I was holding my shotgun in both hands—one hand on the stock and one on the barrel—and I believe this saved me, as the gun caught in the reeds and distributed my weight across the floating marsh edge. I hung there, the icy water an inch from the top of my chest waders, my feet not touching bottom, and I remember thinking, with great clarity and focus, Your next move is very important.

If I lost my grip on the shotgun, or slipped from the edge, the water would pour into my waders and be absorbed by all my heavy clothes, and I'd go down like a sack of sand. There was a chill just south of my pancreas that had nothing to do with the temperature of the water. I remember thinking they'd never find me. I would become Chippewa County's own Kennewick Man. A bog mummy in camouflage waders.

I held my position for a while. Like Jonah, his elbows braced against the jaws of the whale. I tend to yammer sometimes about accepting death as peace, and hanging there that morning, I did achieve a sort of Zen clarity, but it had nothing to do with acquiescence. Unprepared to make the Mission to Big Peaceful, I instead commenced the most delicate, cautious pull-up, ever so slowly drawing my chest to my elbows, firmly suppressing the urge to flail at the fragile marsh-fringe like a spasmodic monkey. Inch by slow inch I slid my body up and over, until I was back atop the floating mattress. I took a very deep breath then, and grinned out there all alone. In time, I thought. In time. But not today.

The time came when the people who bought Snook's Store couldn't make a go of it anymore. I used to try to buy something in there every couple of weeks, a can of mushrooms, some orange juice, the homemade frankfurters. But it was negligible commerce in the face of all I toted home from the supermarkets and Wal-Mart. For the first time since the Depression, the store closed. They reopened it recently, as the Sunshine Café. I've been over there for biscuits and gravy, and there are cars parked there pretty regular in the mornings and around meal time. I hope it works out. The local school principal bought Snook's yellow sign. He plans to hang it on the wall in the student commons area, surround it with old pictures and local artifacts. Give the kids a chance to expand their vision of a place they see and yet don't see every day. If you can find a way to strike a balance between ignoring the past and clinging to it, maybe just *recognize* the past, then I guess you've got something.

There is this photograph down at the fire hall, taken February 25, 1984. The old high school, built in 1906, is in flames. Raging. Smoke so big Betty Lou Ruud saw it clear out from Curavo's hill when she drove into town to help Snook at the store that morning. The fire department is there, all nineteen members. They're lined up in two rows, backs to the flame, posed and grinning as if they're at a family picnic. The old school was grand in its day. Two stories tall and capped with a louvered bell tower. In a picture taken the morning it opened, the three original teachers are posed out front in long pleated skirts and broad-brimmed hats decked with flowers.

The fire department uses old buildings like this for practice. We call it "having a burn." You start the fire, put it out, start it, put it out, and then eventually you let it go. Usually it's an old farmhouse, or a barn out in the country. Shortly after I joined the department, we burned the feed mill where my father used to grind feed. I remember sweeping the corncobs out of the bed of his blue pickup, watching them dance and shatter in the maw of the gravity-fed grinder. It was a little strange to crawl around in the smoke on the floor where I used to stand waist-high beside Dad while he paid the feed bill. Someone took pictures of the feed mill burn, and I looked through them while I was working on this chapter. It's not dramatic, but it is lightly ironic: You join the fire department under the pretext of putting out fires, and you wind up burning your own history.

———

Life is a preservation project. Our instinct for preservation plays out in everything from the depth of our breaths to an affection for bricks. Even as we flail and cling, trying to bottle time, to save it, we live only through its expenditure. Memory is a means of possession, but eventually, the greatest grace is found in letting go.

———

At a small farmhouse deep in the country, a small woman meets us at the door. "My husband shot himself," she says. I put my hand on her shoulder, look straight into her eyes, and ask a terrible question. "Are you sure he is dead?" I am groping for the tone of voice that will allow me to ask this cosmically insulting question and yet convey concern and regret and sympathy and respect, and I am feeling mightily inadequate. I am only asking because it will not do if the coroner arrives to a heartbeat, with us standing around. "I think so," she says. "He is in the granary."

He left the first note on the barn door. It was brief and instructive. *I am in the granary*, it said. *Don't come in. Call the sheriff's department. They will know what to do.* Below, he had written the fire number, and the name of the road that ran by the farm, and he said another letter, a longer one—she would find it by his body—would explain everything else. She didn't see the letter on the barn door, and she walked into the granary and saw him there, slumped against the wall, the gun still in his hand.

I steel myself and open the granary door, only to see a narrow passageway back to another doorway. My heart is kicking pretty hard as I walk down the passage. You have this dread, and it gets worse with time, because like with Trygve and the cat, I have a pretty good idea what I'm going to see. You are setting your senses up for assault. When I get closer, I see the man's feet, just sticking out the door. I take another breath, and put my head around the door.

He is seated, his legs extended. His upper body is leaned against the corner of the granary, his shoulders resting in the vee of the walls, his head tipped forward, his mouth open, his chin on his chest. His arms are crossed across his abdomen. The pistol, an old flat black .38, is still cradled in his left hand. The gun is upside down, his thumb is still in the trigger guard. His mouth is a dark blossom of blood, and the front of his flannel shirt is stained with the bleeding. A small, neat exit wound showed on his scalp, and I remember this absurd sense of relief, because most exit wounds are an expulsive mess. I reached out to palpate the top of his foot, to feel for a pedal pulse. As I pressed my fingertips against his instep, a drop of blood fell from his mouth to his chest, and I felt a familiar, deep drumming in his foot. Oh, no, I remember thinking. This man has so obviously and carefully chosen to die, the idea of having to "work" him horrifies me. I readjust the position of my fingers, lean in more closely, and just as quickly, realize the pulse I felt was my own. My fear has betrayed me, pounding clear out to my fingertips.

Jack hands me a stethoscope. I straddle the man, put the silver bell of the stethoscope over a dry spot on the flannel, and listen long and hard. The man's face is close to mine now. His skin is waxen. It looks moldable. I am satisfied there is no heartbeat.

The wife is in the kitchen, reading the second letter. It is several pages long, with messages for her, for the children, for the agent that holds his life insurance policy. It begins simply: *I'm so sorry.* When he came home after the last CAT scan, he writes, and told his wife the cancer had been eradicated, he was only trying to spare her. The tumors have threaded their way deep into the liver. *I no longer possess the strength nor the fortitude to continue.* Fortitude. The word sounds so considered.

We stood with the wife for a long time, waiting for the coroner to arrive. She told us a little about the man she married, and we looked at family pictures. There he was, burly beside a hay wagon, waving from a tractor, cradling an infant daughter, him in his overalls, she in frilly footies. The face in the granary kept superimposing itself, and I strained to equate them.

Back home, when I step through the door and toss my keys on the chair beside the door, I notice the house has an echo and a chill to it. The call came in at 2:45 A.M., and now it is after five A.M., and I have friends coming to visit at nine A.M. I want to get what sleep I can. All the way up the stairs and into my bedroom, even as I shuck my clothes and roll into the sheets, I keep seeing the figure in the granary. It's a healthy and natural part of the accommodation process, I imagine, this constant reviewing of the image, but it just kept presenting itself, and I found myself reacting the way I always have after one of these calls: pondering the irrevocable nature of death, fighting the desire to call loved ones, wake them up and ask them, Do you realize how thin the thread is? That maybe tomorrow we don't wake up? That sometimes the soul votes to tear the body down? I wasn't terror-stricken or freaked out, just unsettled. And so finally I got up, threw on some shorts and a T-shirt, went down-stairs, turned on some music, and mixed up a batch of bread. It took me about twenty minutes, and I set the timer, so that when the alarm woke me just three hours later, the sun was dazzling in the giant sugar maple outside my window, and the house was filled with the smell of fresh bread, risen and baked while I slept.

11

Oops

Somewhere in a Kodak Carousel Transvue 140 slide tray stashed on a shelf in my parents' house, there is a photo of me visiting the zoo. It's the early 1970s, I'm about eight years old, I'm wearing a red-white-and-blue striped shirt, I've got a cowlick springing up through my bangs, and I am lost in thought before a penful of piglets. The index finger of my right hand is jammed knuckle-deep up one nostril. I reckon there's a lot of metaphorical potential to a picture like that, what with the pigs and the picking. While my finger burrows away with the industry of a coal drill, the rest of my body remains utterly relaxed, and my gaze has dissolved to a midrange trance. Upon closer study of the image, one reaches the conclusion that the pig pen boy is a bit drifty, a tad self-absorbed, and prone to low-key episodes of public mortification.

So I was, and so I remain. In pretty much everything I attempt, even when things are downright serious, I am conscious of a little voice suggesting that I am loosely moored, that I'm just two degrees from goofy, that at any moment circumstances will catch me with my metaphorical finger up my metaphorical nose.

So if you ever see me out there, in my fireman's hat, or kneeling at someone's bloodied head, trying to sort through everything that needs to be done, trying to keep it together, to recall all I have been taught, understand that I don't feel heroic.

Pigpen boy is never far away.

I hadn't been on the department long. It was the heart of winter, after midnight; a woman's voice was on the phone. Cabin fire. Way out in the tules, lakeside. When we got there it was an incandescent stack of Lincoln Logs. Two of us pulled an attack line and moved in. We tried to work together, but we were wading around in six inches of water over a bed of ice. Mostly, we looked like a pair of hockey goalies wrestling an anaconda. A lieutenant beckoned, pointing back over his shoulder. He turned to lead the way, I swung the hose, forgetting to shut it down first, and it got away from me. A torrent of water as thick as a blacksmith's forearm lifted the lieutenant's helmet and smacked him in the back of the neck. He was drenched and frozen. By the time we got back to town, it was dawn. At the lone convenience store, the locals were picking up coffee for the drive to work. I waited in line to sign for diesel, and one of them turned to look at me.

"Fire?" he asked. I was wearing sooty bunkers, a fire helmet, and my shirt was soaked.

"Yep," I answered.

"Where?"

"Out north a ways."

"Stop it?"

"From spreading."

You put on a uniform, or a jacket embroidered with the Star of Life, or even just a helmet, and suddenly you are imbued with authority. No matter that five minutes ago you were doing dishes, or singing in the shower, or drooling in your sleep.

I don't like uniforms. For one thing, a signal joy of writing for a living is the freedom to clear the closet of everything but two old pair of jeans and a stack of T-shirts. For another, I rarely feel as if I can live up to what a uniform implies. But whenever possible—even when we make first responder calls in our street clothes—I try to throw on a jacket or a cap that gives some indication that I am affiliated with the fire department. The issue is not so much to establish authority, but to provide a touch of order in what is often a chaotic situation. You try to wear the uniform in such a way that it will be a source of reassurance to the person who has called for help. It is not unusual for your patients to feel more reassured than you.

I am looking into the eyes of an elderly lady. She thinks she might be having a stroke, but now she isn't so sure. It's early morning. The page got me out of bed, and I dressed in a hurry. My brother John is on the call with me. The lady is sitting on her couch, and I kneel down so I can make good eye contact. It helps with communication, and I can make assessments, too. I am looking for any little cues that she might be having stroke symptoms: facial droop, slurred speech, problems with orientation, any subtle hint that something may be gone haywire in her brain, some discrepancy of word or action that tells me her level of orientation has been altered. I even check to see how she is dressed—an incorrectly buttoned sweater or mismatched shoes can be a sign of something amiss. Close examination reveals nothing. She seems to be fine. I give her one more look-over, smile benevolently, and we leave. On the way to the ambulance, John points at my chest. "Might wanna fix that," he says. I look down. My shirt. Inside out and backward.

I am in an old man's kitchen. The old man says he had a woozy spell, and so he took some nitroglycerin pills. This is like saying you had high blood pressure so you did your taxes. The nitroglycerin has dropped the man's blood pressure even lower, and now he's really woozy. At the hospital, several of the paramedics are standing around, and so after giving report on the woozy man, I join them and chat for several minutes before one of them says, "So, Mike . . . time for new pants?" I look down to see if I've spilled something on myself. "In back," says the paramedic. I reach around and find a gaping six-inch split. How long I have been strolling around this way, I have no idea. Understand also that it is autumn, and so I am wearing camouflage-print underwear.

It can be argued that one of the nice things about working in the field of fire and rescue is that for the most part, things went to heck in a hand basket before you were called, and so there is nowhere to go but up. This is why I dread the idea of delivering a baby in the field. Give me six bloody people in a crushed van any day; the damage is done, I can only help. With the baby, there is this expectation that you will not only *sustain* life, but *deliver* life. In the last decade, our little fire department has been called on to deliver only one baby. The call was in a farmhouse overlooking a swamp, and the cord was wrapped around the baby's neck. My mom was on the call, and because she had experience as an obstetrics nurse, she took charge. The rest of the firemen will be the first to tell you they basically stood there wide-eyed, handing over towels. There is a little girl over in the grade school now whose arrival in this world is marked by a stork decal just behind the driver's side door of our rescue van. It's a cool thing to be proud of your mom, and I am, but mostly I'm glad it wasn't me. I smile whenever I see the decal, but it also braces me a little. Reminds me we might be required to repeat the performance again someday.

Even when you come through under pressure, there is room for humility. I am way out in the country, in the back of the ambulance with a man experiencing chest pain. I need to start an IV, but he is refusing. He is on dialysis, and his veins are used up. "When I go to the hospital, they have to call anesthesia to get an IV in," he says. "I don't want you trying."

"Well, I have to try," I say.

"I'd really rather you not," he says.

"Tell you what. We're supposed to make two tries. I'll just make one. If I don't get it the first time, I'll quit."

"Weelllll . . . OK."

It's tough. I can't raise a vein for anything. I readjust and tighten the tourniquet on the man's bicep. Finally, down in the antecubital space, on the inside of the elbow, I see a little blue spot. There's a vein in there somewhere. I uncap the needle and probe beneath the skin, expecting nothing. Blood flashes in the chamber. Glory be, I'm in. I hook up the tubing.

"You got in?!?" The man is incredulous.

"Yep." I stay cool. Like I do it all the time.

"Well, you're really something. That's amazing. Even the anesthesia people can't get in half the time, and they're the best in the business. You must be good."

I demur, real humble-like. But I'm thrilled.

One problem. The IV is running, but not as fast as it should. I recheck the tubing, make sure it isn't kinked. I check the roller valve, make sure it's wide open. It is. I check the stick site, make sure it isn't infiltrated. Everything checks out. In the drip chamber, the drops fall tentatively, at long intervals. Better than nothing, I guess.

But it bugs me. The miles pass, and I keep sneaking looks, surreptitious-like. Finally, about a mile out of town, the man notices. "Something wrong?" he asks. "Well," I say, "it's running, but not as fast as I'd like." The man points at his arm. "Maybe if you took that thing off?"

My face goes hot. I undo the tourniquet. The drops patter through the drip chamber like a one-note rainstorm. If they were striking a tin roof, you could hear them: "*Idiot . . . idiot . . . idiot . . . idiot . . .*"

I was on jury duty recently. A man was fighting a drunken-driving charge. During voir dire, the plaintiff's attorney asked me if I was able to look at a person in uniform and see a human being, capable of making mistakes just like anyone else. I said I could. I'm not sure he believed me. He had no idea, really. Rarely do I cherish my uniformed cohorts more than when they draw the screwup spotlight away from me:

1. My partner, Flip, parks the ambulance and runs to an accident victim. The ambulance gathers speed slowly but is tooling right along by the time it T-bones a brand-new squad car. Parking the ambulance and *putting* it in park are separate issues.

2. Palpating the foot of a man with a broken leg, Scooter Southern surprises everyone by announcing that he has detected a fetal pulse.

3. A man has been ejected from his car on the interstate. He is lying in the median. He is conscious, and isn't complaining of any significant problems. I am suspicious, though, because it is rare to be thrown this far and escape serious injury, and the man is a little disoriented. The state patrolman on scene is young, crisp, and efficient. He wouldn't have to, but he helps us arrange a blanket over the man on the ground. He straightens up and jots some notes in his report.

   The man cries out. "Ow, ow, ooow!" I bend to his face, quickly. "What is it, bud?"

   "Ohh! Ohh! Down there!" He points with his eyes, because we have him all swaddled in gear. I do a quick survey. Can't see anything. I flip the blanket back. The state patrolman is standing square on the man's fingers.

   I have to tug the patrolman's pants cuff twice before he notices. He pulls a silent-movie *ooops!* face and yanks his foot clear. I think the man on the ground never knew why the pain stopped.

   But I know. That I am not the only goofball in a hero suit.

· · ·

It isn't always the patient who suffers the brunt of screw-ups. I am on a call with Donna. There is a frail old man on the cot. Donna is not very big, and so, thinking I have to compensate, I execute a clean-and-jerk move with the head end of the cot, hoisting it way too high, way too fast and pushing it over center, causing the folding legs to collapse. The full weight of the patient shifts to the foot of the cot, yanking Donna to the ground and slamming her fingers between the rails. She is in great pain, but for the sake of the patient, she acts as if nothing has happened. I feel oafish and cloddy, but I am holding up the head end of the cot, and can't apologize until we have gone all the way to the hospital and the patient is out of earshot.

Sometimes the goofy moments are sweet and funny. My brother and I picked up an elderly lady on the Alzheimer's wing of the nursing home. She had become agitated and attacked another patient. She was being transferred to a psychiatric hospital for evaluation. She was very nervous and worked up, asking me the same questions over and over. "Where are you taking me?" "Don't you hurt me!" "I want to see my doctor!" "Who is my doctor?" I answered her gently, over and over, the same answers every time. "We're going to the hospital." "No, Betty, no one will hurt you." "We'll see your doctor as soon as we get to the hospital." "Your doctor is Dr. Jackson."

She repeated the cycle of identical questions about fifteen times. Each time, I answered exactly the same, and always maintained eye contact. It seemed to reassure her. She became calmer. About ten minutes into the ride, she started the cycle again. "Where are you taking me?"

"We're going to the hospital."

Something changed in her eyes. A little slyness, a little exasperation.

"Well, I *know*," she said. "You said that *fifteen times* now!"

I do not limit my ignominy to rescue work. I was on a bike racing team for a while in the '90s. I was mediocre. Except for one race. I was off the front alone, and opening a sizable gap. I had only to maintain for a few more laps and victory was mine. I remember swooping into a corner. I remember right in the apex of the curve the speedometer said 27.5 miles per hour. I remember I thought I might be taking the corner a little wide. I remember a tremendous thump, as if maybe Barry Bonds took a swing at my clavicle. I remember waking to the sky. What I have done here, is drive straight into a concrete bridge, completely unassisted. Today, one of my shoulders rides lower than the other. It twinges sometimes when I pull fire hose, or load the ambulance cot. I feel the twinge and remember that for a few laps there, I was god of the Peloton.

Sometimes you get set up. A man is trapped in a crumpled car. It takes us a very long time to get him out. It is so cold that chunks of blood are freezing in his hair. There is a lot of blood. He spits it by the mouthful. It's all over my goggles. My turnouts are spattered. My helmet is dotted. We can't find the source. The chopper is coming. The firefighters peel the roof back. Then they winch the steering wheel over the dash, off the man's lap. We stick him in the ambulance and ride to a landing zone set up in the parking lot of a bait shop. I grab a penlight, lean over the man, frog around in his mouth with my gloved fingers, trying to locate the bleeder. The surge and pulse of the blood tells me there's a severed artery in there somewhere. Blood has a way of looking like far more than it is, but still, I'm nervous about how much he might be losing. I keep probing, until a red stream the diameter of a pencil lead sprays from the man's mouth. It arcs over his chest and retreats, then pulses again. I trace the stream back to a small gash inside the man's lower lip. I wedge a fat piece of gauze in like a wad of chew, and it flushes red in an instant. So I grab another piece of gauze, tell the man this might hurt, and pinch his lip, hard. It's the only way I can get the bleeding to stop. I hear the chopper land, and the flight nurses come in the back doors. I hand off the patient, and jump out the side door, into a four-foot free-fall. The rig is parked with the door overhanging the ditch. From my vantage point—in a heap, down in the weeds—I see Tee Norman and the chief, peeking around the side of the ambulance and giggling. "Figured that was gonna happen," says Tee.

Part of the trouble there was that after pulling the man from the car, and locating the bleeder, I got caught up in the idea of Myself as Heroic Rescuer. When I jumped out of the ambulance, I thought I was wearing a cape. I don't always listen to the little warning voices in my head. Last winter we fought a ravenous warehouse fire. Leaping flames, rolling smoke, the water freezing over everything like a glass shell. To get a better angle on the fire, I climbed atop a ten-foot pile of ice-coated bricks. You can see it coming, but not me. I noticed the photographer from the local paper skulking about. I am suspecting I cut quite a figure atop these bricks, all icicle-fringed and silhouetted against the banks of smoke. I am thinking this will make a noble picture for the *Chetek Alert*. These thoughts are still in my mind when my boots shoot out behind me and I perform a credible quarter-gainer, terminating at the base of the brick pile in a full-frontal face mask smash. Lieutenant Pam is watching. She can't see too well, because ten minutes ago I managed to blast her in the face with a fire hose. Her eyes won't be right for a week. But she can see well enough to tell it's me, face first at the bottom of the pile, and perhaps she is thinking there is such a thing as karma.

Sometimes you have to get preemptive. The final morning of our biannual refresher class, I got overexcited on a page-out and screwed up in a way that left evidence dangling in the ambulance bay. Everyone would be sure to see it when they walked in for class. So before anyone arrived, I went to the dry board at the front of the classroom, and aping the style of our instructor, wrote the following:

Basic Refresher Item 1 for Sunday, 9/9
- *Yes, someone took off in 245 without unplugging the landline.*
- *No, the pigtail did not detach.*
- *Yes, the main cord ripped itself out by the roots about 30 feet up.*
- *No, Mike Perry would really rather not discuss it.*

Could be worse. Three years ago Tee Norman roared off to a fire in Pumper One, inexplicably failing to observe that all the equipment doors—which open up and out like wings—were open. Peeled them all off on the garage-door frame. Damage in the four figures, easy.

Could be sillier. The chief once directed a fire scene for several hours before he realized he had forgotten to put on his pants and was parading around in his long johns. He once threw the wrong lever on the pumper and sent water coursing into one of the hoses still accordion-folded in the hose bed. The hose exploded like one of those fake snakes in a peanut can. Took an hour to untangle. I incorporated the incident into a piece of humorous fiction. The chief functions under the weight of the knowledge that if he screws up, he will likely hear about it on a public radio variety show.

Ultimately, you leverage dress, demeanor, and terminology in an attempt to project an aura of calm and control. The true hero is steady in the maelstrom, one hand tending the victim, the other pointing the way to definitive succor. You will need, sometimes, to squeeze your eyes shut real tight to maintain this image. To say nothing of your nose.

I am backing the car out of the driveway when the pager goes off. I intend to meet the grunt novelist Mike Magnuson for a training ride south of Eau Claire. My bike is in the backseat, and I am wearing Lycra biking shorts, a light blue racing jersey, matching ankle socks, and cycling shoes. Man unconscious in a barn, the dis-

patcher says. I have no intention of going on the call, but figure I can
open the fire hall doors, find the fire number on the map, and get
the rig started and ready to roll for whoever shows up. I tug off my
cleats and pull on my steel-toed Caterpillar boots. I leave them un-
laced. They flap around my ankles when I run.

I get everything ready, and still no one has shown up. I take a
quick look up and down the street. No one. Looks like I am the only
first responder in town. It's the last thing I want to do, but I jump in
the rescue van and take off.

It's hot and muggy, and the air in the barn is heavy and wet, sweet
with the smell of manure. The farmer is lying across the cement
walkway. He was milking a cow when it stepped sideways and
pinned him against a waist-high pipe stanchion. He thought he heard
something pop. When the cow swung away, the man tottered to the
walkway, then suffered a Valsalvian reaction (a precipitous drop in
blood pressure subsequent to increased intra-abdominal pressure pre-
venting normal blood flow to the heart) and fell to the floor, cracking
his head. He's on his back now, head lolling over the gutter. In order
to assess his airway and take cervical stabilization, I have to step right
into the gutter channel, into a slick of creamy green manure. At my
back, stretching away to either end of the barn, a horizon of black-
and-white cow rear ends. I grew up on a dairy farm, and I know what
effect excitement has on the Holstein bowel. Excitement = Excre-
ment. Tails are already cocking up and down the walk. I glance over
my shoulder and wince. Two big hocks and the back end of an udder.
I'm really not worried about getting kicked—unlike horses, cows
kick more powerfully to the fore than the aft—but when I turn my
eyes upward and see Bossy's greasy tail twitching between a pair of
dung-stained thurls, I ask the hired man if he can find a tarp or something. He hustles off and returns with a square of plywood, which he
holds between me and the cow's rear end. I put my hands on either
side of the farmer's head to stabilize his cervical spinal column and
check his breathing. I'm locked into this position now—once you take
up manual C-spine stabilization, you are not to release it until the pa-

tient is definitively immobilized, usually after being strapped to a long board and secured with head blocks.

He was unconscious for about five minutes, says his wife. He's semiconscious now. "Can you hear me, Jerome?" I ask, and there is no response. "*Jerome! Can you hear me?*" Now his eyelids flutter, and he mumbles something affirmative. Later, filling out the report, I'll check the little boxes next to "verbal" and "confused" and "sleepy." I'll also write a little note including the fact that he was originally unconscious. It's basic stuff, but we try to record as much information as possible, have it ready for the ambulance crew. It establishes an important baseline. As the farmer is passed up the line to more definitive care, his status can be gauged against what we found when we first got to him. I have some help now—Tim, one of our new first responders, has arrived in his private vehicle. I hold my position at Jerome's head, and Tim continues Jerome's assessment. Pupils equal and reactive to light, albeit sluggishly. No visible bleeding or cerebrospinal fluid discharge from the ears. No Battle's signs (bruising behind the ears indicative of a basilar skull fracture). Hand grips equal bilaterally, movement in both lower extremities. Subaxillary breath sounds present bilaterally. No obvious chest or abdominal injuries. No tracheal deviation that might signal a collapsing lung. I don't have my handheld radio, but the ambulance should be getting here soon. Tim is taking Jerome's blood pressure. Jerome is able to tell us his head and belly hurt. Behind me, some stop-start splashes, then a cascade. The cow is peeing. The urine hits the concrete and spatters across the gutter. Jerome is getting spritzed. I clamp my legs together and shift to shield his face. Hot pee soaks my shorts and dribbles down my calves. The hired man has wandered off. I can see the plywood square leaning against the wall at the far end of the barn.

The ambulance is here now. On their way out, they put the chopper on standby. Based on the fact that Jerome is talking now, they cancel the chopper. Then, concerned when he seems to be losing consciousness again, they radio back and give the chopper the go-ahead. I keep my position while Tim and the paramedics carefully package Jerome and attach him to the longboard. Now the cow behind me jacks her tail and lets go a loose stream of feces. The bulk of the volley misses me, but I can feel the warm patter of the ricochet dotting my back and legs.

Once Jerome is affixed to the board, I run out of the barn to set up the helicopter landing zone. A freshly mown hay field behind the farmhouse looks like it will do nicely. I point the rescue van south and park it with all the strobes lit and spinning. Then I do a quick walkaround, making sure there are no loose objects in the area that might become airborne in the rotor wash. Back in the van, I hear the fire base trying to contact me. Some of the other firefighters have returned to town, and seeing the van out, wonder if I need any help. Now that Jerome is all set and the landing zone secure, I tell them no, but they are already on their way, and so will continue. And somewhere along the line, a group of first responders from Sanderson has headed our way.

You hear about turf wars in EMS, but we're blessed. We get great support from neighboring services. A little overlap happens now and then, but it's mostly viewed as welcome help. So the fact that the Sanderson crew was coming out of its area wasn't an issue. In fact, I suspect they got started when they didn't hear me responding on scene. They were being neighborly.

But they were led by Lorraine.

Lorraine is flat surly. Somewhere along the line, a particularly tenacious bug has burrowed up her transverse colon and taken residence, sideways. She throws equipment on scene. She cusses her own EMTs. She's been known to kick an ambulance cot and send it careening down a hallway. She wears cowboy boots and dresses like a man. She also happens to hold a position of some power in local EMS circles. So one must be circumspect. It's a shame, really, because Lorraine has given years and years to the ambulance service, no doubt often for no thanks. And yet, the most reward this public service appears to have given her is a lemon wedge in each petulant cheek.

So you dread Lorraine.

Everyone arrives at once. The Sanderson contingent, in several pickups. A couple of our guys in pickups. Our fire truck, with lights flashing. The chopper. I radio the pilot, tell him the landing zone is over here, south of the flashing lights. He sees the lights on the moving fire truck, and radios back. "A moving landing zone . . . that's a first!" I jump back on the air, redirect him to the flashing lights on the stationary rescue van. He brings the craft in nicely.

Jerome is loaded. The chopper departs. I've been busy, but now I have a moment to catch my breath and look around. There are trucks and flashing lights everywhere. A platoon of firefighters and first responders. And Lorraine, headed straight for me. I wince. She pulls up and asks if that was me on the radio, telling the firefighters I didn't need any help. "Yeah, we pretty much had everything covered by then," I say. Lorraine lights into me. "You don't *ever* land a chopper in a field without a fire truck standing by!" I don't remember hearing this in any training session, and suspect Lorraine is just target shooting, but I let her go.

And she does. For quite a while, right in my face. She wants her pound of flesh, which is apparently grafted to my ass. And so I am standing there, on this hilltop in this fresh-mown field, in the center of this circle of friends and strangers, my bare shit-spattered legs stuffed into my clodhopper boots, my skintight shorts reeking of cow piss, and Lorraine is yip-yapping, and I am looking her right in the eye and just taking it, because she might have a point with the fire truck thing, but mostly because I figure the gas she vents might take the pressure off the colon bug and get us all some relief, and I'm thinking, if I had gotten up three minutes earlier this morning I would be on my bike right now, pedaling past sunny meadows just like this one, and thinking, what a glorious day is this . . .

Later, much later, I think for a very long time about this scene.

I am disgruntled. Long after the fact, I come up with assorted repartee. I indulge in revenge fantasies. In the most straightforward, I grab Lorraine by the ankles and troll her up and down the gutter.

In another, I stand tall in the rotor wash and improvise a series of rude limericks, each beginning, "There once was a narwhal named Lorraine . . ." In another, I compose a list of terms detailing Lorraine's anatomy, limiting myself to adjectives ending in *-ic*, *-erous*, or *ematous*. In my favorite, I say, well, at least I look good in biking shorts.

I chewed it over for a while.

Then I smiled.

Everything said and done, what you had here, was your Supreme Heroic Moment.

Springtime. A farmer calls. He's been planting corn near a swamp. His orange tractor has backfired, the sparks have lit last year's bleached canary grass. By the time I get there, the brush buggy is parked at the edge of the field. The lieutenant I drenched at the cabin fire last winter is handing down backpack cans. I run around the front of the buggy and he hits me right between the eyes with a stream of water.

"Know what that was for?" He's grinning wide.

Sure do.

12

PENULTIMATE

ALL JACK MOST WANTS is someone to tell him what's the deal with his rock. The rock is a legend now. Jack's constant companion. He's lugged it in and out of every bar and restaurant from New Auburn to Bloomer and back. At the firefighter banquet we gave him a tube of super glue. Told him to stick the rock on the hood of his car to avoid the trouble of dragging the thing in and out of the trunk all the time.

Jack found the rock on a Saturday. His "day off." He runs the feed mill all week, grinding corn, mixing mineral, making deliveries, bulling the heavy bags around. On the weekend, Jack and his twin brother Mack generally split and haul loads of firewood, but on this particular weekend, Jack had been hired by some lake ladies to build a fieldstone fence. That Saturday, he was gathering material for the fence, picking rock at his folks' farm. Depending on how the glacier treated your farm, picking rock is a rite of spring here. When we were growing up, the farmers used to hire gangs of kids—some, like the ten Jabowskis, were a gang unto themselves—to slog along behind hay wagons in the plowed fields, pitching rocks on the wagon bed until it sagged and the wheels pressed deep in the dirt. When it was full, the farmer hauled it to the end of the field or the edge of a swamp and dumped the load. You can still see these cairns all around the county, the smooth brown and pink and tan stones in mounds the size of a Volkswagen.

Jack picked the rock on Saturday, but it wasn't until Sunday morning, when he was turning it in his hands to determine how it might best fit the wall, that he noticed the paw print. The rock is about the size of a bowling ball, and countersunk on the surface is what appears to be the paw print of a large cat—a central pad surrounded by five toes. The print is an inch deep and crisp. It could be covered maybe by a large pancake. Jack pulled the rock from the wall and told the women he was working for he'd be keeping that one. He got a lot of opinions that first day, mostly from guys drinking beer. He stopped at my house and pounded on the door. I looked the rock over and took a couple of pictures. It was strange, all right. Sure looked like a big old paw print. "Whadd'ya think?" said Jack. "Saber-tooth?" I said. It was the only thing I could think of.

Jack was on a mission then. He'd take time off from the feed mill, or from cutting wood, and he'd set off with his rock, trying to find out what he had. He showed it to everybody local—neighbors, the science teacher, strangers at the Gas-N-Go—but then he started seeking out experts. People with qualifications. First place he tried was the Science Museum over in St. Paul. "They said it was a sedimentary rock," says Jack. Then he left it with a geologist in River Falls for a week. "He said it wasn't sedimentary, it was volcanic," says Jack. A geologist on staff at the university in Eau Claire agreed that it was a volcanic rock, but didn't clear up the mystery of the print. "He said no cat could have put a print in a rock like that," says Jack. "He said it would have been too hot, and an animal would not step on a hot rock." Some experts suggested the print was formed by chance, others said it was carved by man. "But the geologist in River Falls told me no way, because that rock was too hard," says Jack. He took a day off work and went to the Field Museum in Chicago.

Took his daughter with him, and I would like to have been there to see old Jack come stomping through the doors with that rock under his arm.

"The lady there gave us free passes all day," he says. "She came to the conclusion that, yes, it was a mammal print, but, no, it wasn't, because the rock was too old. No one carbon-dated it or took a sample of it, but they said it was about two million years old."

Jack followed another line of inquiry. "I said I'd like to see a saber-toothed tiger if they had one, so I could match it up. And the lady there said, 'Well, a saber-toothed tiger has a bigger foot than that.' And I said it could be a kitten. Sometime in its life it had to have a smaller foot than a full-grown cat. She said that made sense, but that was as far as she would go with that."

Jack and his daughter had a good day at the museum. But nothing definitive came of the rock with the paw print. He says he's going to keep searching. He got someone to make a wax casting of the stone, so a friend could make a plaster mold of the print for a rockhound in Arizona. He tried a creation scientist. "He used to be a science teacher for fifteen years," says Jack. "Now he just preaches and he says the Bible says the world and everything in it is only six thousand years old and everything was made at the same time."

Jack does get some ideas in his head sometimes. And I imagine somewhere in his conversations with the experts he finds a way to let them know how much firewood he cut last week. So they probably get a little chuckle from his visits. But you'll forgive him if he begins to think his theories are as reliable as any expert's. "Nobody has agreed with each other," he says. He thinks for a minute. "I just took it all in, and I'm just kind of curious about who is right and who is wrong."

Not long after I moved here, I noticed my backyard was sinking. Indentations, scattered throughout the grass. I stuck a rake handle in one and it dropped in four feet. I got to entertaining notions about what might be down there. Most of the notions were of your boy-who-just-read-*Treasure Island* variety. I figured maybe something important or valuable had been buried back here, or that I'd un-earth the New Auburn equivalent of the terra-cotta army from the ancient Chinese Qin Dynasty. I know when they dug the basement in the lot next door, they found a lot of old beer bottles. So one day a friend and I grabbed a shovel, a sifter, and a notebook and went ar-chaeological. In every hole, what we found mainly were huge rotted roots infested by platoons of red ants. Later on, Durlin Baker, the old-timer who lives out back of my place, across the alley, told me, Yep, there used to be giant elm trees in my backyard, but they cut them all down when the Dutch elm disease came through. Sure enough, when the lady down at the Gas-N-Go lent me some old newspaper clippings, I found a photo of the original schoolhouse taken in the 1930s from such an angle that my house—freshly built—was visible in the background, and the yard was sprouting with elm saplings. We dug up two of the holes and kept a list of what we found in the sifter:

- bits of charcoal

- piece of green glass

- porcelain chips with orange pattern

- nail, rusted, attached to piece of board

- plastic bead, red

- oval chunk of cement, or lime

- candy wrapper (Jolly Rancher)

Not much, but something. Signs of previous inhabitants. "Sure," said Durlin Baker, later. "They used to burn their trash out back there."

• • •

If we're going to settle in a place, we like to dig around a little, get a sense of what came before. The digging reveals things, and even if they were discarded without thought, as was the candy wrapper, they nonetheless represent a fraction of history. That candy wrapper is the husk of a split second. When they dug the footings for St. Jude's Catholic Church down the street, they kept turning up bricks from the old brick factory that used to stand on the ground. When my brother dug out a culvert north of town, his backhoe raked away the blacktop and revealed the cheek-by-jowl logs of the original corduroy road still socked tight in the dirt below. When I had to wait to be waved around a monstrous asphalt grinding machine last summer, I noticed that it was removing the asphalt in layers, and that it had cut the patch beside me on such a plane that the long-buried centerline was visible. I felt a goofy little reminiscent tug when I looked at the yellow paint, thinking that the last time I saw it exposed to the sun I was probably sixteen and riding my bike home from football practice. Silly, I suppose, but it spoke to the ties between the archaeology of a place and the archaeology of the heart.

We dig for threads and echoes, all correlating past to present. If we study the history of a place in order to establish a contemporary context, we are free to make what we will of any resonance, however tangential. A heavy ledger in the back room of the New Auburn village hall contains the handwritten minutes of the first recorded meetings of the village board, including the promulgation on May 28, 1902, of "Ordinance No. 9: An ordinance to prohibit the leaving of animals and teams unfastened in the public streets and for the prevention of cruelty to animals in the Village." Nearly a century later, the photocopied minutes tacked to the post office bulletin board note that during the meeting of March 9, 2000, discussion included "the incident of the shooting of the pig that got loose from Olson's Market."

● ● ●

So we dig. Metaphorically, and sometimes with a shovel. An assignment had taken me on the road for about a week one summer when I returned to find my neighbors scouring their backyard with a metal detector. In between the auto carcasses and defunct lawn mowers, the spotty grass looked as if it had been attacked by a roving pack of gophers. The old man would sweep the detector over the earth, and when it went *whoop*, he'd signal his two young boys to dig. I was on my way out through the backyard to the post office when I saw them, and I thought it was a little strange, but then I got to thinking about it, and knowing how grim their evident financial situation was, I figured, What the heck, good for them if they find anything. That afternoon I had to go on the road again. When I came back five days later, my entire yard—front and back—was dotted with holes. More than forty of them. I was gobsmacked. Never mind issues of trespass and vandalism, I kept thinking, if they *did* find gold doubloons, those were *my* gold doubloons! They're a pretty rough bunch, though, so I just pretended I didn't notice. Indeed, they had gone to the effort of replacing about half their divots. And based on how things continued to look over there—cop cars and junk cars accumulating apace—I doubted they had unearthed the treasure of the Sierra Madre in my dandelions.

We spend this life looking for a center, a place where we can suspend without a wobble. The specific coordinates are elusive, scalable only by the heart. I moved into an old house in this little town on a January night seven years ago. That first night, I switched the lights off and sat for a long time on the wooden floor. A neon beer sign bolted to the roof of the bar up the street filled the empty cube of the living room with soft orange light. I took it for a sort of consecration, and was pleased to note that my heart felt steady.

It was never my intention to live here. By and large, I favor the hermit life, and my plan was to find an isolated place out by the home farm, but nothing panned out. I was on my way back home after another fruitless search when I passed through New Auburn and saw the For Sale sign in front of this house. On a whim, I made an offer and wound up on Main Street. To the extent that such a thing is possible in a town of 485 people, I thought I might feel pressed. But people around here pretty much give you your space.

Which is not to say they don't pay attention. Once a neighbor lady called to tell me a kid was fooling around behind my garage. He ran off before I got around the corner, but there were fresh scorch marks on the siding, so I figure she saved my garage. When I have to go on the road, the women over at the phone company keep an eye on my house. Four years ago, when I was on assignment in Tennessee, my storm door blew open in a wind storm and the latch broke. Bob the telephone lineman came over and wired the door shut. I still think about that whenever I wave at him in his truck. And then I cringe, because I still haven't fixed the door.

There is a fellow in town who does yard work. We often exchanged hellos in the post office, but he had never been to my house. One spring he asked if he could rake my yard, and I said sure. "I'll knock on the door when I'm done," he said. I told him I would be upstairs writing, so he should knock vigorously.

"Yeah," he said. "you've usually got your music on pretty loud."

I was cleaning carp out behind the house one afternoon when the rawboned neighbor guy walked over. He had been fiddling on a junk car. "Nice ones," he said, looking down at the fish. And they were, a bodacious passel of *Ictiobus bubalus,* as my carp-shooting buddy Mills and I like to call them when we're all dressed up in camo on our secret log, sweating in the sun and smelling of fish slime and *Off!*. A little Latin to offset the caveman behavior and stink. Mills got me into bow fishing, and now it's a problem. I sneak off to shoot carp the way some guys sneak off to shoot pool. Mills smokes them up with apple and hickory in his old concrete smoker, but first I have to clean them. The neighbor stood there silent while I sawed off heads and peeled out guts. Every now and then he took a drag on his Marlboro and a pull on his Pabst. Finally, he spoke.

"So. Yer a writer."

"Well, yeah, I mean . . ."

"You do poetry?"

"Well, I'm not much of a . . ."

"I do some poetry."

"I, uh . . ."

"Good shit."

He walked back to his car. We never spoke again.

You cannot foresee the ways a community will make you feel welcome. I was in my second month of residence when the sewer line backed up. If the sewer line plugs between your house and the main, clearing it is your responsibility. But in New Auburn, the responsibility comes with a perk: Anyone living within the village limits is allowed access to the community sewer rod. You need only walk over to the village shop and ask for it. Matt or Mark will lug it down from the storage rack. Before they unhand it, they'll give you a brief overview of fundamentals and technique, outfit you with a pair of rubber-coated gloves, and quite reasonably request that you hose the thing off before you return it, but other than that, you're free to go.

The sewer rod isn't a rod at all. It's a one-hundred-foot chunk of spring steel tipped with an elongated wire bulb. The spring steel is an inch wide and a quarter inch thick, all coiled in a steel bracket. The coil forms a circle three feet in diameter, and the whole works weighs more than twenty-five pounds. Theoretically, it is a straightforward operation: One simply descends to the basement, uncaps the sewer pipe, and feeds in the rod until it reaches and dislodges the offending mass. I unscrewed the sewer cap with a minimum of difficulty. In fact, apart from the resumption of sewage flow, this was the high point of the entire endeavor, as I was able to wield my big red monkey wrench, only recently purchased from Farm & Fleet. Successful monkey-wrench moments are so few and far between in the writing business, and I admit to affecting a certain plumberish saunter as I crossed the bespotted basement floor with the cast-iron tool dangling from one hand. I spun the knurled adjuster ring with one thumb, fitted the jaws to the cap screw, and expertly twirled the cap free. The glory of this moment was muted by the fact that the cap was plastic and, as it turned out, only hand-tight.

I wrassled the monstrous coil into place, placing the tip in alignment with the portal. To advance the tip, a length of strap had to be unfurled from the X-shaped bracket and the entire spool rotated in a reverse manner. This worked for a quarter rotation, at which point certain stored ferrous energies exceeded critical mass, causing the spool to unleash acrobatics of the sort normally reserved for objects animated by paranormal possession. The liberated length of strap iron lashed against my shins like an epileptic black mamba. Consequently, the remaining forty-seven pounds of coil chop-blocked the washing machine, ricocheted off the dryer, and fell flat. The mamba loosed a final spasm, executed a triple rattamacue death dance down my anterior tibial ridge, then went still. Deeply organic words were spoken. I gathered the whole works up again. It was like trying to embrace the spinning beaters of a foul, oversized electric mixer. The tip breached the portal, and the operation recommenced. Bit by bit, the sewer rod disappeared down the pipe. Progress was inconstant, and frequently disrupted by desperate lunging and rants referencing chop saws, scrap yards, and cruel, cruel fate. Tools, I am ashamed to say, were thrown. At one point, I resolved to initiate the permitting process required for the installation of an old-fashioned outdoor biffy. Still, my secret weapon has always been being too dumb to quit, and with less than five feet of the rod remaining, I punched through to daylight, if you will allow the analogy. The residual contents of the pipe gurgled merrily downstream, and I rejoined the ranks of the modernly convenienced.

In the interest of ink, paper, and time, I will leave to your imagination the contortions and vituperations required to re-roll the soiled sewer rod and stow it in its holder. When I presented the neatly swabbed and furled apparatus to Matt, there remained only a slight wild-eyed whiffiness about my person to suggest the Herculean efforts and stevedorean oratory invoked during the repackaging process. And yet, as I walked back to my flushable house, peace ebbed back through my heart, ushered therein by the thought that I had successfully navigated a communal rite of passage. Never mind your cartoony Chamber of Commerce tourist maps. Don't talk to me about city charters or mission statements or public transit or municipal pools. Spare me your block parties and welcome wagons. You want to make me feel at home?

Give me a town that shares its sewer rod.

I didn't assume I'd be happy back here. I had been essentially absent for more than a decade, and knew the whole prodigal returned thing was fraught with the potential for disappointment. It helped, I guess, that I didn't expect to pick up where I left off. I figured I'd have to ease my way back in, and that seems to have worked itself out. The fire department has been the indispensable catalyst.

There are three maps in our humble little fire hall. One is a three-color CAD printout. One is a photocopied enlargement of a plat book page. The largest looks like a giant mimeograph, three feet by eight feet. They're tacked to one wall, and I've already mentioned the rule: When the siren on the water tower goes off, when you come charging in to the hall, all fired up and raring to go, eyes wide, heart charging, you do not, *do not,* leave headquarters without first locating your destination on one of the maps. It does no good to go bugling off like salvation's cavalry if your horses are pointed in the wrong direction. And so more than 100 times each year, some one of us comes huffing through the door, crosses to the maps, and with an extended finger, traces a path from the hall to a fire number somewhere out in the 127 square miles of real estate we cover. If, at the end of every year, those tracings were made visible, you'd see a dense, benevolent web spun one frantic zigzag at a time.

In the summer, when the weather warnings reach a certain level of direness, the chief has us paged and then sends us out in the trucks to watch for funnel clouds. One evening at six P.M., I am at my desk when the windows go dark so suddenly that I am pulled downstairs and out the door. The air is charged and thick. The leading edge of a weather front is passing over, and it has drawn a lowering cover across the town. The clouds are squid-ink black, inverting and churning, a river of pulsing bruises. The thunder begins. When the pager goes off, I'm expecting it. I run for the hall.

I wind up on the overpass, in the brush rig with Jack Most. From up here, we can see it all coming. We are at the center of a giant swirl. South of town, the clouds are twisting to the northeast. North of town, they are twisting to the southwest. We all check in on the radio. One of the tankers is out on Five Mile Road. Lieutenant Pam is out on Highway M with the rescue van. It comes slapping in now, the wind rocking the cab, the first raindrops smacking the window. The traffic slows beneath the overpass. Some of the cars pull to the shoulder. An RV lumbers up the off-ramp, searching for a building to hide behind. Then the rain begins dropping in slabs, and the last thing we see for the next five minutes are hazard lights flashing up and down the interstate.

It goes on for five minutes, pretty much zero visibility. Some hail. The truck is pummeled. Then the rain slacks off and the air lightens. We drive back into town, check for downed power lines and fallen trees. The streets are dark and wet. Green clumps of stripped leaves are flung all around, but the damage has been superficial. We are back at the hall when the pager goes off again. A wire down, draped over the roof of a cabin, arcing. I grab Tanker One. By the time we get there, the power has been cut, and there is no sign of fire. We have a look, check it out, and head back home. We are right at the village limits when the storm comes roaring back. The pumper ahead of me disappears in the rain. I make it to the fire hall. Across the street, the wind is bending Durlin Baker's big spruce trees into semi-circles. This is serious. I can't see to back the tanker into the hall, and I don't think it's safe to make a run for it, so I turn the tanker around, face the big stainless steel rear end into the wind, and settle in. I figure with the weight of the water and the smooth round profile of the tank, it'll be pretty tough for the storm to get a grip and knock us around. Every time the wind whips a space in the rain, though, and I catch a glimpse of Durlin's trees doing toe-touchers, I wonder. I'm respecting nature pretty good when once again the rain slackens and the light returns. We pair off and make a second run of the streets and alleys. This time we find downed power lines, and I hear the chief on Channel Two, calling for a chainsaw over on Columbia Street. We crisscross the village. Between us, we know most of the houses, and stop to check on widows and elderly couples. Over on Pine Street, I knock at the door of a small white house, and at first nothing happens. Then I see a wavering light, and a little old lady approaches through the kitchen. She raises a candle to the door. "I'm OK," she says. We move on. Here in the green half-light of the aftermath, checking on our neighbors, I can't imagine any sweeter place to be.

I am happy here, but my gravitation to place has always been balanced by my need to move. I crave a contrapuntal mix of shiftlessness and stability. In bed at night, I can hear the trucks out on the highway. Sometimes a driver drifts across the white line, and when the tires hit the rumble strip, the rubbery howl makes me want to drive away in the night, fills me with the urge to go west, makes me think the finest sort of freedom is found at sunrise in a South Dakota rest stop. Contentment, it turns out, can be a matter of global positioning.

My grandpa died in the farm yard he was raised in, but during the interceding eight decades he left tracks in every quarter of the globe. "All you need is an apple and a newspaper to sleep under," he'd say, harking back to the days when he saved hotel money by bunking on park benches in Washington, D.C. When I was still a smooth-faced kid, he picked me up at the farm and took me to the city to catch my first Greyhound. When that big bus heaved out of the lot and rolled out of town it seemed I was playing hooky from everything. I talked to a cowboy-booted wino in the backseat and his gentle lies about a fresh start planted a wandering seed in my head. The window glass was cool on my cheek, and Wisconsin slipped away in swipes of white and brown. Motion wed itself to freedom, and from that day forward, I incubated a stray-dog jones for the road. It is a quasi-spiritual thing, in which the pilgrimage is the religion, and movement is the purest form of worship. The altars are harbored in truck stops and train stations, the sacraments are served in foam cups, and heaven glows on the horizon. You will desire hymns performed by the prophets Waylon Jennings, Junior Brown, and Steve Earle.

Grandpa got me started, and to this day my two favorite things in the world are solitude and motion. I've found them in the next county, in a semi crossing the Nevada state line, on a Hungarian train, and on a bus approaching the Guatemalan border. In times of trouble, motion is my morphine. But as much as I love to run, I love even more to come home. At every latitude, my compass swivels to point back here, to little old New Auburn. This place is my true north. A stray dog running, as it turns out, is just circling the rug.

I think I might move, one more time. Out near the home farm, like the original plan. But I am in no hurry. I am deeply grateful for the deep bite of life I've been allowed. The travel, the experiences, the accumulation of miles and places and acquaintance. And yet lately—a slow dawning, perhaps, but nonetheless—I am becoming fixed on the idea of what it means to live deeply in a place, to move about in it, as opposed to pass through it. I have felt the pull of history and place in a hundred places around the globe, and I don't doubt I could have lived a happy life in any one of them. But chance put me here, in a ragtag little village in northwestern Wisconsin, and while I am hardly prepared to mothball the backpack, I find myself more and more content to immerse myself in this place. It is occurring to me that to truly *live* in a place, you must give your *life* to that place. It is a dynamic commitment, but it is also a manifestation of stillness.

The paw print in Jack Most's rock, the detritus under my yard, the metaphysical artifacts, all the things we find when we dig, they fascinate us because they have become imbued with a stillness in time. In one form or another, they have achieved stillness by abandoning themselves to the earth. Is twining yourself into a place so different? "I think heaven is perfect stasis/poised over the realms of desire," writes the poet Mark Doty in the poem "Tiara," and every once in a while I offer a little prayer that this might be true. I am getting hints—yes, even here in this spavined place—that if we work at it, we can learn to achieve stasis in the moment, even as time ripsaws by. We can live in the sweet green half-light of the aftermath, even as the storm drops its thunder all around us.

13

SARAH

IT WASN'T INTENDED as a coming-out party, but when my brother Jed walked into the annual fire department banquet with a blond farm girl on his arm the night of February 3, 2001, every head in the Sundial Supper Club turned to look. He didn't say much, he never does, just went to his seat and started in on his chicken, but the New Auburn Area Fire Department—the only social circle in which he travels with any regularity—had just received their official introduction to Sarah Ann Posey.

The fire department banquet puts a ribbon on the year. We drag out our uniform shirts, put on our pins and name tags, and meet up the road at the Sundial. We eat buffet-style, queueing at the steam tables for chicken and ham and green beans and a slug of mashed potatoes drowned in fluorescent yellow gravy sold in tin cans the size of your head. It's heavy food. Filling, the way you crave it here in Wisconsin when the dirt is frozen two feet down and you saw your last local green leaf sometime back in September.

We eat, and then we have a little awards ceremony. The chief hands out service pins in five-year increments. Last year I got my five-year pin. This year Bob the One-Eyed Beagle gets his twenty-five-year pin. Amazing to think of him answering the siren, the phone and the pager twenty-four hours a day for a quarter century. Several of us receive a certificate and embroidered patch for having completed wildfire suppression class. Funny to think of brush fires tonight, with the dead leaves buried under a foot of snow and the chimney smoke laying flat in air that ices up your nose hair with every inhalation. And yet I have stood outside this very supper club, shoulder to shoulder with these dumpling-scarfing yahoos, fighting like mad to turn a brush fire north.

The chief asks the members of the fire board to stand, so we fire-fighters are reminded of the citizen volunteers who oversee the de-tails of jurisdiction and finance, the necessary drudge so far removed from the excitement of the front lines. He also thanks a number of non-members who pitched in during the year when we were short-handed. Then he hands me the mic, Lieutenant Pam hauls out a box of gag awards, and the fun part starts.

The gag awards are the culmination of a year's worth of pay-back. If you bent a mirror, backed the pumper into a popple tree, or killed the tanker at a stop sign, you can bet someone took note, and that at some point in the weeks leading up to the banquet, the list was reviewed by an ad hoc committee of conspirators, who then fanned out and cobbled up a boxful of commemorative mementos. The guy who backed over his $300 pager with a tractor gets a dime-store pager filled with bubble gum. Tee Norman, who looks like the Pillsbury Doughboy's backwoods stepchild, receives a bottle of Gatorade in commemoration of the day he sprinted all the way from North Star Implement to the fire hall—nearly three-quarters of a mile—in his cowboy boots, only to find he had responded to a test page. Tony Barker is one of the calmest and most reliable members of the department, and we couldn't get any better loyalty out of him unless we mounted a hose and pump on his beloved Polaris, and so he gets the next-best thing—a toy snowmobile with a fire nozzle attached. At a factory fire last winter, Matt Jeffski and I accidentally sprayed Lieutenant Pam full in the face with the two-and-a-half when she came out of the smoke. It messed up her eyes for a while, and it wasn't funny then, but tonight she gets a pair of swimmer's goggles. When the chief ran out of gas on the way to a two A.M. medical call a couple of months ago, he just disappeared from the radio and never did show up. He was found out, of course, and is presented with a survival kit including a gas can, a chocolate bar, and a pair of running shoes. It goes on this way for the entire department, no deed unpunished. Backing the big pumper into a trailer fire, a new guy missed the driveway and found himself stuck in the ditch at a forty-degree angle, contemplating the stars—he gets a miniature pumper and a promise from the rest of us to lobby the village board for an ordinance widening all driveways. At a high-line fire, I happened to be watching when Rusty, a seasoned truck driver, missed a gear and killed the engine on Tanker 3. He has been known to wince visibly when I crash second gear in search of fourth, but tonight he has to stand there, red and grinning, as I hand him a certificate redeemable for six hours of driving and shifting instructions from the Mike Perry School of Truck Driving. Looking for a brush fire in the dark, Lisa turned north instead of south and not only got lost but kept going—we give her a compass and announce that the department has entered into an agreement with the six counties to the north to post signs along all northbound roadways: Lisa—Turn Back! The reddest face of the night is that of Brianna, who, at a monthly meeting several months ago let slip that she once dropped her pager in the toilet. She gets an aquarium net.

When the awards are all done, and we've drawn for all the door prizes, everyone moves to the bar. Jed and Sarah and I lag behind in the dining room and talk for a while, catching up. Jed's been on the road pretty much nonstop lately, running logs, stopping home just long enough to do his chores. We're joined by Jed's friend Max. Max started showing up at our farm when he was a youngster, and just sort of never left. Today he's married and milks cows up the road, and he and Jed share equipment and labor regular. Jed was the best man at his wedding. After we visit a little while, Jed and Sarah slip out the door. I move across the hall to the bar area. Everyone wants to know about this Sarah. I don't have much to tell, because I don't know much.

We share it with frogs and geese and water buffalo, the desire to pair off. We are responding to the usual animal juices, but we also crave a companion, a witness to our living. Someone with whom to accrete an intimate history. Comes a time when you hope to look back, and when you do, you'd like someone to share the sight line.

I have been single for thirty-seven years now. It feels good, like an old shirt. I come and go as I wish, I disappear for as long as I want to, go for days without speaking to anyone. I do the dishes when I need them, peel me some Ho-Hos for breakfast if that's what I want. If I like something and want to look at it, I nail it to the wall. I first began living alone when I was sixteen. Over two decades, I have become absurdly selfish of time and space, and I know it. I cannot pretend otherwise. And in fairness, I cannot imagine anyone who would put up with such self-indulgence. And so I have never married.

I think it is fair to say Jed is the best firefighter on our department. He has the build, for one thing. He stands about five feet five, carries less fat than a celery stick, and his back and arms pop and roll with muscle. He loves to tear into a fire. He is not fearless, because he is not a fool, but the place he goes to, you can see fearless from there. We use him a lot, call him a fire rat, because his strength and size can put him places the rest of us cannot go.

It's fun to see his eyes on the fire scene, see that demented grin and know he's ready to charge in as tight as he can get, because for years and years, he was my silent brother, mostly playing alone and not saying much. I used to build him scale-model sawmills and miniature hay hoists, but his age put him a stage or two behind my brother John and me, and so we never really hung out together. It is a long-standing family joke that none of us remember Jed speaking until he was fourteen years old.

He's still quiet and still mostly a loner. No bowling league, no softball or favorite tavern. As far as I know, joining the fire department is the closest he's ever come to being part of any group outside the family. He wanted to farm from the time he could walk, and he's been working at it since grade school. It was all my folks could do to get him through high school. He graduated, but only through a combination of home-schooling and a work-study arrangement with the local feed mill. He's thirty-one years old now, and into his second decade of fieldwork. He runs his machinery hard and he runs himself hard, going from dawn to dark and beyond. When he's not farming, he's logging, and through the worst stretches of winter he hires out as a log truck driver. He is a silent grinder, and if you try to keep up with him, he will quietly work you into the dirt.

I have never married, and my brothers have never married. We have noticed that to certain people, a single person represents a project. They can't rest until they tuck you in place, like you're a tag hanging out of a collar. We hear it a lot: "When are we going to get one of you Perry boys married?" We just grin. You're missing out, they say, but whenever someone really pushes the point, I become suspicious. Seems like they're determined I wind up in a fix identical to their own.

Of the three of us, Jed has most wanted a wife. We've talked about it now and then, leaning against the tailgate of his pickup, or in the barn at night, waiting for a pig to farrow. He's happy living alone, he says. The bachelor life suits him as well as it suits me. But then he allows that the big old farmhouse gets lonely, and what he really wants is a farm girl, someone who loves the land and animals the way he does. A woman who doesn't mind a little mud on the porch.

I usually needle him a little bit. "Well, at some point, you're gonna have to climb down off that tractor. Ain't no girls on the back forty." I was wrong, as it turns out. Sarah Ann Posey grew up right around the corner. When she first started coming around, she was sixteen. Jed sent her away. Too young, he told her. She was persistent, though, and when she turned eighteen, he was ready to take her seriously. They began to talk about what they hoped for in life, and a lot of it matched up. The night he brought her to the banquet, he was thirty, and she was still in high school. Legal and all, but you can imagine the buzz.

Back in 1978, Waylon Jennings recorded "A Long Time Ago," a song containing the lyric, "Women been my trouble since I found out they weren't men." Note the onus here is not necessarily on the women. I've done the calculations, and in my case, the ratio of me-at-fault to her-at-fault comes in at roughly 14:1. It's an oxygen thing. It seems the day always comes when the Significant Sweet Other says something, or casts a certain gaze, and as if someone bumped a toggle switch in the bathyscaph, all the oxygen shoots from the room. Perry's Law: Once the oxygen leaves, it never returns. And so time after time, I find myself short of breath, and time after time, I hit the road. Anoxia is the bane of bliss.

    I try to convince myself to hang in there, to try harder. Sometimes people tell me I will die lonely, and I think they might be right. But the most earnest pro-matrimony chatter cannot overcome this image: I am on a road trip, stopping for gas at a station somewhere in South Dakota. Just me, running solo. It's a hot day. I'm filling the tank when a minivan pulls up on the other side of the fuel island. As the doors pop open, I catch a last-gasp feral snap between the husband and wife. The kids are belted in and sullen beneath their headphones. Mom steams away to the rest room, and Pop pumps the gas with a twitch in his jaw. I may be a stocky guy in steel-toed boots, but I feel so free I could spin pirouettes all the way back to the Wisconsin state line.

• • •

In the Sundial bar, the pool balls click and the pinball machines ring. The karaoke list is booked solid. The men stand wide-legged, bellies out and relaxed, yukking and blustering and drinking beer. The women are mostly arranged along the barstools, laughing and confiding and blowing smoke at the ceiling. Several card games are going, and at one table, Cubby Rimes and Chief Ernie are taunting each other over hands of euchre. Six years ago the two men knelt together over Cubby's daughter, thrown from her tumbling car on Jabowski's Corner. After the chopper whisked the girl away, Ernie put Cubby in his truck and sped to the hospital. Tracy Rimes died that night, and I wonder, what is the distance between that black hour and all these bad jokes and happy cussing? You cannot see one spot from the other, and yet somehow you find the way. Time is both the traverse and the means of traverse. Cubby laughs, and those of us surrounding him hear his laughter in the context of that journey. The simple history of a small community's fire and trouble leads to a shifting nexus of shared experience that, for this night, pulses in the bar of the Sundial Supper Club. There are husbands and wives and lovers and cheaters and friends and kin in this place tonight, but most of our lives intersect only at the fire whistle. History alone accounts for our being here. In this room tonight are marriages that won't last the year, lovers bound to stray, and friends destined to run afoul, but for these hours we are knit tight in the name of something as fundamental as a volunteer fire department. Laughing and drinking and singing, we are flush with the camaraderie of people who stand the same ground. "The world is filled with hidden running water," wrote poet Kenneth Rexroth, and the ground we stand is cut with subterranean currents that modulate every belly laugh, provide the punch line to some jokes, warn us away from others. But tonight, flush with beer and reflection, we tip our heads back and let loose, and the ground feels solid.

Bob the One-Eyed Beagle has had a few beers, and he's ready to karaoke. He grabs the microphone like a cleaver, squints up his one good eye, hones in on the pixelated lyrics. He has selected George

Strait's "All My Ex's Live in Texas," and he lights into it with the emotive delicacy of a drunken cape buffalo. Even the card players stop to watch. When he hits the chorus, he brings the house down with a ham-fisted improvisation. *"All my ex's,"* he bellows, *"work at the Gas-N-Go!"* Exactly true. It's a public-domain inside joke. He gallumphs through the chorus one more time, and we cheer and hoot and holler.

I have no ex-wives, but I'm at the tail end of yet another relationship. This one is winding down strangely, a long platonic slide sustained by the fact that the woman in question is strong and good and kind and worthy and nearly breaking under the strain of a custody battle. Seven years ago, when her ex-husband shoved her backward over a chair, she took the two babies and got clear. Put herself through school, kept her position as a nurse, constantly juggled her schedule to avoid putting the children in day care, and just when she was getting her feet under her, and was only months from finishing school, the ex-husband hired a lawyer and came after her. It's been nearly two years now, and the court dates are drawing near. In the meantime, through a series of legal maneuvers, he has wangled enough temporary custody to stick the kids in day care for the first time in their young lives. Every other week they live with Daddy, and he hires a driver to run them to school—an hour's commute each way—and because of the driver's schedule, they sit in day care before and after class, ten minutes from their mother's house. This woman and I are no longer lovers, but I admire her, and her children are a bright spot in my life, so I have hung around, running errands, going to school plays, helping make connections and hand-offs. I've had a front-row seat on how the fruits of human attraction can be strung up on the rack of bastardized legalities. I am in up to my neck, having given depositions, faced his blistering vituperations, and now am waiting to testify in the court case. Every day begins with a sinking feeling. Every phone call trips the heart. For months, my guts have felt like steel wool soaked in acid, and if this is how I feel through observation and empathy, how must it feel to be her? And so tonight, when I hit the subzero air of the parking lot at one A.M., the cold jolts me into remembering my friend's ongoing battle, and I wonder if she's sleeping, and I realize that the last six hours have been an oasis, a break from the constant low-level gut burn one feels as a helpless witness to evil. Fire department to the rescue, again.

My friend Frank is getting married. We began our friendship a decade ago. He had just gotten divorced and stopped drinking. Not necessarily in that order. We met when I sold an article to a regional magazine he edited. One night I stopped to drop some work off at his apartment. We got into a discussion about poetry and were reading James Wright when the sun came up. Frank led me through my early writing days patiently, feeding me a steady dose of poets, reading my stuff, and rapping my knuckles as needed. Today he simply points to weak passages and says, "You know better." He is a renaissance man. I have known him, in the space of a day, to declaim a Sharon Olds poem, install a toilet, edit an essay on the cultural implications of the Star Wars trilogy, perform at a poetry reading, and hand-milk a small herd of goats. Once he was very sick and broke, and in desperate need of an expensive antibiotic. After a little research, he deduced that the veterinary equivalent was much cheaper. He went to Farm & Fleet and bought a bottle of calf medicine. Referring to the weight chart on the label, he calculated his dose, and was shortly recovered.

But now, suddenly, after a decade of bachelor friendship, Frank is getting married again. To a woman he met when he and I were delivering a joint creative writing lecture at the local university. I am happy if he is happy, but I keep thinking of the invariable changes to come, and this jealous little voice emanating from somewhere near my spleen keeps asking, "What's in it for me?"

• • •

Clear back in 1989, the litany of failure that is my romantic history reached such proportions that my friend Gene chef'd me up a mix tape he titled, *Easy Listening for the Lonely Guy*. It was a ninety-minute tape. He squeezed twenty-nine songs on there. "Lonely Love," by the Harmonicats. "By Myself," Johnny Mathis. "Sergeant Pepper's Lonely Hearts Club Band," the Beatles. "Lonely Street," Boots Randolph. "Lonely Room," from *Oklahoma!* "Don't Want to Know if You Are Lonely," Hüsker Dü. From the *Against All Odds* soundtrack, "El Solitario." And so on. Gene gauges the state of my love life by how often he finds me sleeping on his couch. Every time I find a new girl, my visits tail off. Once I had begun dating a woman in Minneapolis, and I apologized to Gene for not being around as much as usual. He drew himself up like a long-suffering cuckold. "Oh," he sighed, "you'll come crawling back . . ." (Earlier this year, with me adrift yet again, Gene presented me with a new mix tape: *The Lonely Guy Box Set*.)

Gene is the dearest sort of friend. Kind, brainy, easygoing, a dead-lock match to my sense of humor. A gentle and erudite physical therapist, he can recite your cranial nerves, and yet he is hooked on *Monday Night Football*. Introduced me to basement darts and the music of John Prine. Late one night in his kitchen, I told his wife, "Paula, if Gene was a woman I would marry him." I believe she snorted.

Now it's late April. Jed and Sarah are standing in my living room. Jed is hugging on Sarah tight, his head about even with her shoulder. When he speaks, it is in his usual matter-of-fact monotone.

"Ahh . . . yer probably gonna be hearin' some stuff around town . . ."

Sarah giggles, and he smiles up at her, then turns back to me.

"Ahh . . . we're gettin' married."

"Ah!" I did not see this coming. I hardly know the girl. I have a flurry of thoughts, chief among them, What is he *thinking*? "When's the happy date?"

"Ahh . . . probably next Thursday. Or Friday."

Very little time then, to intervene. It seems hasty. So I say, "Ah!" I keep hoping "Ah!" sounds neutral.

"Yah. We're gettin' married in a rush." Now he looks me dead in the eye. "Not because we *have* to. Because we *want* to."

I would prefer to watch him pack up and run into a burning barn.

I am not a marriage grinch. Growing up, my brothers and sisters and I had a front-row seat on one of the all-time great marriages. I understand my parents had to work at it behind the scenes, but what we saw was a gentle touch now and then, a kiss after supper and before chores, but above all, an abiding respect. The day arrives when you realize you have more past than future, and when you get it right from the beginning, as my parents did, you have this beautiful swath of time to look back on, right back to the youthful edge of adulthood. And so, when it comes to my marital phobias, let me exculpate my parents. My trepidation is more a function of the sheer odds against it going right. And the unbelievable ways it can all go wrong.

Mack Most runs a mobile slaughter service out of the meat market here on Main Street. He drives a rumbling big truck, and if I'm upstairs writing, the window will rattle and I'll look up just in time to see him headed out of town. One day he waves me over behind the meat market and swings the big truck doors open. "Look what I got here!"

There are two huge bird carcasses hanging from the hooks. Turkeys, they look like, turkeys the size of pandas. Mack steps back, swings one door a little wider to give me a better view of the forbidding interior.

"Emu!" He beams a *top-that!* grin. "Guy who owned 'em is gettin' divorced. They was at his mother-in-law's, so he told me to go out there and butcher 'em. Yep. The in-laws weren't too happy. Asked me to wait awhile so they could walk down the road, outta earshot." He pauses to grin again. "Shot 'em in the head with a twelve-gauge."

The meat is dark and glistening. "Good for your hands, emu fat," Mack says. "Absorbs into your skin—ain't greasy."

But I'm hardly hearing him, because I'm standing there, peering into the square cavern of that rolling abattoir, at old oil barrels filled to the rim with hairy cow parts, at the dark streaks of dung and blood on the floor, at the two skinned birds, and I am thinking about the quest for love and how it triggers convolutions of sublimity or despair beyond our wildest reckonings. A girl looks left instead of right, and six weeks later, a boy's heart is still broken. A man breaks his leg, and six months later, marries his orthopedist. A man buys a woman a drink, and six years later, a traveling butcher shotguns the hell out of a pair of emus.

The last time Jed and I fought a fire together, it was fall, and I saw the smoke from Chetek, where I was just finishing an ambulance shift. As the page was going off, I radioed the fire hall and told them to bring my gear to the scene. Then I drove the backroads, homing in on the growing column of smoke. When I came around the last corner, the pumper and brush rig were just pulling up. I parked well clear of the staging area and ran up the road. While I pulled my gear from the pumper and tugged it on, I sized up the fire. Two-story house, long and narrow, running north-south, with an attached garage at the north end. Flame showing in the southwest corner. Wind from the southwest, moderate. Shed pine needles carpeting the lawn, forming a slick rusty yellow carpet right to the woods—we'll have to watch for ground spread.

Matt Jeffski and my brother John are the two "red hats" on scene, and since Matt is running the pump, John will be directing the attack. He sends Jed and one crew to the seat of the fire, at the southwest corner, where they can take advantage of the prevailing wind and attempt to throttle the throat of the fire. Then he tells Max and me to pull an inch-and-a-half Mattydale and swing around to the east side of the house. There is some danger in this, as we will be fighting into the wind and into the fire, but it is a calculated move.

We aren't just going in blind. We're making some assessments and judgments. If we time everything just so, if we hit it just right, we can beat back the ballooning whorls of flame, knock the fire down to its basics, and then chase in after it, put it out at the roots. It's also important that we stop it from advancing. Most of the house is a loss, but the garage is still intact. What little the family will save from this fire is in that garage.

There was this wonderful moment when I saw it all. The smoke was rolling and the flames were snapping, and the pumper throttle was open wide, and the people were gawking, and the firefighters were running, and suddenly I felt in possession of it all. I could see the house as a whole, and I could see the fire as a thing with tendencies and characteristics and predictability, and for that one instant, I realized that amateur as I am, I have learned something over these six years, and I turned to Max, and I grinned through my Scott mask, and I said, "You ready?" He nodded and in we went.

We charged in close and about ten feet out from the big picture window, I turned loose a straight stream of water the diameter of a pop can. It hit the hot glass with 120 pounds of pressure and just as we planned, the big pane disintegrated. I immediately kicked the nozzle over to fog stream and we charged even closer. Staying low, I reached up and stuffed the nozzle over the windowsill, fed in about three feet of hose, and then whipped the nozzle around and around.

This is a beautiful moment, where you've got a lot of things working for you, things you learned off a chalkboard one Wednesday evening years ago, only here they are in 3-D and thirty feet tall. First of all, you always have to think about backdraft, but when I did my size-up, the flames shooting from the roof told me the fire had already vented itself. When I looked through the picture window and saw the flames working through the black smoke, I knew the fire was hungry for oxygen, but it wasn't starved for oxygen—another source of backdraft. You still have to think about things like flashover, and what's gonna happen when you break that window and dump a load of fresh oxygen into the superheated interior. But you also know that if you act fast, if you snap that nozzle head around with a left twist and pump that fog stream straight into the heart of the inferno, the water is going to do something magic.

In fog stream position, the nozzle takes the soda-can-sized fire stream and cuts it into tiny droplets, sends them off the lip of the nozzle in a cone-shaped curtain. And here's where the magic starts. When those droplets hit the superheated air, they explode into steam. Even as we're crashing the window, I am visualizing the cartoony little water droplet in Figure 10.2, page 312, *Essentials of Firefighting, Third Edition*, with its caption: "Water expands to 1,700 times its original volume when it converts to steam." In the cartoon, the droplet puffs into a bank of stippled gray steam. The expansion is so rapid it displaces smoke and gases, including oxygen, and many smaller flames are smothered. Almost immediately, the steam condenses, drawing cooler air into the room and dropping the temperature of available fuels below ignition temperature. In an instant, a roomful of flame becomes a dripping gray cavern. When it all works, it's a tremendous trick.

You have to move fast, use that contained heat. Wait too long and the broken window will become a vent, drawing the fire toward you, disrupting the thermal balance, rendering your fog stream useless. And so Max and I tipped our faces away from the heat and fed that fire all the fog we could bring.

And it worked. Just like they said it would on page 312. The steam stomped that fire like a giant soggy slipper. You can't sit around and admire your work, the fire starts right back at you, but me and Max, we allowed ourselves a little whoop, then went in through the door, to get at the base flames. I stopped at the sill, and checked the ceiling. It was sagging pretty bad. I turned and hollered to Max. "We're gonna have to work from the door!" Your voice comes out all flat and compressed behind the mask, but I could see him nod. I twisted the nozzle back over to straight stream, and began picking off what flames I could. Over on the other side of the house, trying to get at the second-story flames, Jed had melted the top off his ladder. The ladder hangs in the fire hall now, and we have a rule: If the high end of your ladder melts, stay on the low end. At the banquet in February, he is presented with a commemorative miniature ladder.

After the ladder melted, Jed and his crew had to rethink their attack, but they slowly got the upper hand, and then we had the main fire pinned down between us. There was a lot of water pouring into the second story, and at one point, the sagging ceiling collapsed. Against my better judgment I had eased through the doorway a little, and when I heard the drywall loosening, I threw my butt in reverse, and the push of the hose drove me out the door, off the steps, and clear back to the second pumper. I nearly landed in the reservoir. I looked up at Dougie, the firefighter running the hoselines. "Man, I found the reverse in this thing!" I said.

"Never even heard yer backup beeper!" he said.

After we got the seat of the fire shut down, we made a three-man interior attack on a fire burning at the top of the stairs. I had a fresh bottle of air, so John and I and a firefighter from Chetek went in. The stairs had been burned through, so we had to wrestle a ladder over the soggy debris on the floor and stick it up through the landing. I grabbed the hose and started up the ladder, but every time I tipped my head back, a piercing pain shot deep into my left ear. I made three tries, but every time, the pain was the same. I was baffled. "I gotta get out," I yelled to John. I went to the pumper and found Dougie. Gingerly peeling my Nomex hood from my head, I asked him to look in my ear. He reached up and pulled out a dry pine needle.

It was long past dark by the time we cut the last hoseline. Much of the house was a soggy, steaming heap, but we had kept the garage and its contents intact, and were able to salvage some baby clothes from an upstairs bedroom. It had been the usual long slog, digging, tugging, and shoveling through the debris, hunting down every hidden hot spot and soaking it down. You smell of damp smoke for two days. At the end I sat next to Jed on the tailboard of the brush buggy, eating a sandwich under the halogen scene lights. I told him how it went on our side, how those first five minutes were the best

I'd ever had on a scene, how satisfying it was to realize in the thick of the whirl that Max and I were fighting fire not just with adrenaline, but with awareness. I told him about the pine needle. He told me about the ladder. He said they got him another ladder, and while he was climbing that one, the TV antenna fell off the roof and hit him on the head.

I went carp shooting the morning Jed and Sarah were married. It was perfect carping weather, clear and sunny, low wind. I lost track of time out there on my log, and had to hustle to make the ceremony, but I did. On the second floor of the Eau Claire County Courthouse, Sarah stood at the front of Chamber 3, country-girl beautiful in a calf-length pale green skirt and a white sleeveless top. Jed wore black jeans and a shirt he borrowed from me. Found a hole in it right before the ceremony. He looked scared and happy as the vows unfolded, and Sarah cried a little, but we all laughed later at the sight of them up there, Sarah tall and blond at five nine, Jed dark tan and half bald at five five, and the judge coming in at somewhere around five two, smiling up between them like an over-achieving altar boy. Sarah's mom took some pictures out in front of the courthouse, and I popped the trunk and dug out my carp camera, a disposable job I bought on rebate at a Menard's Home Improvement store. There were already a couple of pictures in there of me hoisting a channel buffalo, so I shot up the rest of the roll like some cut-rate hillbilly wedding photographer. I even got them to sit on a bench with their hands on Sarah's knee so I could get the requisite ring fingers shot. While we were milling around, a man started yelling at his wife in the parking lot. She had a handful of papers and was trying to get into the courthouse. The man yelled louder and louder, until a bailiff appeared and escorted the woman into the courthouse. Left in the lot, the man slumped to the sidewalk and hung his head. Jed and Sarah took off for their weekend trip up north, and right at the end there I got a shot of them walking away in the courthouse crosswalk, hand in hand, and that picture is just so sweet.

Brother John and I were so disoriented by the whole deal we took off the next day and went fishing.

Commencing the following Monday, there were changes. Jed's big old farmhouse got a thorough going-over. No more dirty jeans on the living room floor or tractor parts in the sink. Suddenly there were sunflower curtains on the windows. Potted ivy on the windowsill. A herd of Beanie Babies where the equipment sale fliers used to pile up. A second Adirondack chair in the yard. Flowers planted down by the pond. A garden no five people could hope to maintain. I saw those changes in the first week, and I wondered how it was going.

Several weeks later, a friend and I stopped by the farm, and Jed was leading a doe-eyed Jersey milk cow into the barn. He was holding it by an embroidered purple bridle—another sign that someone new was doing the shopping at Farm & Fleet. The Jersey was the only milk cow on the place. Jed had rustled up an old Surge milker and got the wheezing vacuum pump back in running order so that he and Sarah could have fresh milk. I leaned against the pen rail and watched as Jed hung the milker from the belly strap, then swung the inflations into position, one by one. *Whoosh-shlup*, they sucked themselves into place over each teat. The moment all four inflations were in place, the Jersey raised a dainty rear hoof and kicked them to the manure. Jed silently pressed his head into her flank and repeated the process. She kicked them loose again. Still quiet, Jed was positioning the inflations a third time, when the cow kicked yet again. Sarah had come in the barn and was leaning against the rail beside me. She had been to town, and was wearing tan slacks and white open-toed sandals. When the cow kicked the third time, Sarah clambered over the manure-caked rail and strode across the cow pen as if she were wearing wellies and overalls. When I left, she and Jed were kneeling side by side at the flank of the Jersey, the milker in place, the milk coursing into the bucket.

• • •

Late June. I'm on the road to Lincoln, Nebraska. My friend Gene
has been offered a position at a hospital in Scott's Bluff, but first he
must take a test on Nebraska physical-therapy law. During the trip,
Gene reads me passages from the study guide, and it seems to me
Nebraska physical-therapy law boils down to definitions of good
touch/bad touch and proscriptions against advertising the way car
dealers do. The state requires that the test be taken in person. Gene
has only two days off work to make the trip, so I'm helping him
drive, out and back, hammer down. In a minivan, but still. We have
road music—Dave Alvin, Lightnin' Hopkins, Emmylou Harris,
Peter Tosh, the Clash, Bad Livers, Steve Earle, Koko Taylor—and
we entertain ourselves with stories from the old days, back when we
first met while working on the same neurological rehab unit. I tell
the one about the time I looked down the hall and saw all the sad little stroke ladies, waiting to be trundled off to therapy in their wheel-
chairs, and I decided to dance for them, a show-tune sort of thing. I
had a stainless steel bedpan in my hand, and as I high-kicked down
the hall, I doffed the bedpan like a tricorn hat. They laughed and
laughed. A little too much, I noticed, then I turned and saw the staff
psychiatrist following two paces behind me with his notebook.

We hit it off back then, and we hit it off now. It's the mystery of
compatibility. If he passes the test, he gets the job, and I'll see him
maybe once or twice a year. Somewhere on I-80, still in Iowa, westbound, mile marker 13, a little overpass, a blackbird teeters on a
wire, flutters against the crosswind, and just as we pass beneath, he
allows himself to be swept aloft and I think, these are the moments
that fine-tune the spin of the earth. Later that night, in the Motel 8,
while Gene studies, I write a letter to a friend, and I include the observation on the blackbird.

Gene took the test the next day. All that driving, the test took
twenty minutes, and he passed. Before the summer is over, he'll be
gone to Nebraska for good. His wife, Paula, will be happy. Her family are all in Nebraska, and it has been years since she has been near
them. Gene has mixed emotions about the move, but he is a Ne-

braska boy himself, and he understands the pull of family and geography. "It will be nice for Paula," he says, and I love him for the unqualified understanding in his voice. But I will miss him. And I wonder if Frank will leave when he gets married. And I still haven't quite figured out how to act around my brother Jed when he is man and wife.

I dropped Gene off at home and came in off the road on the morning of June 29, 2001. I drove into New Auburn and made my customary lap around the block, cutting over to Elm Street rather than driving straight up Main, so that I could see if the trucks were out. The fire hall was closed up tight, but Jed's pickup was parked on the street out front. It didn't make sense, but perhaps he was in working on equipment, or had been dropped off at home after a fire. It didn't quite add up. I pulled into the lot and let myself in the hall. It was cool and dark. No one around. I crossed in front of the engines, through the garage to the meeting room. The run logs were in a clipboard on the chief's desk. I paged back through them to see what I had missed, starting with the day I left for Nebraska. A couple of medical calls, nothing out of the ordinary. Then I flipped up the bottom sheet, the most recent call. The crew log showed that ten members had been out, and they had been logged in for four hours. Unless it was a structure fire, that's a long time to be out. I looked at the description form. "Accident" had been circled. There is a column down the left side of the form with the heading, "Driver Information." In the box titled "Driver, Vehicle 1," someone had written *Sarah Perry*.

I went straight home. There were fifteen messages on my machine. The first three or four were hangups. Then there was my brother John. He was on a cell phone, calling from the ditch along Five Mile Road. His voice was haggard but straight. Sarah was just killed in a car accident here at Turkey Corners. The rest of the message was static.

Jed was feeding heifers when his pager went off. When the dispatcher gave the location he recognized it as an intersection less than three miles from his farm, and he knew Sarah had to make that intersection on her way home. He grabbed his gear and jumped in his truck, a little extra nervous, as we all are when a call comes from an area frequented by family. Just down the road, at the home farm, Mom pulled out in front of him in her big old Lincoln. They arrived at the scene together. Jed didn't recognize Sarah's car at first. It was that badly damaged.

Mom thought I would want to know how it went, and so the morning after, she took me through the scene. The car had been shoved from the roadway into the ditch, but was still right-side up. Sarah looked as if she had simply reclined her seat. Her hands were at her sides. Jed saw the damage, the passenger side crushed clear into Sarah's right side, and immediately he thought of her in a coma. She wasn't breathing, but her heart was beating. Mom suctioned blood from her throat with a tube, and Jed gave her several breaths. Then the fire and rescue trucks began arriving, and Jed remembers seeing the familiar yellow paint and then a feeling of gratefulness, gratefulness that the people spilling from the vehicles were his friends, and that Sarah would not be in the hands of strangers. Max had arrived in his pickup, and he pulled Jed away now, took him down the ditch, and, not knowing what else to do, held him.

It unfolded the same as it always does then, the ambulance arriving, driven by more friends, and the fire crew fanning out to reroute traffic, mark out the helicopter landing zone, help Mom and the EMTs with medical care. John was on an excavation job fifteen miles away, but when he heard the call and location, and then radio traffic mentioning a first responder's wife, he dumped his trailer and headed to the scene. Almost unnoticed, one of the first responders and EMTs were treating the driver of the other vehicle, preparing her to be transported to the hospital for evaluation. Chief Ernie had ordered the chopper the moment he sized up the situation, and shortly it was settling into a nearby cornfield with its familiar thunderous buzz. The flight nurses came on the run, and Mom says it was something to see, the way they worked, inserting chest tubes to relieve the pressure on Sarah's lungs, running through their resuscitation algorithms, placing tubes and setting IV lines. They handed the IV bags to two firefighters and told them to squeeze, as if they could force life back in her veins.

At the end, they made the call right there in the green grass. Jed has told me he is thankful for this, for it left him with no questions. He wasn't called to some emergency room cubicle, or to some morgue, didn't have to stand and wait for someone to pull back a sheet. Instead, on his knees, touching familiar ground, he bent to his young wife, gave her his very breath, and knowing it wasn't enough, gave her into the care of friends, stepped back, and turned to face the desolate traverse.

Jed had hay down, and so the day after Sarah was killed, I baled it. We embraced and wept deeply that morning, and then we got to work. We don't ask why, my brothers and I. These things happen every day. This time, it happened to us. Still, when I bring the tractor back from the hayfield, I see my brother, his tough little body sagged with grief, and I am overwhelmed with the journey he faces. Returning to the field with a forklift, I gather up the fresh bales, stacking them against a future guaranteed to no one.

At the wake, it was her hands that made me cry. I would look at them and think of them touching my brother. I thought too of the poet Frank Stanford, or more specifically, eight beautiful, desolate lines of his "Blue Yodel of the Lost Child":

> *A letter to the condemned,*
> *You came too late*
> *Like the snow*
> *Who calls you his wife now,*
> *And your breasts will never be*
> *Heavy with milk,*

And your voice like an owl
On every fence post.

At the funeral, we brothers stood and spoke in turn. John went first, told about Sarah's goofy little laugh, told how he used to roar past her yard in his dump truck and hit the air horn, and he would see her blond ponytail bobbing as she waved. I went next, and said something about how I reckoned we aren't given this measure of grief without first being given an equal measure of love. I said I had done the math, and between the three of us, Jed's wedding had brought an end to 102 combined years of bachelorhood. That got a little laugh. Then I told the story of Jed and Sarah milking the cow.

And then Jed stood, and we were amazed at his strength, him facing the wall-to-wall church, speaking slow but strong about how every time Sarah went to the sale barn she came home with an orphan goat or a calf or three chickens, and how they were going to have to have a husband/wife discussion about the financial implications of perpetual animal rescue, and then he said neither he nor Sarah had much time for organized religion, but they got married because they loved each other and wanted to do the right thing before God, and I was at once stricken and proud.

Hud Simpson and Nick Tuggle washed and buffed the fire trucks in the morning, and the department turned out in uniform shirts—the first time they'd been off the hanger since the awards ceremony in February. Chief Ernie led the procession to the cemetery, while several members of the department shut down traffic and then brought up the rear in the other trucks. John and I made the procession in his dump truck, put it right in there a couple of vehicles behind the hearse, his dog Leroy between us on the homemade booster seat. It's an eight-mile drive to the cemetery, over the skid marks in the intersection where Sarah was killed, past her childhood home, past the house she and Jed shared for seven weeks. It is the price and comfort of living in a small place.

We sang a hymn in the sun, then left her to be put in the ground, just a few feet from the graves of my brother Eric and sister Rya. At the end Jed stood by the casket with Mom, and then with Sarah's mother, and I kept thinking of all the slide carousels in my parents' house, filled with pictures of us as children, and how much a mother agrees to stand when she delivers life into this world.

Except for the funeral director, John and I were the last to leave the cemetery. The funeral director is getting up there in years some, and I think we caught him a little off guard, and maybe he thought it disrespectful, but when we pulled even with the casket John hit the air horn good and solid one more time. Then he ginned up the diesel and we turned toward home.

Seven nights after Sarah's death, the entire department met in the fire hall. A team of five volunteers—EMTs and firefighters, led by a minister—took us through a critical incident stress debriefing. The experts will tell you CISD is an integrated system of interventions designed to mitigate the adverse psychological reactions that accompany an event with the potential to overwhelm the coping skills of an individual or a group. What you basically do is get together and talk the whole thing over, with outside supervision and support. It has been six years since our last CISD. We had that one after Tracy Rimes was killed on Jabowski's Corner. I'm not one for group therapy. But I saw some powerful good done in the session we held for Tracy, and now I'm four-square behind the idea. We sat in a circle, and the minister got us started, and that's all I will say. CISD is only effective if everyone speaks freely, without fear of chatter. The first thing the group leader does after closing the door is bind everyone in the room to complete confidentiality.

The doors were closed for two hours. When we came out, someone had a pot of coffee ready, and we leaned around on the trucks, smoking and dunking cookies, and we made the sort of small talk you make when you're finding your way back to the trail. I thought back to the night these folks all met Sarah. The mood in the Sundial

Supper Club was festive, the mood here in the trucks is grave. But the nut of the thing is the same. At some point over the last twenty-five years, each of us walked in, took a seat at the back of the room, and offered to drive these yellow trucks to trouble. And because of that, we now stand in the midst of a small cluster of people privy to a history written in places the outsider does not see.

For my brother, there are dark days ahead. The house, suffused with her memory, the most perverse sort of tease. Her horses, her pet goat, her empty saddle in the hog shed. This buddy of mine called, and I think he put it well. "The tough times start," he said, "the day the last casserole dish is returned."

Out there running Jed's baler, looking ahead to line up the windrow and back to check the ties, I feel centered on the earth, the way I always feel when I'm doing something fundamental in a familiar place, the same way I feel when I grab a hose and try to put out a neighbor's fire, or hold an old lady's hand while Bob or Jack gets the oxygen set up. Captive of my heart and feet, I'm a wandering fool, but I've got the sense to keep returning. On this land, in this place, with these people, I am where I belong.

I have a new girlfriend. She lives on a farm and sleeps in the back of her pickup. She has been tending Sarah's garden. We are lying on our backs in the truck bed, looking up at the sky. A goose-bump wind sends clouds scudding over the face of the moon. I watch the whiteness wax and wane, and I am thinking, little brother, how long will you have to sleep beneath the cold moon before you can feel the sun again?

About the author

2   Meet Michael Perry

About the book

4   Population: 562

Read on

14   An Excerpt from Michael Perry's
     Truck: A Love Story

17   Have You Read?
     More by Michael Perry

Insights,
Interviews
& More...

Meet Michael Perry

MICHAEL PERRY is a humorist, and author of the bestselling memoir *Truck: A Love Story* and the essay collection *Off Main Street: Barnstormers, Prophets & Gatemouth's Gator.* Perry has written for *Esquire*, the *New York Times Magazine, Outside, Backpacker, Orion*, and Salon.com, and he is a contributing editor to *Men's Health*. His essays have been heard on NPR's *All Things Considered*, and he has performed and produced two live audience recordings: *I Got It from the Cows* and *Never Stand Behind a Sneezing Cow.* Perry lives in rural Wisconsin, where he remains active as a volunteer firefighter and emergency medical responder. He can be found online at www.sneezingcow.com.

© 2002 by J. Shimon and J. Lindemann

Raised on a small dairy farm, Perry equates his writing career to cleaning calf pens—just keep shoveling, and eventually you've got a pile so big, someone will notice. Perry further prepared for the writing life by reading every Louis L'Amour cowboy book he could get his hands on—most of them twice. He then worked for five summers on a real ranch in Wyoming, a career cut short by his fear of horses and an incident in which he almost avoided a charging bull. According to a series of informal conversations held around the ol' branding fire, Perry still holds the record for being the only working cowboy in all of Wyoming to attend nursing school, from which he graduated in 1987 after giving the commencement address in a hairdo combining mousse spikes on top, a mullet in back, and a mustache up front—otherwise known as the bad hair trifecta. Recently Perry has begun to lose his hair, and although his current classification varies depending on the lighting, he is definitely Bald Man Walking.

Perry has run a forklift, operated a backhoe, driven a truck, worked as a proofreader and physical therapy aide, and distinguished himself as a licensed cycle rider by careening into a concrete bridge completely unassisted. He has worked for a surgeon, answered a suicide hotline, picked rock in the rain with an alcoholic transvestite, been a country music roadie in Switzerland, and worked as a roller-skating Snoopy. He can run a pitchfork, milk a cow in the dark, and say "I don't understand" in French, Greek, and Norwegian. He has never been bucked off a horse, and contends that falling off doesn't count. He is utterly unable to polka. ∿

> **"** Perry equates his writing career to cleaning calf pens—just keep shoveling, and eventually you've got a pile so big, someone will notice. **"**

Population: 562

THESE DAYS, the sign just off the highway says POPULATION 562. Urban sprawl strikes again, we like to say. Although I also like to point out that when I was in high school, the population was 383. Then it went to 485. So 562 is actually—as the politicians tend to twist it— a *decrease in the rate of increase,* which means we could loop around to 485 again one day.

Some things change, some don't. You can still see the old silver water tower from the four-lane, but over there between the park and the trailer court, they've put up a new tower, one of those slim spheroid deals painted white and trimmed with the school colors, and there is talk of scrapping the silver one. Jamboree Days gets bigger every year, and lately we've been bringing in high-dollar

The new population sign. We are now population 562. Urban sprawl strikes again. The reproduction of the book cover was one of those things that makes you thankful and keeps you humble all at once. Forever and always I am grateful to be from—and of—New Auburn.

All photographs courtesy of the author

bands, but on Sunday afternoon it's still door prizes and polka. Tugg's bar has changed hands time and again, but the folks who emerge just past two A.M. to provide their own boisterous form of street theatre have maintained a consistent dedication to craft and theme.

One of Bob the One-Eyed Beagle's ex-wives still works at the Gas-N-Go. She was none too happy with me when *Population: 485* first came out, with that line where the Beagle says he knew their marriage was in trouble because she wouldn't let him look at the checkbook. One day when I was paying for my gas she stared me down and said, "I told him I'd give up the checkbook when he gave up the *girlfriend!*"

Fair enough, and now you know. ▶

Shortly after Population: 485 *came out, fresh census numbers were released and the village had to put up new signs. They gave me one of the old ones. I can see it from my writing desk, and it is one of my most cherished possessions. Thank you, Nobbern! (It does lack one thing: a bullet hole. Perhaps some day we'll have a special sign-shooting ceremony, so it looks like all the other signs in the county.)*

Population: 562 *(continued)*

In early 2007, they did in fact tear down the old village water tower. I was out of town and didn't get pictures. So now I'm glad I have this fuzzy little snapshot. I keep it in a frame by my writing desk.

The Beagle is still running solo, but his good humor does not flag. Last winter we got paged out to a logging accident. It was below zero, and we could only reach the victim by foot. The Beagle was wearing cowboy boots, and he slipped and slid as we ran down the logging trail. After the patient was packaged and packed out, we made a beeline for the warm cab of the rescue truck. I had to stow some gear, so the Beagle got there first. I could see him in the front seat, peeling off his turnout coat, then his sweatshirt, right down to a sleeveless T-shirt. Cold as it was, it didn't make sense—until I jumped in the back and he swiveled around with a big grin on his face. "Hey Mikey—whaddya thinka *this?*" He was flexing his arm so I could view the lateral aspect of his considerable bicep, upon which was a freshly-inked depiction of a beagle hound. "I got the picture off the Internet," he said. "When I told the tattoo lady what I wanted her to do, she said, 'You're the guy from that book!'" He turned a little more, to give me a better view.

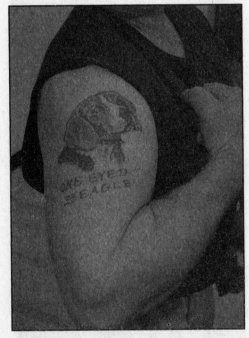

The Beagle's new tattoo

What a privilege it has been, to write about a place I love. Even more, to write *from* ▶

Population: 562 *(continued)*

that place. My fellow citizens have been very tolerant, and I thank them. They didn't ask for this. *Population: 485* is not *the* story of New Auburn. You could say it is one of at least 485 versions. I did my best to get the facts straight (the checkbook), but everyone has their take (the *girlfriend!*). You can't get it all in there. The most common complaint I've received, to date? "Why am I *not* in the book?!" This little essayistic update of mine is all well and good, but for the truly contemporary good stuff, I suggest a

66 My fellow citizens have been very tolerant, and I thank them. They didn't ask for this. *Population: 485* is not *the* story of New Auburn. You could say it is one of at least 485 versions. 99

The new water tower. You can see it from the four-lane. During Jamboree Days, it will serve as a beacon guiding you to the beer tent.

three-pronged attack: breakfast at the Corner Store on Highway 40, lunch at the Sunshine Café on Main Street, and dinner at TJ's Food-N-Fun. (Where, if you get huffy about the delay on your Tubby Burger, Goldie will say what she always says: "This ain't McDonald's!") For the complete experience, schedule a perm at the Wig-Wam and drop in for coffee at North Star Implement—although to make it legit, they'd prefer you buy a manure spreader.

But really, it doesn't have to be New Auburn. When *Outside* magazine asked me to contribute a few paragraphs on small-town life, I wrote:

> Approach any small town with a reverence for what you can learn. Memorize the population sign. Small-town people love to out-small each other, and you must be prepared. Go to the café, order quietly, and eavesdrop shamelessly. Wander the local cemetery. Study the headstones. Notice which names recur. Note the spans of birth and death. These stratifications of time compose the foundation of the town. Browse the community bulletin boards and all announcements taped to the gas station door. In short order you will have clues to who has what, who wants what, who can fix your deck, who can stuff your deer, and who can save your soul.
>
> Drive the outskirts. Consider the look of the town in the rearview ▶

mirror as opposed to through the windshield, and think about how you feel. More to the point, if you find yourself trapped behind an old man doing thirty-five in a forty-five, don't figure out a way to pass him, figure out a way to *be* him. And for the love of Pete, don't moo at the cows. This is the habit of outsiders.

What a smile it puts on my face, to be in California, or New Hampshire, or Mississippi, and have a reader from a town of twenty thousand people say, "Your town is just like our town." There is something in play here that goes well beyond geography or a number on a sign. And based on correspondence from readers, even the biggest cities and broadest suburbs are filled with people not so far removed from rural or small-town life. America picked up and moved to the big city generations ago, and we've been second-guessing ourselves ever since. For every stifled small-town kid champing at the bit to split, there are a thousand grown-ups yearning to return—even if only for a weekend.

66 And for the love of Pete, don't moo at the cows. This is the habit of outsiders. 99

Twelve years have passed since I moved back to New Auburn, meaning I have spent twenty of my forty-two years in the same zip code. That's about to change again. I have a little family now, and we're moving—not far, but outside the fire district—to the country. (I describe how this all came to be in the book *Truck: A Love Story*.) We have been given the opportunity to keep farmland in the family, so inside my head the decision was easy. My heart is not yet convinced. I am centered in New Auburn, so content when I see that green sign come into view that I wonder what I am giving up. I would go on, but this world groans with armies of souls in forced march, driven by everything from foreclosure to genocide, whereas we are simply easing down the road a piece.

Instead, my sense of place evolves, and perhaps it will expand. It has been subzero cold here in our first week of residence on the farm, and I have been hauling firewood in Herbie Gravunder's ice-fishing sled. I got the sled at Herbie's auction (the same day I bought his hovercraft), and when I drag it full of split oak, I feel like I'm drawing something of New Auburn along with me.

I shall also maintain the rent on New Auburn Post Office Box 85, and as we shuttle back and forth with our moving boxes, I keep my fire pager switched on. Last week I snuck over and stood among the trucks. I breathed in that quiet firehouse fragrance (it's a *still* smell . . . dampened notes of rubber, diesel, and concrete, all of it cushioned by undertones of smoked canvas), and I was comforted when the moment brought back the words in chapter 2:

> The community is the constant.
> Volunteer firefighters come and go.
> The old-timers hand down equipment
> and stories, show up occasionally
> when we're shorthanded, but most of
> all they help us recognize that time—
> our time—is transient. ▶

> 66 I breathed in that quiet firehouse fragrance (it's a *still* smell . . . dampened notes of rubber, diesel, and concrete, all of it cushioned by undertones of smoked canvas). 99

Population: 562 (*continued*)

The new fire district is looking for first responders. When I get all the pictures hung, I'll see if they'll have me. But dragging Herbie's sled reminds me: no matter where I stand when I say it, I am forever gratefully from—and of—"Nobbern."

People want to know about Jed. I wrote the last chapter of *Population: 485* with his permission. I remember sitting in his kitchen surrounded by sunflower curtains, sunflower dish towels, sunflower hot pads—Sarah's sunflowers everywhere—and asking if it would be all right to tell the story. I had already written a final chapter for the book (essentially a slightly different version of the eventual chapter 12), and I told him if he said no, I would never mention it again. He sat there quiet for a long time. Then he said, "I guess it's okay. I trust you. Go ahead and write it. But I don't think I ever want to read it."

After a long haul on a black path, Jed is back in the light. He has a little family now—a daughter, a son, and a wife who honors Sarah's memory while living strongly as her own person. In a gentle closing of the karmic circle, Jed was introduced to his second wife by Sarah's mother.

As a writer, I have no more claim on a higher purpose than any other person working a job. Likely less, as some of my abler critics have established. It's a craft. You work at it. You write what pays the rent. But in rare moments you feel like maybe the typing transcends the electric bill. Sometime after his second wedding,

❝ As a writer, I have no more claim on a higher purpose than any other person working a job. ❞

Jed wrote me a note. Said he had set himself a goal to read the book. The last chapter was very hard, he said. But he approved. I read the note twice and then put it away.

For Sarah. That is enough. ⌒

An Excerpt from Michael Perry's *Truck: A Love Story*

IN AN EFFORT TO HELP ME arrive at the age
of eighteen alive and financially solvent, my
parents quite wisely forbade me to buy my
own car while I was in high school. Which
meant I did a lot of dating in the F-100.
By the time I got my license, the truck was
entering its second decade of hard labor. The
side panels were ragged with rust and flapped
like buzzard wings. When you gained speed,
they flared. The truck pulled drastically to the
right. I'd hang off the left side of the steering
wheel to keep it moving on a straight line.
The transmission, originally three-on-the-
tree, had been replaced at some point and
converted to a stick shift accessed through a
hole cut in the floor. No one is clear on why,
but the mechanic put the new transmission
in backward so that the gear selection pattern
was reversed. You had to go far right and back
for first gear and shift against your intuition.
There was a gap in the floorboards beside the
clutch through which you could gauge your
speed based on the road-blur. When it rained,
my pant legs were mud-spittled. On the
sharper turns, sheep ear tags and fencing
staples shot across the dash. The brakes were
inconsistent. Sometimes the pedal was soft
as squishing a plum. Other times the brakes
caught so abruptly empty vaccine bottles
rocketed from beneath the seat and smacked
you in the ankle bone.

Naturally, the windshield was cracked.

The heater was passable, but in the
summer you'd rely on what a laughing

> **❝** No one is
> clear on why, but
> the mechanic
> put the new
> transmission
> in backward so
> that the gear
> selection pattern
> was reversed.
> You had to go far
> right and back
> for first gear and
> shift against your
> intuition. **❞**

bus driver once described to me as a "2-80" air conditioner: "Roll down two windows and go eighty miles an hour!" There were vents on either side of the cab at shin level, but to open them was to unleash a cyclone of alfalfa chaff and dehydrated horseflies.

Picture your date perched beside you on a summer's day, her lips glistening with Bubble Gum Lip Smackers and the cab charged with the scent of Gee, Your Hair Smells Terrific! shampoo. You're running fifty miles an hour down a gravel road when she grows overwarm and bends down to crack a vent. When she rares back, she appears to have emerged from a polluted wind tunnel. Her hair is frosted with feed dust and she's got pine needles stuck in her banana clip. Her lips are dotted like twin strips of flypaper, and there is a June bug in her braces.

You're young. You kiss her anyway.

I spent so much time dating in that old truck I didn't now how to act in anything nicer. Once my grandfather lent me his Ford LTD. It was a beauty. Bloodred paint job with a white vinyl top and air-conditioning. Power steering, power brakes, and a fully automatic transmission. I was dating a farmer's daughter with the cutest button nose. I had coupons, so we got dressed up and went to Pizza Hut. After dinner I pulled out of the parking lot, merged into traffic, leaned back expansively, and draped my right arm across the back of the seat. The girl smiled up at me sweetly. She had grown to tolerate the farm truck, but as we picked up speed, I could see her luxuriating in the smoothness of the LTD. At which point, out of reflex and forgetting ▶

> ❝ I spent so much time dating in that old truck I didn't now how to act in anything nicer. ❞

An Excerpt from Michael Perry's
Truck: A Love Story (continued)

I was driving an automatic, I went for second gear, instinctively mashing what should have been the clutch but in the event was the power brake. I had my seatbelt on. She did not. The image that endures is of her flailing elbows as she fought to unwedge her button nose from that pinch point where the windshield and dashboard meet. ॰৹

Have You Read?
More by Michael Perry

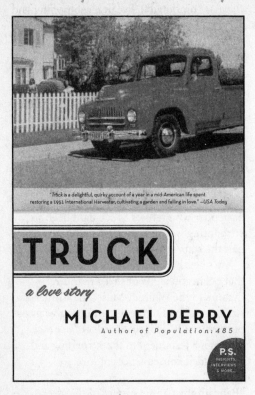

"*Truck* is a delightful, quirky account of a year in a mid-American life spent restoring a 1951 International Harvester, cultivating a garden and falling in love." —*USA Today*

TRUCK
a love story
MICHAEL PERRY
Author of *Population: 485*

P.S.
INSIGHTS,
INTERVIEWS
& MORE...

TRUCK: A LOVE STORY

The author of *Population: 485* returns, delivering a truckload of humor, heart, and . . . gardening tips? Think *Zen and the Art of Motorcycle Maintenance*, complete with stock cars, sexy vegetables, and a laugh track.

"All I wanted to do was fix my old pickup truck," says Michael Perry. "That, and plant my garden. Then I met this woman. . . ." *Truck: A Love Story* recounts a year in which Perry struggles to grow his own food ("Seed catalogs are responsible for more unfulfilled fantasies than Enron and *Playboy* combined"), live peaceably with his neighbors (one test-fires his black powder rifle in the alley; another's best Sunday shirt reads 100 PERCENT WHUP-ASS), and sort out his love life. But along the way, he sets his hair on fire, is attacked by wild turkeys, takes a date to the fire department chicken dinner, and proposes marriage to a woman in New Orleans. As with *Population: 485*, much of the spirit of *Truck: A Love Story* may be found in the characters Perry meets: a one-eyed land surveyor, a paraplegic biker who rigs a sidecar so that his quadriplegic pal can ride along, a bartender who refuses to sell light beer, an enchanting woman who never existed, and half the staff of National Public Radio.

By turns hilarious and heartfelt, a tale that begins on a pile of sheep manure, detours to the Whitney Museum of American Art, and returns to the deer-hunting swamps of northern Wisconsin, *Truck: A Love Story* becomes a testament to the surprising and unintended consequences of love.

"Beneath the flannel surface of this deer-hunting, truck-loving Badger is the soul of a poet and a man at work balancing his masculinity against his softer urges toward food, sentimentality, and literature. It is this tension, this misfitting of parts, that creates a delicious tautness in his potent memoir. . . . Perry takes each moment, peeling it, seasoning it with rich language, and then serving it to us piping hot and fresh." —*Chicago Tribune*'s "Books"

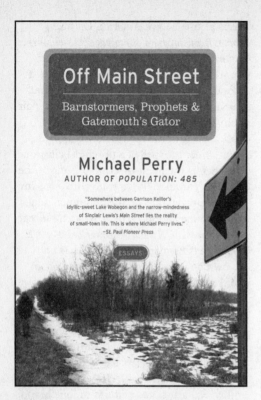

OFF MAIN STREET: BARNSTORMERS, PROPHETS & GATEMOUTH'S GATOR (Essays)

Whether he's fighting fires, passing a kidney stone, hammering down I-80 in an eighteen-wheeler, or meditating on the relationship between cowboys and God, Michael Perry draws on his rural roots and footloose past to write from a perspective that merges the local with the global.

Prior to writing the beloved memoir *Population: 485*, freelance journalist Michael Perry wrote essays on such diverse topics as big-rig truck driving, country music, butchery, farming, nursing, and the many facets of small-town America. *Off Main Street: Barnstormers, Prophets & Gatemouth's Gator* is a collection of Perry's offbeat reporting, and is confirmation of his one-of-a-kind worldview and deeply personal and humane insights.

In "Branding God," we witness Perry working on a cattle ranch and recalling time spent under the spell of a fire-and-brimstone preacher by the name of Brother Timothy. In "Rolling Thunder," Perry rides with a convoy of Vietnam veterans on their chopper-rigged march to the nation's capital. In such pieces as "A Way with Wings," "Swelter," and "Manure Is Elemental," Perry reflects on his own boyhood spent in rural Wisconsin amid everyday characters of the American Midwest.

Ranging across subjects as diverse as lot lizards, Klan wizards, and small-town funerals, Perry's writing in this wise and witty collection of essays balances earthiness with poetry, kinetics with contemplation, and is regularly salted with his unique brand of humor.

"Michael Perry is like a sensitive, new-age Hemingway." —Salon.com

Don't miss the next book by your favorite author. Sign up now for AuthorTracker by visiting www.AuthorTracker.com.